Community Organizing in a Diverse Society

FELIX G. RIVERA
San Francisco State University

JOHN L. ERLICH
California State University—Sacramento

ALLYN AND BACON
Boston   London   Toronto   Sydney   Tokyo   Singapore

To Vicky,
Sophia and Olivia
To Kathleen
and
Lynn, Kathy, John and Megan
To people of color
struggling to achieve their rightful
share of the American dream
and
their own dreams

Executive Editor: Susan Badger
Series Editor: Karen Hanson
Series Editorial Assistant: Deborah Reinke
Cover Administrator: Suzanne Harbison
Manufacturing Buyer: Megan Cochran
Composition Buyer: Linda Cox

Organizing with people of color : changing and emerging communities /
  [edited by] Felix G. Rivera and John L. Erlich.
      p.   cm.
  Includes bibliographical references (p.   ) and index.
  ISBN 0-205-13295-2
    1. Community development—United States.   2. Minorities—Housing—
—United States.   3. Community organization—United States.
  4. Neighborhood—United States.   I. Rivera, Felix G.   II. Erlich,
John L.   III. Title.
  HN90.C6074   1991
  307.1'4'0973—dc20   91-758

Printed in the United States of America
10 9 8 7 6 5 4 3   96 95 94 93

Contents

Contributors

Carlos B. Cordoba, Ed.D., is an Associate Professor in the School of Ethnic Studies, San Francisco State University, California, where he teaches in La Raza Studies. He has published numerous articles on refugee issues, including a portfolio of his photographs taken in El Salvador.

Felipe de Ortego y Gasca, Ph.D., is a Professor of English at Arizona State University. He has taught English and Chicano literature in various universities. He is a long-time activist.

Wynetta Devore, Ph.D., is a Professor at the School of Social Work, Syracuse University, New York, where she teaches practice. Dr. Devore is the co-author of *Ethnic Sensitive Social Work Practice.*

Daniel E. Edwards, D.S.W., is an Associate Professor at the Graduate School of Social Work, University of Utah. He is a member of the Yurok Tribe, and a long time Director of the American Indian Social Work Program at the university. His varied publications reflect his broad concern for Native American cultures.

Margie Egbert-Edwards, Ph.D., is a Professor of Social Work, Graduate School of Social Work, University of Utah; she is the former co-director of the American Indian Social Work Career Training Program.

John L. Erlich, A.B.D., is a Professor in the Division of Social Work at California State University, Sacramento where he Chairs the Child and Family Services Concentration and teaches child and family macro practice courses. He has worked as an organizer in New York City, Michigan and Sacramento. Professor Erlich has served as a planning and organizing consultant to numerous community-based organizations. He has published extensively in the areas of community organization and planning, social change, emerging minority communities and burnout. Among the books he has co-authored or edited are *Changing Organizations and Community Programs, Tactics and Techniques of Community Practice,* and *Strategies of Community Organization.*

Lorraine M. Guitiérrez, Ph.D., is an Assistant Professor, School of Social Work, University of Washington. She teaches courses in Community and

Organizational Services and in the Concentration on Women and Minorities. Dr. Guitiérrez has extensive experience organizing against violence against women, particularly within urban, multi-ethnic communities.

John Duong Huynh, M.S.W., is an ethnic Chinese born in Cholon, Vietnam. He left Vietnam for France in 1968, and arrived in San Francisco, California in 1980. He is a child welfare specialist, working with refugee populations at the Department of Social Services. Mr. Huynh is an activist for Southeast Asian refugee and immigrants' rights.

Isaiah C. Lee, D.P.H., is a Professor in the Social Work Department at California State University, Long Beach, California, where he teaches practice and minority issues. Dr. Lee has been chair of the department. His publications are quite diverse, reflecting his many interests in social work.

Edith A. Lewis, Ph.D., is an Assistant Professor at the School of Social Work, University of Michigan, where she teaches practice. She has done research on social support systems and low-income mothers, and role strain in African American women. Her publications cover such diverse topics as students of color, socialization and social supports as a prevention strategy.

Miguel Montiel, D.S.W., is a Professor in the School of Public Affairs at Arizona State University. He has served as Assistant Vice President for Academic Affairs at A.S.U. and has taught social research and Chicano issues in social work at the University of California, Berkeley, and at Arizona State University.

Julio Morales, Ph.D., is a Professor at the School of Social Work, University of Connecticut. A long-time activist, he has been instrumental in founding Puerto Rican Studies Projects and numerous social service agencies and programs in New York, Massachusetts and Connecticut.

Kenji Murase, D.S.W., is a retired Professor from the Department of Social Work Education, San Francisco State University. His areas of teaching and Community involvement are minority issues, research and program planning and development, to mention a few. He is noted for his teaching, research and grantsmanship skills, and many publications pertaining to Asian American communities.

Antonia Pantoja, Ph.D., has taught at the schools of social work of Columbia University and the University of Puerto Rico. She has also taught at the New School for Social Research, New York. She has been responsible for the development of such organizations as the Puerto Rican Association for Community Affairs, The Puerto Rican Forum, Aspira, and Boricua College. In 1984 she began to work with residents to organize PRODUCIR, INC., a community economic development corporation in Canovanas, Puerto Rico. Dr. Pantoja's publications reflect a broad-based commitment to multicultural approaches to social change and community development. She is also a consulting editor for the *Journal of Progressive Human Services*.

Wilhelmina Perry, Ph.D., was a faculty member at The School of Social Work, Stony Brook, N.Y. Dr. Perry has been adjunct faculty for students in alternative educational programs, such as The Union Graduate School, Rural Development Leadership Network and The Western Institute for Social Research. She, with Dr. Pantoja, resigned her tenured faculty position at the School of Social Work, San Diego State University, to organize, administer and teach in the Graduate School for Community Development, a private alternative educational institution working with low-income and people of color learners from communities around the U.S. She helped establish, with Dr. Pantoja, PRODUCIR, INC. She is a consulting editor for the *Journal of Progressive Human Services*.

Felix G. Rivera, D.S.W., is a Professor in the Department of Social Work Education, San Francisco State University where he Chairs and teaches in the Social Development Concentration. He also teaches social and evaluative research. Dr. Rivera has been a grass-roots organizer. He has worked with numerous community-based organizations as a planner, program developer and evaluator. His research and numerous publications range in subject from emerging and changing communities of color, and social change, to the application of Bushido (martial arts) strategies to community organizing and decision-making. He is a consulting editor for the journal from the National Association of Community Organization and Social Administration, the *Journal of Progressive Human Services* and the *Humboldt Journal of Social Relations*.

Vu-Duc Vuong, M.A., M.S.W., J.D., is the Executive Director and economic development specialist with the Southeast Asian Refugee Resettlement Center. He was born in Nam Dinh, Vietnam and came to the United States in 1968. Mr. Vuong is highly visible throughout the refugee communities in the San Francisco Bay Area both as an economic developer and social activist. Mr. Vuong was the first Vietnamese-American to run for political office in San Francisco, California.

Preface

Maybe it was the smells.

Perhaps even more than the sounds and sights, the neighborhoods where we grew up were defined by smells. Aromas of frying pork and plantains, simmering pasta and sausage announced a homecoming as we returned to our apartments after school or from a game of stick ball in the street.

The streets were alive with people and movement—playing, talking, walking, or just "hanging out." Children were admonished from front windows by observing parents, grandparents, aunts and uncles in Spanish, Italian, Yiddish or variously accented English. While not always delivered with a full appreciation for who had done what to whom, the comments on youthful misbehavior were delivered with commanding vigor and directness. It was some variant of "Stop, or else!" (and the "or else" was likely to be embarrassing, to hurt, or both). We didn't have much privacy, but each of us felt a deep and abiding sense of belonging.

We were privileged to see all different ages and kinds of people: very old and very young; tradespeople, winos, and numbers runners; brown, black, and white. The city blocks of the easily identified geography of our youth had natural rhythms of time and place. It made sense to us, and there was a power to it that we somehow shared.

The idea for this book has been part of each of us since the 1950s. Growing up in New York City's Spanish Harlem and Upper West Side, we did not know what special communities we shared. Indeed, it was the resurgence of community organization in the 1960s and 1970s and our own involvement in it—as organizers, consultants, and teachers—that led us to take a careful look at our roots. We recognized that these roots, despite the problems of poverty, racial conflict, and drugs, had been a major source of nurturance, strength, and validation for us both.

In each of our neighborhoods, part of what made them places of identity and empowerment were elements of ethnic solidarity. Aspects of religion, similarity of economic status, and life situation contributed to this solidarity. The contempt of more affluent surrounding communities also contributed to defensive, but supportive efforts of mutual aid.

There was a sense of continuity and meaning in these communities—a sense only rivaled by what we saw in the 1960s and 1970s (and knew to be there in the 1980s despite the lack of public recognition), and what we are now seeing as the 1990s emerge. In the most important sense, this book is about what communities of color are doing to protect their integrity and build their power. But it is also about two kids growing up with an immeasurable feeling that people can come together to enrich their lives and increase their influence with the forces that control their destinities.

Felix G. Rivera

John L. Erlich

CHAPTER ONE

Prospects and Challenges

FELIX G. RIVERA   JOHN L. ERLICH

Introduction

There was nobody we could talk to. If we had an idea or even a question, it was met with deaf ears. When you're up against the power structure, how can you get them to listen if they don't see you as equals?*

Waldo Rodriguez was describing the town he grew up and lived in with his family—Watsonville, California. Although about half the town's pre-earthquake (1989) population was Latino, the seven-member city council was all Anglo. Despite the efforts of 9 Latinos to win a place on the council between 1971 and 1985, not 1 was elected. After almost four years of organizing and litigating against the city for violating the Federal Voting Rights Act, the U.S. Supreme Court ruled that Watsonville's at-large elections discriminated against Latinos by diluting their voting power. Single-member voting districts would have to be drawn. However, the vast devastation caused by the earthquake hit the poor Latino community hardest, with hundreds leaving and many remaining homeless more than a year later. A renewed organizing effort is now underway. But if the recent past is a reasonable predictor of the near future, this organizing effort will go largely undocumented and unrewarded.

Indeed, there is very little written material available to guide such efforts among people of color. A book on community organizing with people of color does not seem to exist. The reasons for this deficiency are multiple, complex, and interwoven. Racism—political, economic, and social—is at the core of the problem.

---

*Sacramento Bee, April 2, 1989

1

A community-based program, The Center for Third World organizing in Oakland, California has put together a resource manual consisting of a variety of papers looking at the tactics and techniques of organizing.

Some of the papers address communities of color. Although the manual is not specific to social workers' concerns, it is an excellent example of the kinds of material available from grassroots organizations. The document may be obtained by writing the center at 3861 Martin Luther King Jr. Way, Oakland, CA 94609.

At the same time, societal interest in the problems of the poor has sharply declined, especially in the 1980s. Despite all the research evidence to the contrary, the disenfranchised are again being forced to bear the major burden for their oppression. The problems of drug abuse, crime, inadequate housing, alcoholism, AIDS, teen pregnancy, and underemployment have had their most devastating impact on poor communities of color. The lack of resources to combat these problems falls most heavily on the same people. The growing national debt has served conservative forces well as an excuse for not meeting the urgent need to expand services in these areas.

As if their many problems and needs were not enough, the incredibly dramatic population increases is sobering testimony to the daunting challenges ahead for us all. Census Bureau preliminary reports show an increase in all populations of color. Out of a total of over 248 million people in the United States, almost 30 million are African American, representing 23 percent of the total population and an increase of 64.6 percent over the 1980 Census figures. Native Americans, Eskimos, and Aleuts share .08 percent of the population with almost two million people, representing an increase of 33.7 percent from the last census. Asian and Pacific Islanders, over seven million strong, represent an increase of 144.9 percent from 1980, with their 2.9 percent representation; Latinos share 8.9 percent of the population with over 22 million people, an increase of 87.3 percent from the 1980 census.[7, 8]

These figures are far from being fixed. A heated debate is going on about the problems of undercounting, especially in communities of color. The Census Oversight Committee claims that over two million African Americans have not been counted. They state that the undercount is between 5.5 percent and 6.5 percent, compared to an undercount of 5.2 percent in 1980. Other critics of the Census claim the undercount is as high as nine million people. Whatever the final count will be, these statistics are a reminder of the enormous amount of work that needs to be done by agents of social work. The challenge is unparalleled in this nation's history.[2]

The government's pro-Contra and anti-Salvadorian rebel role in Central America, the invasions of Grenada and Panama, and the vast commitment to the Persian Gulf, however justified they may have been, have contributed to a decline in our commitment to racial equality. In a curious twist of logic, the withdrawal of support for communities of color at home is partly justified by resources demanded abroad because peoples of color cannot manage their own affairs.

Our priorities in foreign affairs, along with a realignment of domestic preferences has sharply reduced not only support for community-based human services but the resources necessary to provide training for people to work in these services as well. One result is decreased interest in and demand for trailing in community organization and community development. In many cases, the rhetoric of working along multicultural lines has been a smoke screen to avoid funding programs for desperately underserved ethnic enclaves. All too many joint police and community antidrug efforts, for example, make good copy for the six o'clock news while deflecting public attention away from underlying problems of poverty and racism.

The fact that community organization has been the most resistant of the social work methods to consistent definition has further exacerbated this situation. As Erlich and Rivera have noted, community organization has evolved from being the general rubric under which all social work practice beyond the level of individual, family, and small group was subsumed—including grassroots organizing, community development, planning, administration, and policy-making—to being the smallest sub-segment of macro level practice (where it exists at all). This definitional difficulty is well-illustrated by one of the better contemporary definitions of community organization:

> *Community Development* refers to efforts to mobilize people who are directly affected by a community condition (that is, the "victims," the unaffiliated, the unorganized, and the nonparticipating) into groups and organizations to enable them to take action on the social problems and issues that concern them. A typical feature of these efforts is the concern with building new organizations among people who have not been previously organized to take social action on a problem.[10, 20]

However, by any definition, it was not until the 1960s that large numbers of schools of social work were willing to regard it as a legitimate concentration. Majors in community organization in graduate schools increased from 85 in 1960 to 1,125 in 1969, or from 1.5 percent to over 9 percent of full-time enrollments.[11]

By 1989, the number of students nationwide training to work as organizers had declined significantly. The Council on Social Work Education's most recent statistics demonstrate that there were 154 master's degree students (1.8%) in Community Organization and Planning, 417

(4.9%) in Administration and Management, and 101 (1.2%) in a combination of C.O. and Planning with Administration or Management. Given the fact that there are now many more schools of social work than in 1960, the trends do not augur well for community organizing. Despite growing acceptance as a legitimate area of study in social work, urban planning, and labor studies, community organization and planning has been held hostage by the political and social vagaries of a society that has never accepted its strategies as tactics, especially if methods like public demonstrations and boycotts caused disruptive embarrassment to those in positions of political authority and power.[24]

From an educational standpoint, the result has been a diminished community organization curriculum—few field placement opportunities, few courses, and sparse literature. This is particularly surprising in light of the important, documented successes of community organization and development during the 1960s and early 1970s.[12]

Community organizing and community development by people of color have been virtually ignored. Isolated electives and rare articles in the professional journals have done little to fill this void. Work of a multicultural nature has received only slightly more attention. No book is available which addresses a broad range of the organizing efforts currently going forward in diverse minority communities. This book is a first effort to remedy that situation.

What is the status of community organization practice this book attempts to address? The civil rights gains of the 1960s in voting rights, public accommodations, and job opportunities, for example, were tempered by the belief that the African-American community had gone too far, that its gains were based on unacceptable levels of violence. Quickly forgotten by the white community was the continuing history of violence experienced by African Americans and other communities of color. "What more do they want?" was more than mere inflammatory rhetoric. These gains seemed to threaten white job security, community housing patterns, and long-cherished social interaction networks. The bitter residue of racism remains, and the resentment experienced throughout much of the United States has been part of the conservative backlash we are witnessing (as everything from Skinheads and antiminority high school violence to English-only public school curricula poignantly illustrates).

Similarly, efforts toward enfranchisement of new voters, changes in immigration laws, and women's and gay rights have also suffered from the schism between methods deemed acceptable and resulting "reasonable" benefits. As long as "someone else" did the social protesting, and as long as it was far enough away from their homes and places of work, most white people did not complain actively, or publicly resist slow, nondisruptive changes.

A concomitant shift has marked the reluctant acceptance of the "worthy" among each ethnic minority (largely dependent on whose economic interests are being threatened) while at the same time rejecting those without education, job skills, or at high risk for drug problems and sexually transmitted diseases.

Not surprisingly, with the emergence of reverse discrimination as a legitimate response to the enfranchisement of people of color, a new consciousness permeated schools of social work whose espoused philosophy was that of commitment to aiding poor and oppressed populations. It was no longer fashionable to invite a Black Panther as a speaker for a seminar on social action, or a Young Lord from New York's Puerto Rican community to discuss how they initiated the movement against lead poisoning in New York's slum tenements, or have Angela Davis address the systematic exclusion of women of color by the women's movement in key policy and strategy sessions. Instead, the invited ethnic "leaders" tended to focus on issues like creatively funded drug education programs, multicultural day-care and pre-school efforts, and the demographics of rapidly expanding minority populations around the country.

As funding sources evaporated, people of color began being relegated to the not-so-symbolic back of the bus once again. The rapacity with which affirmative action was attacked became trendy. Ethnic studies programs were closed or cut back at alarming rates throughout the country and many community-based agencies in ethnic areas were forced to close their doors. The Supreme Court's chipping away at civil rights legislation seemed to be a culmination of much of the backlash being experienced.

People of Color and Organizing: A Troubled Alliance

Why has community organization not been more successful in working with people of color? What happened to some of the cross-cultural efforts that appeared to be so productive in the 1960s and early 1970s. Traditionally, much of the writing on community organization attempts to be color blind. Organizers work with specific strategies and tactics applied to different situations, but the methods that combine them rarely—if ever—change.[5, 13]

Alinsky's mobilization model is a good case in point (Horwitt 1989). Too often the level of analysis of a community's problems has been determined by an organizing strategy that identifies a particular strata of people or social problem for intervention. By doing so, the racial and cultural uniqueness of the community is ignored. These organizers are not conservative or even liberal community organizers but well-intentioned, progressive thinkers who have been victimized by what may be termed "organizers' myopia" because of their single-minded organizing ideology or preordained methodology.[19]

One thing that becomes readily apparent in the chapters in this book is the absence of an easily identified "radical" or "progressive" ideology along class lines. That does not mean the book is apolitical; far from it. What it does point out, however, is the fact that issues surrounding race, culture, and their attendant problems are often more urgent concerns than social class that has often been historically conceptualized by white theoreticians apart from the dynamics deemed more critical to the self-determination of communities of color by communities of color. Middle-class Asians, Latinos, or African Americans are still viewed as minorities because of a most easily identifiable characteristic: skin color. Good clothes and an elegant briefcase are not much help when you need a cab in the middle of the night in Chicago or Washington, D.C.

People of color have traditionally been caught between the polarized struggles of conservative and liberal theoretical forces. Too many liberal community organizers have emphasized class issues at the expense of racism and cultural chauvinism, relegating them to "logical" extensions of the political and economic structure. Much of the neo-Marxist literature has treated race from a reductive, negative posture: "super-exploitation", and the "divide and conquer" strategies of individual capitalist employers. On the other hand, many conservative thinkers have emphasized a kind of uniqueness of each community which divides it from other communities of color, as well as separating those who can "make it" from those who cannot.[3, 21, 26]

These perspectives largely disregarded many questions, including the fact that racism existed long before monopoly capitalism was institutionalized. The logic fortunes of race relations are not necessarily coterminous with those of capitalism, as the persistence of racial antagonism in post-capitalist societies (like Sweden) demonstrates. The structural analysis that leads to a unified ideological interpretation of racism is thus deficient.

What too many organizers fail to consider is that there appears to be little or no history or contemporary evidence to substantiate that relations established and legitimated on the basis of race were or are identical to those established and legitimated on the basis of class. For example, the increasing violence against students of color on our college campuses cannot be explained primarily as a class phenomenon, especially when one recognizes that many of these students of color are economically similar to the white students attacking them. By continuing to look at racism as a mostly broad structural issue, organizers are underestimating the roles played by schools, churches, social welfare agencies, and other institutions in negatively influencing and changing race relations.

How might we best define the equality and liberation struggles being waged by the African-American communities? The Native-American communities? The Chinese-American and Vietnamese communities? The communities of women of color? The immediate reaction of most oppressors is based on skin color and other physical characteristics, language, culture, and lastly, class. The oversimplification of the struggles of people of color has led to unwarranted generalizations about their economic, social, political, and cultural behaviors and attitudes as groups.

Writers criticize the tendency of mainstream and radical theorists to divide society into separate domains culturally and structurally. They argue that this arbitrary bifurcation promotes tendencies toward essentialism (single-cause explanations) in contemporary thinking about race. Race and culture cannot be separated as "things in themselves."[25] They have to be linked to other social processes and dynamics operating in a society that continues oppressing communities because of skin tone. At least three dynamics—race, class, and gender—are significant in understanding oppression and the roles played by social welfare institutions in that process. None are reducible to the others, and class is not necessarily paramount.[25, 18]

The phenomenological day-to-day realities of race, language, class, gender, and age help to shape ideological perspectives and give force to the hostilities with which one lives (as well as the strengths that make survival possible). The resulting process is difficult to analyze because it manifests itself differently from one community to another across the country, thereby making the task of organizing against these attacks that much more difficult a challenge. These realities do not lend themselves easily to simply categorizations by agents of social change or schools teaching community organization practice. The need for a more integrated and receptive social change paradigm in working with communities of color must be a main goal of organizers.

The conservative tradition in community organizing—especially within social work education—has also had an impact on the way organizers of color and their communities view the political implications of the social change efforts in which they have been involved. The conventional perspective that education should be ideologically value-free and politically nonpartisan has been especially evident in community organizing. Typical textbooks on organizing have avoided clear political and moral positions on issues.[9, 27] These books were guided by a "professional" and largely mechanistic value base.

Fisher[11] notes:

The social work tradition views the community essentially as a social organism; it focuses on social issues such as building a sense of community, gathering together social service organizations, or lobbying for and delivering social resources. It assumes that basically the community's problem is social disorganization. The organizer functions either as an "enabler" to help the community gather itself together or as an advocate to secure additional services for the community. The strategy is gradualist and consensual, which means that organizers assume a unity of interest between the power structure and the neighborhood and assume a willingness of at least some in power to meet community needs.

In contrast, Freire proposes:

> ... one cannot be a social worker and be like the educator who's a coldly neutral technician. To keep our options secret, to conceal them in the cobwebs of technique, or to disguise them by claiming neutrality does not constitute neutrality; quite the contrary, it helps maintain the status quo.

Many professors of macro practice still resist the systematic inclusion of discussions on analyzing power and confrontational empowerment, the development of critical consciousness and racism as fundamental components of community organization. The lack of attention to critical consciousness—that is, how personal and political factors interact with each other and one's work, as well as how values, ideas, and practice skills are influenced by social forces and, in turn, influence them—is both particularly noteworthy and undermining. This neoconservative stance has had the net effect of leaving students of color (as well as white students) confused about their potential roles in their communities and how far they might go in fighting racism and social injustices.

While the rhetoric of self-determination implies that students are intended to be agents of social change, the reality clearly calls for modest improvements that do not seriously upset the status quo. The tools that might help lead to more fundamental change through a thorough questioning of what is happening and what it means to a community and a person working there are largely absent from the curriculum. Indeed, as a totality, the picture is not very promising.[14]

A Paradigm for Organizing With People of Color

The different racial and cultural characteristics present in oppressed and disadvantaged communities represent an unprecedented challenge to organizers of the 1990s. We are defining culture as a collection of behaviors and beliefs that constitute "standards for deciding what is, standards for deciding what can be, standards for deciding how one feels about it, standards for deciding what to do about it, and standards for deciding how to go about doing it." A recent history of benign or belligerent neglect has required people of color to mobilize their skills and limited resources in creative ways that challenge prevailing community programs. Although they get little attention or help from mainstream society—indeed, in some areas, overt opposition is more typical—many of those communities are trying to tackle their problems with strategies unique to their situations.[17]

For example, the African-American community of West Oakland, California has attacked the drug problem head-on, with many community leaders making themselves visible enemies of major dealers. Also, nearby, an African-American first-grade teacher has promised to pay for the college education of her entire first-grade class if they maintain a "C" average and go on to college. The teacher annually saves $10,000 from her modest salary for this fund. In the rural mountains of Eastern Puerto Rico there is an exciting revitalization of the community through an energetic community development program. Southeast Asian communities in Boston, New York, Houston, and San Francisco have organized legal immigration and refugee task forces to help fight the arbitrary deportation of undocumented workers. Derelict neighborhoods in New York, Chicago, and Philadelphia are being revitalized through cooperatives and community development activities. Native-American tribes are attacking problems of alcoholism through indigenous healing rituals which utilize the sweat lodge ceremony as its core. Success rates are often dramatic. In the village of Akhiok, Alaska 90 percent of its adults were chronically drunk. After Native treatments, at least 80 percent were able to sustain sobriety. The Latino community in Boston has a very successful grassroots health program called "Mujeres Latina en Action which has successfully integrated Third World health models that include the concept of the extended family in health care delivery systems. A cultural- and gender-sensitive model of community organization is used to reach women in the barrios.

Traditionally, communities of color have not been involved in issues related to ecology and the protection of the environment. For many neighborhoods, these are among the last priorities when the many problems people face are listed. However, one example bears special attention for it may well be a model for similar actions across the country. In California's East Los Angeles, which is predominantly Mexican American/Chicano, a group of Latina mothers was organized by a parish priest in the mid 1980s into militant urban ecologists. They call themselves Mothers of East Los Angeles. They have successfully mobilized against threats to their community, such as (1) the construction of a state prison in a residential area near neighborhood schools, (2) an above-ground oil pipeline that would have cut through their middle-to-low income barrio while avoiding much more

affluent coastal towns, (3) the local use of dangerous and potentially pollut-
ing pesticides, and (4) local construction of a large incinerator. They believe
in peaceful tactics and wear white kerchiefs as a symbol of their nonviolent
philosophy. They are often seen pushing strollers during demonstrations,
and they lobby the state capitol, engage in letter writing, and serve as paceset-
ters of a growing environmental movement in the Los Angeles area among
people of color.

From an ethnic sensitive practice perspective, organizing strategies in
the Vietnamese or Laotian communities (and with different ethnic groups
within these communities) cannot be the same as in Puerto Rican, African-
American, Native American or Japanese-American enclaves. The experience of one of the editors illustrates this point. In the early 1970s he was
organizing in a Mexican-American barrio. One of the outcomes of the
struggle was the establishment of a storefront information and referral center. In furnishing and decorating the center, several political and cultural
posters were displayed—much to the anger of some of the viejitos (elders) in
the neighborhood. One particular poster featured Emiliano Zapata, and the
staff was told in no uncertain terms that the poster had to come down because
Zapata was still perceived as an enemy. Several fathers of the viejitos had
fought against Zapata during the Mexican Revolution! Although the editor is
a Latino, he is not of Mexican decent. However, he does know the conflicting
loyalties of Mexico's revolutionary history and should have checked with the
community to be sure none of the posters would be offensive. This apparently
innocuous mistake set the organizing effort back many months and required
the staff to work doubly hard to regain the community's confidence.

Unfortunately, the history of organizing is replete with such examples.
Certainly organizers of color must accept a share of the blame. However, the
overwhelming majority of organizing writers and practitioners are white
males, many of whom come from liberal or radical traditions, and who most
often got their theoretical and practice feet wet in the social upheavals of the
1960s. Their apparent successes seemed destined to be color blind. From a
community perspective, white radical groups were often more enamored of
their political ideologies than they were committed to the needs of minority
neighborhoods. The Detroit-based battles of African-Americans within the
United Auto Workers is a prime example. Frequently hovering on the fringes
were white radical groups looking to make the struggle their own. They were
very critical of the efforts of people of color, accusing them of being culturally
nationalistic and methodically not progressive enough. Too often we forget
that experiencing racism, economic deprivation and social injustice are the
key relevant politicizing forces in most urban areas. Indeed, it was this kind
of elitist attitude that caused many minority organizers to shy away from pre-
determined ideological postures that seemed to define peoples *for* them.

Even many liberal white groups seemed to disdain poor whites in favor of more visible organizing efforts in communities of color.

Thus, it is not sufficient to identify the three classic (and presumably "color blind") models of community practice—locality development, social planning, and social action—as being the foundation within which community organizing with people of color takes place. Factors that must be addressed are (1) the racial, ethnic, and cultural uniqueness of people of colors; (2) the implications of these unique qualities in relation to such variables as the roles played by kinship patterns, social systems, power and leadership networks, religion, the role of language (especially among subgroups), and the economic and political configuration within each community; and (3) the process of empowerment and the development of critical consciousness. (This is in contrast to what Freire has called "naive consciousness," or a tendency to romanticize intense, satisfying past events and force the same experiences into the future without taking fully into account such multidimensional elements as those noted above.) In addition, the physical setting within which the community finds itself is an essential component for consideration as it plays a significant part in the way people view their situation. The need for a new, revised paradigm is clear and urgent.[22, 15]

One of the most critical factors affecting organizing outcomes hinges on determining how strategies and tactics are played out based on the nature and intensity of contact and influence will help to determine the constraints placed on the organizers' (whether indigenous or an outsider) knowledge and identification with the community, and when and how technical skills may be brought into play. This "meta approach" will help organizers arrange their strategies and tactics within parameters that are goal, task, skill, and process specific. We suggest that the degree and nature of contacts is a three-tier process which—for sake of simplicity—may be conceptualized as contact intensity and influence at the primary, secondary, and tertiary levels of community development (see Figure 1-1).

The primary level of involvement is most immediate and personal with the community. It is that level that requires racial, cultural, and linguistic identity. The primary level of contact intensity and influence is the most intimate level of community involvement where the only way of gaining entry into the community is to have full ethnic solidarity with the community. For example, this would not be possible for a Chinese American in a Vietnamese or African-American area.

The secondary level consists of contact and influence that is one step removed from personal identification with the community and its problems. Language—although a benefit and help—is not absolutely mandatory. Many of the functions are those of liaison with the outside community and

Community Levels

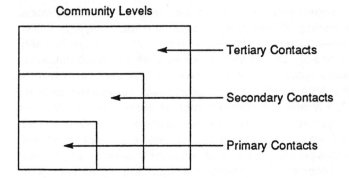

FIGURE 1-1   •   *Organizer's Contact Intensity and Influence*

institutions, and service as a resource with technical expertise based on the culturally unique situations experienced by the community. Examples of persons able to work at this level include a Puerto Rican in a Mexican American neighborhood or a person identified as Haitian in an African-American area.

The tertiary level is that of the outsider working for the common interests and concerns of the community. Cultural or racial similarity is not a requirement. The responsibilities of these organizers will see them involved primarily with the outside infrastructures as an advocate and broker for communities of color. However, their tasks are less that of liaison and more of a helpful technician approaching or confronting outside systems and structures. Clearly, whites and nonsimilar people of color may be particularly effective at this level.

The issue over whether or not organizers should be part of the racial and cultural group with whom they work has been given much attention within and outside communities of color. Alinsky and his Industrial Area Foundation organizers were often in the middle of this question. However, a careful review of these efforts suggests that in most cases, indigenous organizers played key roles in the success of their organizations. Thus, it seems imperative that if communities or color are to empower themselves by giving more than symbolic recognition to the ideal of self-determination and community control, then we must search hard for the successful roles played by people within their own communities and the lessons they can teach outside organizers. Furthermore, many emerging communities of color are underrepresented in the society's infrastructure because their languages and customs make them especially difficult to approach. In the emerging Southeast Asian communities, there are nationalities, ethnic and subethnic groups whose cultures are quite different from one another and where there exists an assortment of languages, dialects, and idioms. An outside organizer simply does not stand a chance of gaining rapid access to such unique and insular community groups. Even the Native American nations, it should be remembered, speak over 200 different languages. Clearly, special care must be taken in recruiting people to work in widely varied Indian communities— on reservations and rancherias, in both rural and urban areas.[6, 10, 12,19]

The knowledge necessary to understand and appreciate customs and traditions in all communities is an incredible challenge. Organizing and social change strategies are complex and stress-inducing enough without further exacerbating the community's problems by having organizers who have very limited (or no) awareness of the customs, traditions, and languages of these communities. That is not to say that persons without some of this knowledge cannot fulfill certain important functions; for indeed, they have served and should continue to serve effectively in secondary and tertiary roles. But we must emphasize that the most successful organizers are those individuals who know their culture intimately: its subtleties of language, mores, and folkways. A white outsider, however sensitive and knowledgeable, simply cannot appreciate all that needs to be considered about a fundamentally different nonwhite culture or subculture. Some newly emerging communities are so well defended that there would be little chance for an outsider to gain meaningful admission to them, not to mention becoming a successful organizer. However, it must be very clear that cultural and racial similarity—by themselves—are no guarantor of organizer effectiveness or community acceptance. Indeed, an arrogant, know-it-all insider may be viewed with more suspicion than a similarly styled outsider.[16]

Despite these difficulties, there are common practice elements that may be identified as prerequisite to successful organizing. These principles are not exhaustive, but if organizers take command of these elements, they can increase the likelihood of being effective change agents in their communities. Knowing when and how to mix and phase these strategies and skill areas is critical to the successful outcome of a struggle. Organizing has to be conceptualized as a process that is educational both for the community and the organizers.

Organizer's Profile

What follows is a summary of those qualities—knowledge, skill, attributes, and values—that are most important in contributing to the success of organizers. It is recognized that the list is an idealized one in the sense that those few who have already fully attained the lofty heights described can probably also walk on water. Realistically, it is a set of goals to be used by organizers and communities together to help achieve desired changes. The careful reader will also note that many of these qualities are addressed by each contributor in describing a particular community. Illustrations and examples of parts of this "model-in-progress" may be found throughout the chapters which follow.

1. Similarly cultural and racial identification. The most successful organizers are those activists who can identify with their communities culturally, racially, and liniguistically. There is no stronger identification with a community than truly being a part of it.

2. Familiarity with customs and traditions, social networks, and values. This dimension of organizing stresses the importance of having a thorough grounding in the customs and traditions of the community being organized. This is especially critical for those people who have cultural, racial, and linguistic identification, but who, for a variety of reasons, have been away from that community and are returning as organizers.

For example, how have the dynamics between organized religion and the community changed throughout the years? Ignored, its effect may imperil a whole organizing effort. Both the definition of the problems and the setting of goals to address them are involved. A number of Latino mental health and advocacy programs regularly consult with priests, ministers, and folk healers about the roles they all play (or might play) in advocating for mental health needs. These mental health activities are very clear about the importance of these other systems—formal and informal—in the community's spiritual life. The superstitions and religious archetypes are addressed by a variety of representatives, thereby making the advocacy work that much more relevant and effective. The Native American nations give deference to their medicine man, with no actions being taken until he has given approval. Similarly, the Vietnamese, Cambodian, and Laotian communities have strong religious leaders who help to define community commitments and directions.

All too often, there exists a cultural gap, as typified by younger, formally educated organizers working with community elders. The elders may be too conservative for the young organizers, or they disagree about tactics. Knowledge of and appreciation for the culture and traditions will help close the gap among key actors, or at least reduce the likelihood of unnecessary antagonisms.

3. An intimate knowledge of language and subgroup slang. We separate this dimension from the one just mentioned to emphasize its importance. Knowledge of a group's language style is indispensable when working with communities that are bi-or monolingual. Many embarrassing

situations have arisen because of the organizer's ignorance of a community's language style. Approved idiomatic expressions in one area of the community may be totally unacceptable in another. Some expressions have sexual overtones in one community while being inoffensive to other communities. Certain expressions may denote a class bias which may be offensive to one group of people or another. The literature on sociolinguistics has done an excellent job in alerting us to the importance of language subtleties and nuances. For a discussion on the role played by the same language in culturally different populations see Harrison.[18]

4. Leadership styles and development. Organizers must be leaders and lead organizers, but they must also work with existing community leaders and help in training emerging leadership. We recognize that there are significant differences in leadership styles from one community of color to another. Many of these issues are addressed in the chapters throughout this book. Indispensable to the composition of a successful leader is the individual's personality, how the individual's roles fit within the organizing task, and how personal values help to shape a world view. However achieved, a leader should have a sense of power that may be used in a respectful manner within the community.

5. An analytical framework for political and economic analysis. This is one dimension where the understanding of the dynamics of oppression through class analysis is paramount. A sophisticated knowledge of political systems with access and leverage points is very important. It must include an appraisal of who has authority within the ethnic community as well as who in it has power (often less formally acknowledged). The sources of mediating influence between the ethnic community and wider communities also must be understood. This knowledge fulfills two needs: (1) it helps to give the organizer the necessary analytical perspective in judging where the community fits in the hierarchy of economic analysis, and (2) it serves as a tool for educating the community, thereby increasing the community's consciousness of the roles and functions of the organizer within broader economic and social systems.[23]

6. Knowledge of past organizing strategies, their strengths, and limitations. It is imperative that organizers learn how to structure their organizing activities within an historical framework. This framework helps them to look at those strategies and tactics that have succeeded and failed in each community in the past. Since so little knowledge-building is evident in the field, it is critical that organizers develop and share an historical knowledge base that helps identify the many mistakes made to finally illuminate those techniques that appeared to have recently worked best in similar situations.

7. Skills in conscientization and empowerment. A major task of the organizer in disenfranchised communities is that of empowering people

through the process of developing critical consciousness. How the personal and political influence each other, and the local environment in which they are played out, is a key to this process. It is not enough to succeed in ameliorating or even solving community problems if there is little or no empowerment of the community.

At the same time, power must be understood as both a tool and part of a process by the organizer. As Rubin and Rubin write ". . . community organizations need not focus exclusively on campaigns to achieve specific goals; they can make building their own power a long-term effort." Power may be destructive or productive in the sense of germinating ideas and concerns, and being integrative, or community-building. Of course, power is typically experienced in poor communities as both a negative and positive. The kind of power which is based on threats is often the most common in disenfranchised areas. When Organizer A makes the Target B act in ways it does not wish to act solely because of the sanctions A can levy against B, typically this becomes an imposed "win-lose" situation. A limited special hiring program usually takes this form.[23]

Power may also be a form of exchange, when Organizer A and Target B involve themselves in a reciprocal relationship or exchange because both parties have something to win from the process. Exchange is an integrative component of power because it involves some degree of trust, where the final outcome may be "win-win." Coalition building often takes this form. Power may also be defined as love—love for community, lifestyle, or family—which should motivate an organizer and the community.

Organizers and communities need to view each other as subjects rather than objects, as learners, and as equals. No organizer should enter a community with a sense that she or he has "the" answers for it. The development of critical consciousness through the process of conscientization may be visualized as a double spiraling helix, where both the organizer and community learn from each other the problems at hand and the strategies and tactics employed.[4]

The phenomenology of the experience is based on praxis, the melding of theory and experience, for both parties which in turn makes them stronger actors because their learning is mutual, supportive, and liberating of any preconceived notions one had about the other.

8. Skills in assessing community psychology. Organizers need to learn about the psychological makeup of their communities—free from stereotypes. Scant attention has been paid to this knowledge area by most community organizers. Methodologies without the understanding of the motivations of the community are a risky undertaking.

Organizers also need to understand what tends to keep a community allied and synergized. What is the life cycle of the community? Is it growing,

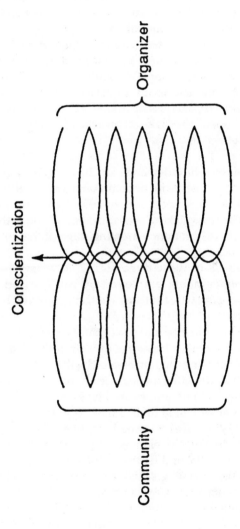

FIGURE 1-2 • Development of Critical Consciousness

mature, or declining? Are there new arrivals? Have they been in the community for generations? Does their language work as a cohesive force, or because of the multigenerational patterns, serve as a problem in getting people together? If the community has experienced a failure recently (like the loss of a valued school), what has it done to the shared psychological identification of the community? Does it feel frustrated and powerless? Or has it served to focus anger? If the latter is the case, what strategies may be employed to mobilize the community to action?

9. Knowledge of organizational behavior and decision making. Knowledge about organizational behavior and decision making are critical to the success of an organizer. The work of Bachrach and Baratz around decisionless decisions and nondecisions as decisions has demonstrated its worth in the field. Decisionless decisions are those decision-making strategies that "just happen" and "take off on a life of their own." Nondecisions as decisions are defined as:

> . . . a means by which demands for change in the existing allocation of benefits and privileges in the community can be suffocated before they are even voiced or kept covert; or killed before they gain access to the relevant decision-making arena; or, fail all these things, maimed or destroyed in decisionimplementing stage of the policy process.[1]

An awareness of these dynamics is necessary both to be able to ascertain strategies being employed by the institutions targeted for change, but also, as a tactic that may also be employed by the community in its organizing.

10. Skills in evaluative and participatory research. One of the reasons communities of color have lost some of their political, economic, and legal victories is the increasing vacuum created by the lack of supportive information that has kept up with growing social problems experienced by most communities. Many communities are being victimized by data and demographics that have redefined their situations in manageable terms as far as the traditional systems are concerned. There needs to be an expanded role for organizers to include developing skills in demographic and population projections, and in social problem analysis. More organizers should develop theories about the declining social, economic, and political base of communities of color, and how people are still managing to survive in times of open hostility and encroachment on their civil rights and liberties. Crime, including drugs, is a major arena for these pressures.

Research continues to be an indispensable and very powerful tool for social change. Organizers should pay special attention to the use of participatory approaches, where both researchers and community people are involved as equal participants in securing knowledge to empower the community.*

Skill in evaluation research is another indispensable tool for organizers. The editors are not just suggesting that evaluative research be used only to assess program outcomes, but more to analyze the success and value of different organizing strategies and their relevance in disparate situations.

11. Skills in program planning and development and administration management. One of the bitter lessons learned from the War on Poverty had to do with the setup for failure nature of the administrative jobs offered to many people of color. Most had little or no administrative or managerial experience. One of the editors, then little-experienced was offered a position that required him to administer a four-county migrant education and employment training program. With crash courses on organizational behavior, information processing, and budgeting, the challenge was met, but there were many mistakes along the way. Needless to say, the mistakes were widely reported by the program's detractors and administrator's enemies.

Many administrators of color have fallen by the wayside because they had not been given the opportunity to sharpen their managerial skills, and thus, a self-fulfilling prophecy of incompetence was validated in the eyes of people who desired to see these programs fail. Organizers must be aggressive in seeking out this knowledge base and not be deterred by the institutional barriers—financial, political, or otherwise—to attaining it.

12. An awareness of self and personal strengths and limitations. Reading through the list above may raise the question, "Does such a super-organizer possessing all the enumerated skills and knowledge exist?" The answer is both yes and no.

There are people throughout the country with these skills, and many who have most of them. We ask that organizers of color know their limitations and struggle to improve themselves. Organizers must know when to seek help, when to share responsibilities, and when to step aside to let others take over. Conversely, skilled and knowledgeable organizers must be open to sharing their expertise with communities and community leaders, especially when such sharing may mean their departure can be that much sooner.

A successful organizer is that individual who gains respect within the context of the actions being taken, not the individual who is (or appears to be) more knowledgeable than another. Honest intentions and abilities are

---

*For example, an entire issue of the *Community Development Journal* was devoted to participatory research and evaluation, thus stressing its international importance in working with disenfranchised and oppressed communities (1988).

worth more than degrees. Organizers also need to understand how to react to stresses. We all have our ways of coping with conflict. We need to know when our coping is no longer working for us, thereby jeopardizing the community. The danger of burnout is too well-documented to be ignored.

Finally, we would like to caution against "doing it *for* the community." Not only is this counter-productive, but it also increases the risk of feeling that one is being eaten alive by the people with whom one is working. All too often this results in another abandonment of a community whose experiences with social services have been much more of good rhetoric than serious social change.

The Readings

The next 10 chapters, written by 15 people of color, represent a wide panorama of history, oppression, and social problems, and organizing and development experienced by their respective communities. While some might be inclined to argue that this book would have been more coherent if each author rigorously followed a standardized outline, the editors have taken a different view. Each contributor (or contributing team) was invited to direct attention to the following areas: (1) the historical context of social problems in the community about which they were writing—including their nature, magnitude, and severity; (2) the current state of affairs in their communities—from a personal rather than objective point of view; (3) what they anticipate happening in this community over the next two-to-five years, especially as it may impact community organization efforts; and (4) whatever final conclusions the writer(s) might wish to offer.

Rather than creating a book weakened by a lack of parallel composition across chapters, the mosaic that follows is strengthened by the rich and unique approaches taken by the contributors. Unlike Oscar Lewis, who believed that poor people were largely the same through his misguided notion of the "culture of poverty," the authors offer a diverse canvas of problems, hopes, dreams, and actions experienced by individual communities.

The authors have placed each communities social problems within an historical context that is political, social, and economic. The structural, leadership, power, fiscal, and human issues that have been responsible for making their communities what they are today are analyzed. They address what they see as the strategies for change in the future: the most effective ways of dealing with their communities' problems and the implications these problems have for community organization practice and, where relevant, social work education.

Chapter 2, "Community Development Among American Indians," by E. Daniel Edwards and Margie Egbert-Edwards presents a structure for working with Native Americans whose values reflect a cultural sensitivity that is necessary to effective organizing with any Native American tribe. They discuss the impact that colonization has had on their communities with special emphasis being given to the roles played by extermination, expulsion, exclusion (the reservation system), and assimilation. The need for self-determination is assessed with examples of how Indian groups are working with their people.

A model for community development is introduced, with special emphasis being given to the identification with "Indianness." They discuss the dynamics of understanding and implementing the community organization process with examples of successful programs in a variety of settings and tribes. The authors conclude by discussing what they consider to be the common characteristics of successful American Indian community development programs, ways of overcoming barriers to change, and a plan for the future.

"Chicanos, Communities and Change," Chapter 3, was written by Miguel Montiel and Felipe de Ortega y Gasca. The authors analyze the nature of change within the context of the Chicano experiences and community. They put the Chicano experience within an historical perspective, discussing the roles played by community-based organizations in sustaining the Chicano ethos. They assess the movement away from community-based organizations to "profession-centered organizations" and the roles these emerging organizations will play in the Chicano communities in the 1990s and beyond.

They assess and reevaluate the continuity of change in Chicano communities by considering the contributions made to that assessment by the difficulties in sustaining meaningful organizations and change, and the importance dialogue must play in creating organizations, jobs, and the development of a courageous vision of action.

Wynetta Devore is author of Chapter 4, "The African-American Community of 1990: The Search for a Practice Method." Devore sets the tone of the African-American experience from the mid-1950s to the present. The role played by social class in community organizing is analyzed by the author, linking it to values and expectations in the community. The dynamics of an emerging leadership, with attendant political ideologies and strategies for change are discussed. The dilemmas confronting African-American communities in the 1990s are presented, with special emphasis being given to political developments, social class, and the strength inherent in the communities.

Devore discusses what she sees as the "social work dilemma" in working with African-American communities, and she introduces a framework for African-American community work in the 21st Century, with special emphasis being given to social work values, community knowledge, social work knowledge in policies and services, self-awareness, and the role played by our own ethnicity. How the profession of social work should respond to new economic realities is also considered.

Chapter 5, "Community Social Work with Puerto Rican Communities in the United States: One Organizer's Perspective," by Julio Morales, introduces the Puerto Rican community's political situation, and its ongoing relationships with the United States government. He discusses the roles played by ideology, values, and social change within the Puerto Rican community, along with the dynamics represented by culture and practice issues.

The significance of such attributes as respect, honor, dignity, and hospitality in the Puerto Rican community are assessed. Similarly, the nature of the extended family, "personalismo," "confianza," and "espiritismo" are analyzed with their importance to organizers evaluated. The dynamics of self-oppression are explored with a discussion of their negative outcomes and their implications for change. "Machismo," " 'marianismo, and other "isms" ' are considered, as well as the strengths inherent in the Puerto Rican community. Finally, Morales introduces the reader to the problems, programs, strategies, and tactics that should be employed by a successful agent for social change, strongly supported by case studies.

A critical look at the feminist movement and the reasons why women of color have been systematically excluded from significant policy-making arenas is taken in Chapter 6, "Feminist Organizing with Women of Color," by Lorraine Guitterez and Edith A. Lewis. They define what they mean by women of color, looking at ethnic, racial, social, political, and economic factors that have helped shape that definition. A distinction is made between the interests of women of color and men of color. Additionally, a feminist perspective is introduced, emphasizing power and powerlessness as an integral part of their perspective, and as a way for women of color to begin assessing their situation in the United States.

The authors define feminist organizing, introducing a model delineating its dynamics. Issues for feminists organizing with women of color are discussed, as is community organizing by women of color, richly illustrated by case examples. Finally, the authors end their chapter with a discussion of future directions for feminist organizing with women of color, listing practice principles that should be addressed.

Chapter 7, "The Chinese American: Community Organizing Strategies and Tactics," by Isaiah Lee portrays for readers the complex multigenerational world of the Chinese in the United States—from fresh off the boat to made in Taiwan, from Overseas Chinese to American Born Chinese. An illuminating historical introduction traces Chinese history from the 16th Century to the present. The author identifies two factors as being very important in keeping the Chinese Americans cohesive as a people: filial piety and family system values. He proceeds to analyze the most significant sociocultural, psychosocial, economic, and political characteristics that are experienced by the Chinese-American community. A discussion of the community's needs follow with suggestions for implementation. The importance and role played by organized religion is introduced, supported by a variety of case examples. In the conclusions and recommendations section, the author emphasizes the importance of social adjustment and cultural adaptation of individuals and families.

Kenji Murase introduces the reader to the socio-demographics of the Japanese in Chapter 8, "Community Organizations and Community Organizing Among the Japanese in the United States." A brief history follows the Japanese immigrants from 1880 to the present. The author points out that historically the Japanese in America had a tradition of establishing formal organizations for purposes of taking action to advocate their interests. The exclusion and internment period is presented and analyzed, including the rebuilding of the community at the end of World War II, with emphasis on the role of community organizations. The redress and reparations movement is also reviewed. Murase introduces some key theoretical perspectives in assessing the Japanese-American organizing experience. The roles played by such dynamics as accommodaton, exceptionalism, (the "model minority syndrome), racial subordination, and the political economy are presented, interwoven with themes of loyalty and patriotism.

The chapter closes with a discussion of problems and prospects for the future. Special attention is paid to the Sensitive issue of relationships with other Asian American communities. Also, the Japanese-American community has an obligation to extend its own boundaries in response to social problems and concerns that affect all Asian American communities.

Chapter 9, "Organizing in Central American Immigrant Communities in the United States," by Carlos B. Cordova, looks at the complex history of the El Salvadorian, Guatemalan, Nicaraguan, and Honduran communities in the United States. He analyzes those economic and political issues that have forced so many of these people to flee their homelands, and the role played by United States politics and the Immigration Naturalization Service. Cordova looks at the structure of Central American communities in the United States, how they function and survive. He analyzes the political power and influence in these communities and the reactions to threats by homeland opponents.

Cordova develops a model of empowerment using Paulo Freire's concept of critical consciousness. And the author looks at what needs to be done in the future in the areas of research, immigration reform, counseling services, education, and medical and mental health needs, especially addressing the problems associated with Post Traumatic Stress Syndrome. Finally, the limits of the literature on community organization with Central

American refugees and the need that exists in developing new models of practice in these areas is addressed, while organizers change and adapt existing models of community and economic development.

Vu-Duc Vuong and John Duong Huynh present a demographic profile of the Southeast Asian communities and the complexities that exist in working with them—both culturally and linguistically—in Chapter 10, "Southeast Asians in the United States: A Strategy for Accelerated and Balanced Integration." Migration patterns are traced and analyzed, beginning with the wealthy elites that left Viet Nam in the mid-1970s to the Boat People of more recent times.

Critical issues for these communities are addressed, dividing them into two main concerns: adaptation and maintenance issues. The importance of community building is discussed, and the authors present a strategy for accelerated and balanced integration into the mainstream of society. Examples of the kind of work being done with the diverse communities is also presented.

An innovative model of activist community development is presented by Antonia Pantoja and Wilhelmina Perry in Chapter Eleven, "Community Development/Community Restoration: A Perspective." They begin by defining what they mean by "community" and introduce a model of analysis that expedites the developmental process. The nature of dysfunctional communities and the implications this has for the community developer are explored. The authors identify the prerequisites to be a successful community development worker, and define their approach to community development/restoration. The major processes of community development are identified, supported by case studies. Inherent throughout these processes, the authors make clear, is the development of political awareness at the same time they are working in the organizing process. One cannot exist without the other.

The editors would like to make special note that a chapter on organizing in the Filipino community was commissioned. However, through a variety of unfortunate circumstances, it was not possible for the authors to complete the chapter in time for this publication. The editors deeply regret this important omission.

In a brief epilogue the editors offer their perspectives on the patterns, trends, and possibilities that have been illuminated by the authors. The diverse and unique histories, racial and ethnic differences, language and cultural patterns are synthesized into a model that addresses the similarities and differences experienced by the communities addressed by the authors, and the implications these have for successful organizing outcomes.

The editors look at the need for coalition building, with its attendant challenges and rewards. In conclusion, the international implications of the struggles by communities of color in the United States are made.

Summary

There is little doubt that the struggle to bring about significant social change at the community level is a Herculean task. Despite widely-heard political rhetoric to the contrary, the gates to social justice are sliding further shut— not open. Increasing numbers of people of color continue to be thrown into disadvantage and poverty—homeless, drug addicted, alcoholic, imprisoned, AIDS-infected, underemployed and unemployed, pushed out of deteriorating schools without marketable skills.

Community organization and development with people of color offers one small vehicle for battling to reverse this trend. The editors join the authors in the belief that organizers can make a difference. The work is not lucrative and is rarely romantic, but it can be critical in helping to meet peoples' needs. Perhaps above all it is about empowerment, an empowerment that organizer and community cna share.

As Zimmerman and Rappaport note:

> Empowerment is a construct that links individual strengths and competencies, natural helping systems, and proactive behaviors to matters of social change. It is thought to be the process by which individuals gain mastery or control over their own lives and democratic participation in the life of their community.[28]

Endnotes

1. P. Bachrach and M. S. Baratz, *Power and Poverty: Theory and Practice* (New York: Oxford University Press, 1970), 42.
2. Felicity Barringer, "Two Million Blacks Not Counted Head of Census Panel Asserts," *New York Times*, March 12, 1991, p. A5–A6.
3. R. Blauner, *Racial Oppression in America* (New York: Harper & Row, 1972), 29–42.
4. Kenneth Boulding, *Three Faces of Power* (Beverly Hills: Sage Pubs., 1989), 25.
5. H. Boyte, *The Backyard Revolution: Understanding the New Citizen Movement* (Philadelphia: Tremple, 1980).
6. S. Burghardt, *The Other Side of Organizing* (Cambridge, Mass.: Schenkman, 1982).
7. Census Bureau Press Release CB91-100, in *Census and You*. April, 1991, 3.
8. "Census Shows Profound Change In Racial Makeup of the Nation," By Felicity Barringer, *New York Times*, March 11th, 1991, A6–A9.
9. A. Dunham, *The New Community Organization* (New York: Crowell, 1970).
10. John L. Erlich and Felix G. Rivera, "Community Organization and Community Development," in N. Gilbert and H. Specht, *Handbook of the Social Services* (Englewood Cliffs, N.J.: Prentice Hall, 1981), 472–489.

11. R. Fisher, "Community Organization in Historical Perspective: A Typology," *The Huston Review* (Summer 1984), 8.

12. R. Fisher, *Let the People Decide: Neighborhood Organizing in America*, (Boston: Twaynne, 1984).

13. G. Frederickson, *Neighborhood Control in the 1970s* (New York: Chandler, 1970).

14. P. Freire, *Education for Critical Consciousness* (New York: Seabury, 1973).

15. Paulo Freire, *The Politics of Education: Culture, Power and Liberation* (Massachusetts: Bergin & Garvey, Pubs., Inc., 1985), 29.

16. J. Gibbs, L. Huang and Associates, *Children of Color*: (San Francisco, CA, Jossey-Bass, 1989).

17. W. Goodenough, Culture, Language, and Society. (Reading, MA: Addison-Wesley. 1971), 21–22.

18. Lawrence E. Harrison, "Underdevelopment Is a State of Mind." Cambridge: *Harvard Educational Review* (August 1988). Special Issue, "Race and Racism in American Education."

19. Sanford Horwitt, *Let Them Call Me Rebel: Saul Alinsky-His Life and Legacy* (New York: Knopf, 1989).

20. R. Kramer and H. Specht, *Readings in Community Organization Practice* 3rd Ed. (Englewood Cliffs, N.J.: Prentice Hall, 1983), 15–16.

21. J. Roemer, Divide and Conquer: "Microfoundations of Marxian Theory of Wage Discrimination," *Bell Journal of Economics*, 10 (Fall, 1979), 695–705.

22. J. Rothman and J. Tropman, Models of Community Organization and Macro Practice, in F. Cox (reds.) *Strategies of Community Organization* 4th Ed. (Itasca, Ill.: Peacock, 1987), 3–26.

23. H. J. Rubin and I. Rubin, *Community Organizing and Development* (Columbus, Ohio: Merrill, 1986), 234.

24. E. Spaulding, *Statistics on Social Work Education In the United States: 1989* (Alexandria, VA: Council on Social Work Education, 1990), 6.

25. E. P. Thompson, *The Making of the English Working Class* (New York: Vintage Books, 1966).

26. W. Trattner, *From Poor Law to Welfare State* 3rd ed. (New York: Free Press, 1984).

27. R. Warren and D. Warren, *Neighborhood Organizer's Handbook* (Notre Dame, Ind.: Notre Dame Press, 1977).

28. Marc A. Zimmerman and Julian Rappaport, "Citizen Participation, Perceived Control, and Psychological Empowerment." *American Journal of Community Psychology* (16, 5, 1988) 725–750.

CHAPTER TWO

Native American Community Development

E. DAN EDWARDS   MARGIE EGBERT-EDWARDS

Community organization and development among American Indians is an important part of their culture. Historically, many American Indian tribes and bands were relatively small in number and culturally bound together by strong individual and community support principles. Decision making was facilitated by considering the opinions of all tribal members through well-developed cultural values.

It is important to note that there are over 500 American Indian tribes in the United States. Each of these tribal groups is distinct and highly individualistic. All tribes have their own language, and some tribes continue to speak their Indian language as their first language. While there are many similarities in the emphasis placed upon the importance of community relationships among American Indian tribes, these values and beliefs are uniquely applied in each individual tribe. Professional people working with American Indians will do well to search for the commonalties and uniqueness of each American Indian tribal group as they seek to facilitate community development approaches.

Community Approaches are Compatible with Native American Values

Each American Indian tribal group takes considerable pride in its uniqueness. American Indian people also value their identification as the first inhabitants of this country. They respect those values that are common among many American Indian tribes. Several of these common values promote a positive community organization and development approach among American Indian tribal groups. Among these values are the following:

1. Belief in a Supreme Being. This value recognizes the existence of a Supreme Being. It also promotes the tenet that everyone should strive to live in harmony with nature and American Indian religious beliefs.

2. Appreciation, Hospitality, and Sharing. American Indians are grateful for all that they enjoy in this life. They offer prayers expressing gratitude for the blessings of nature. Indian people are generally hospitable. They value sharing food and worldly goods. They especially enjoy their associations with other Indian people and look forward to social and religious gatherings.

3. Respect for Individuality. All men, women and children are worthy of respect and autonomy.

4. Responsibility and Industriousness. Responsibility is taught in early years. Industriousness is an important value because each person's contribution is important to the success of the tribe.

5. Honesty. It is important to act in accordance with tribal teachings and avoid bringing shame upon one's self, family, clan, and tribe.

6. Group Consensus and Decision Making. Because each individual is highly valued, each person's opinions and contributions are important to the total group. Group consensus was traditionally sought in major tribal decisions.

7. Knowledge and Wisdom. Throughout each of these values is an expectation that American Indians will strive to attain knowledge to help them live in harmony with nature and in accordance with their religious beliefs. There is also an expectation that this knowledge will be used wisely in support of positive living experiences for the benefit of one's self, family, clan, and tribe.

When these expectations are operationalized, community togetherness and support are achieved. Each person is valued. Decision making is accomplished with a community organization approach. Historically, many day-to-day interpersonal experiences promoted community togetherness. Many of these experiences continue to be important today and include:

Visiting.   Indians make time to visit with one another. This is particularly true on the Navajo Reservation. Many families live in close proximity to one another. Since they belong to the same clan, their homes and hogans are located in the same general area or "camp." When representatives of educational programs visit the Navajo Reservation the word quickly circulates among the "camp," and many clan members will participate in the visit. They want to know of the educational experience of their clan members. They want to meet the people with whom their "brothers" or "sisters" are associating. Second or third visits are even more warmly received. As people become better acquainted, offers to join in family meals are freely given. Visitors bring gifts of food for such occasions. These visits are often accompanied by positive feelings and open discussions and exchanges of humor.

Sweat Houses.   Sweat houses are common components of many Indian cultural traditions. Social, cultural, and religious ceremonies take place in sweat houses. The sweat houses of the Yurok Indians provide for the cultural and religious instruction and socialization of both men and women in separate sweat house activities. Interestingly, the Yurok sweat house is built with a rather small entrance, reinforcing the Yurok value of physical fitness and a trim body. Overweight people would be prohibited from entering the sweat house because of their size. The exit opening is even smaller. Some tribal members may have to lose some weight in order to exit the sweat lodge.

Comradery.   Many Indians enjoy relaxed, positive interactions with one another. The pace of life is appropriate for the value they place on each person's existence. There are few reasons to hurry. When one lives life in accordance with cultural expectations, a balance is achieved and there is no cause for hurry or worry.

There are many occasions when laughter and open exchanges of humor are typical of American Indian interaction. This is especially true at family gatherings, reunions, and even funerals of valued family members who have lived long, successful, and positively influential lives. This was exemplified at one Yurok family gathering following the funeral of the patriarch of the family who had lived well into his 80s. Family members recounted a number of positive interactions they enjoyed with their father and grandfather. Many of these happenings were humorous in nature. The laughter provoked tears of emotional release, comradery, and closeness as family members validated positive experiences with their father/grand-father and other family members.

Advice Giving.   One of the strengths of the Indian community system is the value it places on every person's contribution. All tribal members, and especially the elders, are encouraged to offer their opinions on decisions facing the family, clan, or tribe. In many tribes, there are expected procedures that are used to request advice from elders. This protocol is especially important in seeking input from valued community members. Advice is usually not given unless requested according to well-defined cultural procedures. Upon request, each person's input is welcomed, even when people share and restate opinions that have previously been offered. There is sufficient time to listen and weigh everyone's suggestions before decisions are reached.

Marriages, naming ceremonies, and healing rites offer opportunities to celebrate and receive advice from elders and other interested tribal members. The advice-giving adds to the importance of the ceremony and is a valued contribution to the process. Many modern-day ceremonials have incorporated these traditions into their rites and rituals. An example of this can be seen in the "Eagle Feather Graduation Ceremonies" practiced by some American Indian tribes. When American Indians graduate from high school, vocational, or higher education programs, they participate in an "Eagle Feather Graduation Ceremony." An important component of the graduation ceremony is the involvement of American Indian elders. Several tribal elders are invited to address the graduates and their families and friends regarding the cultural significance of the eagle in the lives of Indian people and the symbolization of the eagle feather. Graduates are encouraged to care for the eagle feather and to remember the effort they expended to achieve graduation. The eagle feather serves as a symbol of their growth and accomplishment. It also serves as a symbol of what lies ahead for them and what they can accomplish with similar effort. The eagle feather is a tangible reminder of the support they have received from their tribe and their Creator in reaching important goals. The ceremony serves as an inspirational challenge to the graduates and their families and friends. As previous graduates attend the eagle feather graduation ceremonies, they are reminded of their past and present accomplishments and their future goals.

Decision Making.   Much individual, family, and community deliberation is acceptable in the decision-making processes of American Indians. Community meetings are often accompanied by potluck dinners. Comradery and good feelings are reinforced throughout the decision-making processes.

Each of these American Indian values and rituals promotes togetherness, acceptance, and community support. The value of each person and the importance of their contributions to the success of tribal governments contribute to the community support network that promotes community organization and development.

The Impact of Colonization on American Indian Communities

Colonization of the United States greatly affected the lives of American Indians. Throughout the early colonization years, American Indians were subjected to the control of the dominant groups that settled within their homelands. Trappers, explorers, land speculators, and miners influenced the lives of American Indians. European settlers enacted governments based on those of their homelands. Policies were often established for the benefit of their "mother" countries. Religious groups were interested in proselytizing and establishing religious organizations for the benefit of controlling and "civilizing" American Indians.

With the emancipation of the colonies from England, federal legislation was enacted to address issues related to American Indians. Initially, American Indians were governed by the War Department. Later, the responsibility was transferred to the Bureau of Indian Affairs (B.I.A.) within the Department of the Interior. With the emancipation of the colonies from England, federal legislation was enacted to address issues related to American Indians.

Historically, numerous federal policies have influenced the population, lifestyles, geographical locations, and general well-being of American Indians. Detailed descriptions of American Indian and non-Indian relations in this country are covered in considerable detail in B. Berry's book, *Race and Ethnic Relations.*[1]

It is important to note that each of the more than 500 American Indian tribes in this country has experienced the implementation of fedeal policies differently depending upon a number of variables including the location of the tribe; the desirability of tribal natural resources; and the attitudes, values, and cultural solidarity of both Indians and non-Indians. Throughout the implementation of these policies, issues of trust and distrust have been important to the establishment of Indian and non-Indian relationships.

Five major governmental policies have been identified by Berry as being most influential. They are (1) extermination, (2) expulsion, (3) exclusion (reservations), (4) assimilation, and (5) self-determination.

Extermination

Historically, extermination has often been used as a method of handling conflicts between races. Disease, war, alcohol, and slavery are examples of extermination methods. Disease was one of the most effective extermination practices utilized against American Indians who were particularly vulnerable to smallpox, measles, and chicken pox.

The most prevalent reason for the extermination of American Indians was the unrelenting desire for Indian land. Since American Indians did not utilize deeds and written agreements, there were no records of ownership, and the land was easily usurped by non-Indians.

Expulsion

As the nation's westward movements expanded, American Indians were forced to leave their homelands for more remote western areas. The removal of the Cherokee and the resultant "Trail of Tears" is an example of this policy. The Homestead Act of 1863 opened valuable Indian lands to purchase or for homesteading. Many non-Indians viewed expulsion as a more humane way of resolving the "American Indian problem" and advocated expulsion in lieu of extermination.

Exclusion (reservations)

Under this policy, American Indians were removed from larger geographical areas to well-defined "reservation" lands. Goals of the reservation system were to conform, control, and civilize American Indians and to convert them into "white men" by teaching farming and ranching skills. (Historically, American Indian people were expert farmers domesticating approximately 50 percent of the vegetables enjoyed throughout the world.)

Reservations were strongly resisted by most American Indian tribes. The final removal of Indians onto reservations was completed after the massacre of the Sioux at Wounded Knee in South Dakota in 1890.[8]

Many negative sanctions and restrictions were imposed upon Native Americans living on reservations. They were often denied use of their language and participation in religious ceremonies. Whatever the reservation system represented, it did not acknowledge the American Indians right to live and retain land and it did not allow for the maintenance of their identity and the many components of their culture.

Assimilation

After the reservation system was accomplished, many politicians encouraged enactment of laws to promote the termination of federal programs and trust relations with American Indians. The Dawes Act, or Land Allotment Act of 1887, was an example of this legislation. This Act provided for the allotment of plots of Indian lands to "competent" Indian individuals. In many cases, Indians sold their lands to non-Indians. This Act continued for nearly 50 years. Before the Dawes Act, American Indians owned 188 million acres of land through the federal government. After the Dawes Act, American Indians were left with the possession of 47 million acres.

Another assimilation policy, "relocation" (currently employment assistance) was enacted in 1952 by the Bureau of Indian Affairs. Under this program American Indians were recruited for off-reservation employment. Estimates indicate that approximately one-half of the American Indian trainees returned to their reservations. They lacked the support systems necessary to their adjustment in large urban environments.

In 1953 Congress passed a resolution declaring termination of Indian reservations to be the official federal policy. In the next 5 years, the trust status and federal programs of 60 Indian tribes and groups were terminated. This policy was reversed in the early 1960s because of the detrimental consequences that resulted from the termination policy.

Self-Determination

Since 1960 greater understanding and acceptance of Native Americans has led to more positive legislation allowing for American Indian self-determination. These achievements came as American Indians joined other ethnic minority groups to promote understanding of the extent to which poverty and racism influenced American Indian living situations and possibilities for future development.

The American Indian Movement (A.I.M.) actively engaged in promoting a number of American Indian happenings that called attention to the plight and needs of Indians. Some of these events led to notoriety and conflict. The most publicized event was the "Wounded Knee" confrontation on the Pine Ridge, Oglala Sioux Reservation. A nation-wide gathering later united Indian and non-Indian people in Washington, D.C. to bring attention to the "Trail of Broken Treaties."

At the same time these events were taking place, American Indian people were organizing and actively mobilizing support for a number of their professional groups and causes. The National Congress of American Indians (N.C.A.I.) was founded to bring together Indian leaders from rural, reservation, and urban areas for problem solving and lobbying efforts in behalf of American Indians. Other professional organizations were formed, including the National Tribal Chairmen's Association; the National Indian Youth Council; the American Indian Medical Doctors Association; the American Indian Nurses Association; the American Indian Lawyers Association; the American Indian/Alaskan Native Social Workers Association; the America Indian Counselors Association; the American Indian Court Judges Association; and the American Indian Engineers Association. These organizations are working individually and collectively on behalf of many American Indian needs and causes.

Effective Community Development in Native American Communities

Many variables will contribute to the effective development of community organization in Native American communities. Some of these variables are discussed below.

Increased Enhancement of and Identification with "Indianness"

Many Indian people are finding much pride and satisfaction in renewing their identification with their culture and in establishing relationships with Indian people from many different tribes. Reservations are promoting the cultural and spiritual enhancement of their specific tribes. The use of tribal language is being reinforced. Language instruction and cultural education programs are being developed. Urban Indian Centers are located in every major city where substantial populations of American Indians currently reside. Socialization and contest powwows are important components of reservation and urban cultural activities American Indian artists are creating traditional art pieces and designing modern art that is representative of their cultures. Social, recreational, and mental health and medical programs are reemphasizing the importance of cultural and tribal identification in their prevention and treatment programs. The message is very clear and concise: "It is okay to be Indian. There is much pride to be taken in Indian heritage and culture."

Addressing the Uniqueness of Each American Indian Community

Successful American Indian community development projects are those which identify and respond to the specific needs of their communities. In some communities alcohol and substance abuse detoxification centers are being replaced by healing centers that focus on "healing" individuals, families, tribes, and communities. These programs are reinforcing the natural and cultural support networks that are readily available in American Indian communities.

Many American Indian people are beginning to recognize the pain and trauma they have suffered as children of alcoholics. Indian people have sustained multiple losses from alcohol-related fatal accidents. Much grief work is being accomplished by professional and lay people who have been trained to work with children of alcoholics.

Some Indian communities are identifying and talking openly about their problems with family violence and child abuse and neglect. These communities are seeking solutions and resources to address these problems.

Strengthening Indian leadership is a priority in some Indian communities. Lay tribal members are assuming more responsibility for participating in tribal government meetings. In some tribes women, children, and elders are demanding that tribal leaders support programs which will be in the best interests of the tribe. Some tribal members are insisting that tribal council members who are substance abusers consent to treatment. As more Indian people participate in community involvement roles, Indian government will more closely resemble the traditional leadership systems which required community support and participation in the decision-making process.

In reservation and rural settings, unemployment rates range from 30 percent to 70 percent. Private employment opportunities are limited on many reservations. Because of these problems, many American Indian people are moving to urban areas in search of employment. Alcohol and drug abuse are common occurrences in urban cities as Indian people miss their associations with family and friends and seek relationships to support their transfer to new communities. The establishment of Urban Indian Centers is important to the adjustment of Indian people from rural and reservation settings to municipal locations. Substance use and abuse prevention and treatment centers are also important urban services for American Indian people.

Positive spiritual and cultural programs are being developed in many Indian communities. Indian people are being encouraged to support one another in their religious and cultural affiliations. Many Indian people are seeking strength in their cultural and tribal identities. They are identifying their clan names. Those who were not given Indian names or who have forgotten their Indian names are participating in appropriate naming ceremonies. A wide variety of cultural and spiritual activities are being developed throughout urban and reservation communities.

Some Indian communities are actively supporting the education of their youth and adults. In areas where dropout rates are especially high, Indian youth have much free time. Alcohol and drug abuse are often attempts to promote socialization and deal with problems of boredom and inactivity on reservations. Many Indian communities are recognizing the need for trained Indian professionals in every discipline. Scholarships and other support services are being offered to Indian youth and adults who wish to attend professional programs to prepare themselves to work more effectively within their Indian tribes.

Enactment of Federal Mandates

The Indian Reorganization Act implemented by the Roosevelt administration paved the way for Indian people to assume more responsibility for their government. Since then, emphasis has been placed on helping tribes become economically self-sufficient. More tribal businesses are in operation today. Where leadership has been properly trained, many of these organizations are successful.

Under contracting systems, former Bureau of Indian Affairs and Indian Health Service programs are operated under the jurisdiction of American Indian tribes. Social welfare and health programs are examples of such services.

In 1978 Congress enacted the Indian Child Welfare Act. In 1980 Congress enacted the Adoption Assistance and Child Welfare Act. Both of these Acts were actively supported by American Indian leaders, professionals, and lay people. These Acts provide procedures to ensure that Indian children receive child welfare services to safeguard their rights to family stability and tribal jurisdiction over Indian child welfare matters. In 1988, CSR and the Three Feathers Associates conducted a national study on the status of Indian child welfare after ten years' experience under the Indian Child Welfare Act. A summary of this research appears in *Children Today*. The researchers report that progress has been made in the implementation of the Indian Child Welfare Act and Adoption Assistance and Child Welfare Act. Compliance, however, is uneven. Increased resources and professional staff must be made available to ensure that the intent of the Acts is achieved.[7]

American Indian people are becoming more adept at utilizing the legal system to advocate for their tribal and individual rights. Legal suits have been filed to resolve issues regarding land claims, water rights, and hunting and fishing policies guaranteed under the provisions of their treaties. The Indian Child Welfare Act is a result of considerable lobbying of the congressional bodies.

Inmates in prisons have filed suits to contest policies that deny them the right to wear their hair in the longer, more culturally accepted styles of their tribal groups. Prison inmates have also filed for the right to participate in sweat lodge cultural and religious ceremonies.

As more Indian people are educated in professional schools, more appropriate services will be provided on their behalf. Young Indian people are becoming increasingly aware of the important roles being modeled by competent Indian professionals. More Indian professionals are being educated to continue this important work.

Understanding and Implementing Community Organization Processes

Contemporary writers are currently reporting on community approaches which address the problems of American Indian people.[2, 3, 4] This approach relies heavily on the active involvement of all components of American Indian communities. According to Beauvais and LaBoueff an important first step is to create an awareness and understanding that a community problem exists, and that it is substantially impacting the American Indian community.[2] This awareness can be accomplished in a number of ways. An individual or family crisis may be of substantial concern to a community. Community members may look deeper within their community to see if other community members are experiencing similar crises. An accident or tragedy may affect virtually all community members to the extent that a united community effort may be directed toward attacking the particular issues that contributed to the accident. An example of such a community crisis occurred in a midwestern Indian community. A tragic automobile accident resulted in the deaths of several Indian youth. Virtually every member of the tribe was affected by the tragedy. Since the accident was alcohol related, considerable support was generated for alcohol prevention and treatment programs following the tragedy.

Research and needs assessments are appropriate for use in many Indian communities. When either technique is utilized, the researchers must be sensitive to the previous research experience of the Indian community. Many Indian people are reluctant to participate in research projects because of prior negative experiences. Every possible consideration should be taken to ensure a positive experience with the current research process.

The Indian community must be made aware of the purposes of the research, the objectives the research hopes to meet, the data gathering and reporting methods, and the projected dates for completion of the research project. To assure cultural relevancy, the researchers should enlist support and input from all tribal members. Confidentiality must be assured. Wherever possible, Indian people from the community should conduct the interviews and participate in the data tabulation and interpretation. All members of the research team should be properly trained to obtain the most accurate data possible and informants should be reimbursed financially for their participation in and contributions to the data collection.

When the data have been collected, tabulated, and analyzed, they should be presented to the entire community. Those problems and prevention and treatment approaches that most often surface should be detailed

with considerable discussion and elaboration. Unique and creative suggestions for problem resolution should be highlighted. Wherever possible,
researchers should identify for the community those American Indian programs which are addressing similar problems with positive results.

Following the community meetings described above, it is important to
assist in organizing the community to address the issues and recommendations identified in this research. It is at this point that task groups may be
convened with responsibility for each of the major community issues
reported in the research. Task group membership should include all professional and lay people with interest and expertise in specific problem areas.
Special consideration should be given to including American Indian youth,
adults, and elders. Task force leadership should include people with substantial community support and leadership strengths to motivate and encourage
identification and attainment of task group goals.

Task group members should include those who have a commitment to
the specific community problems to be resolved. Members should have both
the time and an attitude of willingness to work together. Task members
should have the capacity to support one another and other task groups in
achievement of the overall goals. Members who can see the entire picture
should be included as should members who can see possible pitfalls and are
willing to discuss and address such problems. Some members may be
included not because of the positive contributions they will make but
because if they are not included they will work negatively to defeat the purposes of the task group. Knowing the community, its previous experience
with community organizing, and its potential for successful resolution of
problems is crucial. Knowing the community leadership is also crucial. Some
people must be included for the reputation of the committee to be positive;
others, to accomplish the tasks identified; and others, to maintain the
momentum of the work effort. All these issues and additional ones should be
addressed in order to achieve goals and to maintain positive gains once the
committees are disbanded.

Examples of Community Programs that Work

Many American Indian communities, both urban and rural, are
achieving considerable success in organizing and motivating communities to achieve problem resolution. Several community projects will
be described below.

Tribal Action Plan: Havasupai Tribe

In accordance with the provisions of the Anti-Drug Abuse Act of 1988,
Public Law 99–570, American Indian tribes have been required to formulate

Tribal Action Plans to address the treatment and prevention of substance abuse. This mandate requires the formation of Tribal Coordinating committees which are responsible for (1) surveying the problems and needs of their particular tribes, (2) formulating task forces to address each of these problems, and (3) coordinating all community prevention and treatment programs to combat problems of substance abuse on their reservations.

The authors of this chapter participated in the accomplishment of these goals on behalf of the Havasupai Tribe located at the bottom of Arizona's Grand Canyon. Access to this reservation is by foot, horseback, or helicopter. Over 400 members of this tribe reside at Supai, Arizona, the location of the tribal headquarters.

Assisting in the formation of this Tribal Action Plan was a unique learning experience. Selected members of the community were asked to participate on the task force to accomplish the needs assessment, problem identification, and Tribal Action Plan. This task force included professional and lay community members, representatives from the Tribal Coordinating Committee, and interested volunteers. The task force was directed by the chair of the Tribal Coordinating Committee.

The authors spent one week with the task force committee members. Each day began with a meeting of the task force. Community respondents were identified and interviews conducted with them to obtain needs assessment data. A time frame was established for completion of the project's tasks. Reports of each day's work were entered into a computer word processing program and presented to the task force at the next meeting. Suggestions for modifications and corrections were reported at each meeting.

As the needs and recommendations were identified, task force members suggested individuals and programs to address these recommendations. Where necessary, suggestions for new programs or staff were offered. As the final draft was formulated, goals were identified and consensus achieved in prioritizing these goals. Among the most important goals identified were the following:

1. Hire an alcohol and drug prevention and treatment professional. (This person was hired.)
2. Institute a substance abuse education and prevention program for grades K through 8 at the local reservation school. (A "Positive Action" program was instituted in the spring.)
3. Institute a class for college credit related to alcohol and drug education for adult members of the tribe. (More than twenty adults enrolled in this course, which was taught by the principal of the local school on the reservation.)
4. Organize a Youth Council with appropriate adult leadership. This

Youth Council could assume responsibility for planning and organizing recreational and educational activities for youth and the community.

The Tribal Action Plan was finalized and submitted to the Tribal Vice Chairman by the chair of the Tribal Coordinating Committee. The plan was later presented to the Tribal Council for their endorsement and support.

Children's Cultural Groups

In many communities, American Indian adults are sponsoring native American cultural groups for children. These groups are led by agency professional staff, community lay people, and parents of group members. The groups are usually held on a weekly or biweekly basis. Many of the groups are sponsored by local community schools or Indian centers. The groups often specialize in one of the talents of the group leaders. Both urban and reservation/rural areas are teaching their youth how to bead and make the specific arts and crafts of their tribal groups. Some of the groups focus on American Indian dancing, while others teach the skills necessary to make American Indian costumes. Adult Indian fathers teach their sons and other youth drumming and singing skills.

An example of such a group is the "Little Deer Track Singers"—a group of elementary age boys from the West Jordan, Utah area. The group members are trained by the father of one of the boys. The group meets on a weekly basis for practice sessions. The boys' talents are so well developed that they sing for powwows in the local area. These young men are talented, energetic, and well-trained singers. They attract much attention and admiration and are the favorite singers of many powwow participants.

Another example of such a group included the children of graduate students in the School of Social Work who showed an interest in learning more about their culture. This interest was identified during an activity for their parents and family members at the authors' home. A group was organized on a weekly basis for latency aged American Indian girls at the School of Social Work. The two major goals were (1) to increase the girls' knowledge of American Indians and identification with "Indianness," and (2) to support their adjustment to their new living arrangements. American Indian history topics, current events, and cultural activities were programmed for each session. Community activities were planned to engage the girls in the broader community. Skill development was encouraged with assignments given for the girls to share their knowledge and skills with family members. A dinner/giveaway was planned for all family members to support each group member's growth and achievement. Parents were encouraged to form groups of this nature upon their return to their Indian communities.

Group Living Facilities

American Indian tribal groups are organizing to meet the needs of their children through community projects such as those that establish youth homes on reservations. These homes may be established as alternatives to foster care. Other groups living facilities provide residential treatment services for American Indian youth. These projects are usually initiated under the direction of a community agency. On some reservations, such as the Gila River Pima Reservation, the initial boys' home was established in a residence owned by the Bureau of Indian Affairs under the direction of a community committee which included the tribal judge, the chairperson of the tribal council's social welfare committee, and two social workers—one (the author) from the Bureau of Indian Affairs and one from Indian Health Service. The home, its furnishings, and money for staff salaries were obtained through the support of the B.I.A. superintendent.

Selection of the full-time house parents and substitute, or relief parents required considerable time and careful study and was the responsibility of the Pima tribe committee members. Most small reservations are populated with long-term residents who know each member of their communities. The selection of house parents requires considerable care, since the role of the house parents is crucial in providing for a safe, nurturing environment for their children. When the selection of nurturing parents is facilitated, youth homes are established with considerable community support.

Indian Youth "Drug Busters": Ignacio, Colorado

Capitalizing on a current popular phenomenon, tribal and townspeople of the Southern Ute Tribe developed an educational prevention program designed to enhance youth awareness of drug abuse. This program was reported in *Linkages: For Indian Child Welfare Programs*. The program was developed with the cooperation of two VISTA volunteers, the Southern Ute Tribe, and the community of Ignacio, Colorado. The program is now in its fifth year and, while supervised by adults, is run primarily by youth group members who call themselves "Drug Busters." One of the group supported activities is a 325 mile annual run from southern Colorado to Denver where the youth deliver a message to the governor and legislature relating their concerns about substance abuse and the importance of curbing the problem and providing alternative activities. In addition to this annual run, other activities sponsored by the Drug Busters include: monthly meetings, movie trips to a nearby city, and drug-free parties and dances, including an all night New Year's Eve party. With the help of the community, the Drug Busters have acquired and are renovating an old building which will serve as a "teen center." All work is being volunteered. The youth also sponsor several fund-raisers including garage sales, Navajo taco dinners, and bake sales. A twenty-five minute video has been prepared describing this project and can be obtained from the Southern Ute Tribe, Box 294, Ignacio, Colorado for the cost of the postage.[6]

The Ignacio Drug Busters project effectively describes the efforts of a community task group in identifying a problem area and responding to such needs. While efforts are directed mainly toward youth, the entire community benefits from this program.

Chevak Village Youth Association—Alaska

Another community approach is described by McDiarmid regarding the Chevak Village Youth Association. This organization serves the recreation needs of the entire Chevak village and operates under the auspices recreation needs of the city government. It provides primary prevention services to reduce social problems of the village including alcohol and drug abuse. All youth are considered members of the Association. The youth are responsible for generating the large proportion of their budget. Among the activities offered as constructive alternatives to boredom and substance use are social and recreational activities, including basketball leagues for men and women; western and Eskimo dances; dinners; games; Scouts; holiday celebrations; and bingo games (a source of much of their budget). They also sponsor a Winterfest in March and Tundrafest in August which include native games, athletic events, dances, dinners, and arts and craft shows featuring many traditional crafts. Community service projects are emphasized. An alcoholism awareness day is combined with the Winterfest activities in March.[4]

This is another example of a community program which has been established as an alternative for drug use among young people. The program is responsible for providing recreation, education, and social activities for the entire community. The leadership skill and voluntary service development of the youth are major benefits derived from this community effort.

Soaring Eagles—Minneapolis, Minnesota

The Soaring Eagles organized in 1983 to promote leadership development of Indian youth. They now provide social, cultural, and educational activities for youth from 3 to 20 years of age. Alternative activities to substance use are promoted. Supportive relationships are developed with other Indian youth and adults who do not use or abuse substances. Educational achievement and attainment are positively reinforced. Positive identification with "Indianness" is encouraged. Individual goals are set with each member. Service activities to younger youth and the community are encouraged. Family activities are scheduled on a regular basis. An annual summer family retreat is an important component of this program.

Youth must apply for Soaring Eagles membership. Applicants are screened by program staff who acquaint them with the purposes and expectations of Soaring Eagles group members. There is a long waiting list for new members. The program has been so successful that a Soaring Eagles II group has been formed to provide additional meetings for teenagers as their needs for education and prevention activities increase.

The Indian children participating in this program live throughout the Minneapolis area. Transportation to and from the social center is provided for all youth who require it. Transportation is one of the crucial components of this program. Many Indian families do not have reliable transportation nor the financial or time resources to provide transportation to and from Soaring Eagles activities for their children. Program transportation also enhances the safety of the children as they travel to and from the activities.

Urban Recovery Programs

Many urban areas could profit from the development of urban recovery programs which relate to the needs of American Indian people. Such a program was established in Salt Lake City. Initially, the program was located in a small house. When the condition of the home deteriorated to the extent that it was condemned, the Board of Directors began their search for a new facility. Limited funds required a community approach to attain this goal. Several professional people with sympathetic ties to the Indian community were recruited through this effort. A real estate professional and an attorney (both anglo) were instrumental in locating a new building and preparing the necessary lease documents. Considerable public and private support was engendered to provide furnishings, food, and office equipment. HUD provided funds for remodeling. The attorney prepared the papers with a "first option to buy" clause, and the owner agreed to consider the remodeling costs toward the purchase of the building. Community relationships were expanded to the point that ongoing donations and support continue to be received from these public and private sources. The focus of the recovery center continues to relate to the needs of American Indian people, but people of all ethnic and racial groups participate in their programs.

University Community Development Programs

Universities may be thought of as small communities. They also have the responsibility of relating to and cooperating with their broader communities. When the Graduate School of Social Work initiated its Social Work Career Training Program for American Indians, it involved the university community, Ute and Navajo tribes, the Bureau of Indian Affairs, Indian Health Service, and social work agencies throughout the Intermountain West in a community approach. Support for the program was received from universities and colleges throughout the state of Utah. Social service agencies and American Indian organizations and communities provided consultants to both the Administrative Advisory Board and the American Indian Advisory Board, as well as opportunities for summer work/study positions for American Indian students exploring interests in social work careers. All these agencies contributed to the recruitment, retention, and graduation goals of this project. Since 1974, as a result of these efforts, 112 American Indians have graduated with their M.S.W. degrees and 5 American Indians have attained D.S.W. degrees from the University of Utah's Graduate School of Social Work. As national funding sources have withdrawn their financial support, the University of Utah, American Indian Scholarships, Inc., and American Indian tribes have increased their financial support of the program. Community strategies are being utilized to develop other funding resources to support the American Indian students who continue to enroll in this program.

Common Characteristics of Successful American Indian Community Development Programs

All of these successful programs have several commonalities. One of the most important of these is the programs' emphasis on cultural enhancement and positive identification with "Indianness." All of these programs are effective because they were organized and continue to operate with considerable community support.

All of these projects are directed by people who have long-term, realistic commitments to their programs, goals, and communities. They do not give up easily when problems surface. Program staff members understand the destructiveness that can be caused by criticism and backbiting. There are attempts to meet criticism openly and to hear complaints with a willingness to listen and understand. All of these projects are directed by people who believe in the benefits of their programs.

Enhancing Community Development Effectiveness: Overcoming Barriers

In order to achieve the community support essential to the success of these programs, every member of the community must have the potential for being served by some aspect of the program. Each community development project can effectively be tied to other community projects.

Cooperative relationships are essential on an individual, group, and community basis. It is particularly important to involve all elected tribal officials. They are responsible for the entire tribe. Their potential contributions are invaluable to the success of community development projects.

Community development projects require an understanding and awareness of the variables which accompany change. Resistance and fear of the unknown may be observed throughout all phases of change. Helping people deal with these feelings is an important role of a community organizer. Wherever possible, elders should be consulted and recognized for their advice in planning and developing community projects.

Community development projects take time and patience to develop their potential success. Patience is a required personality characteristic of those working on behalf of community development projects.

Planning for the 1990s

The social work profession has made a considerable commitment to meeting the needs of American Indians. The profession has supported the recruitment and education of Native Americans. It has also recognized the advantages of service delivery by American Indian professionals to American Indians. Culturally, Native Americans know and understand their cultures and are familiar with and often speak their tribal languages. This knowledge and skill is important for meeting the social service needs of American Indian people.

The social work profession has been active in supporting legislation aimed at reinforcing the cultural needs and resolving social issues facing American Indians. The Indian Child Welfare Act was passed with considerable input from Native American social workers speaking on behalf of American Indian family and cultural needs.

The Council on Social Work Education has mandated attention to recruitment and training of social workers from all minority groups of color. The Council has also mandated inclusion of ethnic content in the social work curriculum.

The National Institute of Mental Health (N.I.M.H.) has directed considerable financial support toward ethnic minority social work training programs. Financial support for the University of Utah's American Indian Social Work Career Training Program continued for nineteen years. Funding for other projects of this nature was also made available through this organization. N.I.M.H. recently funded a study coordinated by the authors of this chapter to assess the social work clinical training needs of ethnic minority people.[5]

In spite of the progress identified above, considerable concern is raised by American Indians today who note a decrease in understanding and support of the social service needs of their people. There appears to be considerable apathy from the perspective of the "majority culture" in relating to the needs of minorities generally and American Indians specifically. This apathy is particularly evident in university settings where fewer American Indian faculty members are employed in schools of social work today than in previous years. Decreased financial support for students has also led to a reduction in the numbers of American Indians attending colleges and universities. There also appears to be less emphasis upon curriculum content related to American Indians and a need to provide training for current faculty who have not participated in the development of social work minority curriculum materials emphasized years ago.

There is considerable need for increased attention to the many and varied social problems facing American Indian communities from both university and community perspectives. American Indian and non-Indian students must be educated to address the problems of native Americans in urban and reservation/rural communities. Native Americans are willing to assume responsibility for problem resolution in their communities. They are open to and receptive of professional input. American Indians are asking social workers to help them address their problems through a community development approach. The social work profession is in a strategic position to provide Native Americans with the knowledge base and support services necessary to achieve their goals.

These support services, however, must facilitate tribal and community ownership, identification, and resolution of Native American problems. Traditionally, American Indians believe that the "problems of one are the concerns of all," and equally, "the healing of one is the healing of all." Native Americans have the traditional heritage, wisdom, and ability to assume responsibility for directing their own problem solving efforts.

The 1990s will see Native American community development efforts achieve considerable problem solving success.

The Native American Development Corporation is currently documenting these successes.* This nonprofit corporation is owned and controlled by native Americans. They have published several booklets that describe tribal community approaches to problem resolution. In these publications, tribes are encouraged to take the initiative in studying, planning, implementing, and evaluating their community approaches to problem resolution.

The approach used is similar to that described earlier. It includes the following steps: (1) get people together, (2) define how the problem specifically affects the community, (3) talk about it, (4) ask questions about what is currently being done, (5) identify what needs to be done, (6) develop

---

*Copies of Native American Development Corporation publications can be obtained from their offices at 1000 Connecticut Avenue, NW, Suite 401, Washington, DC 20036. (202) 296–0685.

a plan—coordinate existing and new activities, (7) make assignments, (8) find the gaps—seek training, (9) use outside resources when necessary, but maintain control and responsibility for their use and coordination, (10) document progress, and (11) measure achievements by small steps.

Summary

Historically and culturally, American Indians have taken interest and pride in the positive accomplishments of their communities. Enhancement of community development projects is culturally appropriate and promotes positive identification with "Indianness" for each American Indian. In furthering community development programs, American Indians and non-Indians will witness a cultural resurgence that will promote the positive growth of all American Indians and communities.

Coordinated American Indian community projects have great potential for success. As successful programs are implemented, enthusiasm will build to allow for further risk taking on behalf of American Indian community programs. In order to achieve this success, Indian leadership must be developed continuously as a priority for American Indian communities. Native Americans are in the most strategic positions to formulate and accomplish the goals of their projects. They know their culture, language, and community expectations. They have a personal, family, and tribal stake in the success of these programs. They have made geographical, philosophical, and professional commitments to community development. Wherever possible, youth and adults should be encouraged to complete college degrees to gain knowledge, training, and experience to organize and direct community development programs. Financial assistance and support services must be made available to assist in the attainment of educational degrees. Indian community development should be encouraged in both reservation/rural areas and in urban communities. Wherever Indian people live there should be opportunities for them to identify with and promote American Indian community development.

Endnotes

1. B. Berry, *Race and Ethnic Relations* (Boston: Houghton Mifflin, 1965), 150.
2. F. Beauvais and S. LaBoueff, "Drug and Alcohol Abuse Intervention in American Indian Communities," *International Journal of the Addictions* 20 (January 1985): 139–171.
3. E. D. Edwards and M. E. Edwards, "Alcoholism Prevention/Treatment and Native American Youth: A Community Approach," *Journal of Drug Issues* 18 (January 1988): 103–114.

4. G. W. McDiarmid, "Community and Competence: A Study of an Indigenous Primary Prevention Organization in an Alaskan Village," *White Cloud Journal* 3 (January 1983): 53–74.

5. *Ethnic Minority Social Work Mental Health Clinical Training Programs: Assessing the Past—Planning for the Future:* A Survey Commissioned by the National Institute of Mental Health, SLC. (Utah: University of Utah, 1989).

6. *Indian Child Welfare: A Status Report.* Prepared for Administration for Children, Youth and Families, U.S. Department of Health and Human Services, Bureau of Indian Affairs, and U.S. Department of the Interior. (Washington, D.C.: CSR, Inc., and Norman, OK: Three Feathers Associates, 1988).

7. M. C. Plantz, "Indian Child Welfare: A Status Report," *Children Today* 18 (January/February 1989): 24–29.

8. M. L. Wax, *Indian Americans* (Englewood Cliffs, N.J.: Prentice-Hall, 1971), 65–78.

CHAPTER THREE

Chicanos, Community, and Change

MIGUEL MONTIEL   FELIPE DE ORTEGO Y GASCA

Introduction

The goal of this chapter is to explore the idea of change in the Chicano community and to examine the part played by Chicano organizations in influencing change.

As inexorable as change is, there is nothing more "curiouser" (to use Alice's word) than change. Change is inevitable, but purposive change has to do with the power of "intervention oriented toward improving or changing community institutions and solving community problems." Often, "change" is viewed as being as synonymous with "progress:" movement toward reason and justice stressing equality as the core of justice. Men and women have power to the extent that they influence the circumstances of the time.[8, 12]

Why do some people resist change while, others rush to greet it? William Blake identified resistance to change as "mind-forged manacles." It is true that each of us guards a gate of change most of us are reluctant to open. Nevertheless, each of us makes concessions to change, consciously or unconsciously, with or without consent.[3]

To understand how change occurs in Chicano communities, let's consider what is meant by "community." Community is simply a group of people sharing similar interests and goals. Warren refers to community as action organized to "afford people daily local access to those broad areas of activity which are necessary in day-to-day living." Often towns are referred to as communities even though the residents may not share common interests and goals. In large terms one talks about the Los Angeles community or the Phoenix community. The notions of community—culture, religion, work, education, war, and power—have served "to gratify man's desire for community and for the cherished legitimacy that community alone can give to authority, function, membership, and loyalty."[9, 19, 22, 30]

What has been the process, progress, and direction of change in the Chicano community? What part have Chicano organizations played in change? What are the prospects and projections for Chicano communities and organizations? What needs to be done to make things better? These are some of the questions we will explore.

Chicanos and Community

Chicanos have defied (perhaps not voluntarily) the one-way process of assimilation. Conquest, a distinct language, (Spanish) and to some extent "color" have kept Mexican Americans/Chicanos from full participation in the American experience. The year 1848, when the United States acquired one-third of Mexico's land base, marked the end of an historically Mexican community (of Mexico) and the beginning of a consciousness as Mexican Americans (of the United States).

Only since the Civil Rights Movement of the 1950s and 1960s have Americans realized that 19th Century theories of acculturation have not told the full story of minorities in America. An America founded on a homogeneity of values rooted in the English tradition is giving way to an America founded on cultural pluralism.[15]

The Mexican origin population of the United States is growing rapidly: in 1980 it was 8.7 million, an increase from 4.7 million in 1970. The 1985 Advance Report of the Census Bureau estimated that there were 17 million Hispanics including 10.3 million Mexican Americans. In 1980, 83 percent of Mexican Americans lived in the states of Arizona, California, Colorado, New Mexico, and Texas. The greatest percentage increase in Hispanic population in the 1970s, however, occurred outside these five states.

Compared with the total U.S. population, Mexican Americans are younger (21.9 years versus 30 years for whites); more fertile (3.6 children for women aged 35–44 versus 2.5 for white women), and more vulnerable (16.4 percent female-headed households versus 14.3 female-headed white households). Similarly, there are higher rates of delinquency, dropouts, violent deaths, and alcohol-related diseases among Mexican Americans even though the life expectancy of Mexican Americans is similar to that of Anglo Americans. The "bad will" that existed in the early years of Anglo-American interaction continues to some extent in the form of an "English only" movement which is attempting to outlaw the use of Spanish in governmental settings (except for the courts) and in the sometimes volatile relationships between Mexican immigrants and the immigration service of the United

States government. Although Mexican American males had the highest labor labor force participation of any group, they had relatively higher rates of unemployment. Median income was $4,000 less than white males, and women received the lowest wages of any group except Puerto Ricans.[1]

In many areas of the Southwest, Mexican culture has lingered despite overwhelming dominance of Anglo society. It was in the barrios where the culture was kept alive and vibrant. Louis Wirth described the Jewish ghetto as a transitional enclave that provided temporary continuity to their land of origin. Similarly, barrios and Mexican American organizations have served as havens from the vicissitudes of American society.[31]

A barrio however, is not necessarily a community—that doesn't mean it isn't. The word "barrio" is an imprecise term for a cluster of Chicanos principally because it is fraught with negative perceptions of poverty and impotence. The breakup, or more appropriately the segmentation of barrios, as with ethnic villages, has been created partly because of the movement of the middle class to the suburbs. According to Sennett and Cobb the integration of white ethnics "meant integration into a world with different symbols of human respect and courtesy, a world in which human capabilities are measured in terms profoundly alien to those that prevailed in... their childhood." The same applied to Mexican Americans. Nevertheless, barrios do serve an important function, particularly for immigrants who come (legally) at the rate of 60,000 per year. It is difficult to estimate the number of illegal aliens that cross the border into the United States. There are, however, several million Mexicans now living in the United States.[28]

A Brief History

To understand the nature of the Chicano community since the 1960s and the change that ensued therein one needs to examine the historical record. The period from 1848 to 1960 can be seen as three stages, each contributing cumulatively to the evolution of Mexican American existence and Chicano consciousness.

Early Mexican American Period: 1848–1912

This period is one of transition. While no reliable statistics on the number of Mexican citizens in the territory demarcated by the Treaty of Guadalupe-Hidalgo in 1848 exist, estimates range from 75,000 to 350,000. Additional Mexican citizens were acquired by the United States per the

Gadsden Purchase in 1853. These first Mexican Americans had to deal with becoming Americans in their own land.[17, 24]

In the years between 1848 and 1912, Mexican Americans saw the need for organizational strength to ward off Anglo-American onslaughts. A number of resistance organizations were formed in response to the Mexican War, to the land grabs, and to laws such as the California "Greaser Act" of 1855 that ensued.* In 1894, twelve years before the formation of the NAACP, the first successful organization for Mexican American rights was formed in Tucson, Arizona under the banner of Alianza Hispano Americana. Its mission was to defend Mexicans against the bad will extant in American society.

The massive land transfers, legal and illegal, from Mexican to Anglo hands and the conversion of Mexican people into a pool of cheap labor were the tangible effects of discrimination. This is what set the agenda of the times. In addition to the many mutual aid societies like the Alianza were radical organizations. One such organization, *El Guante Negro Mutualista*, was a secret organization dedicated to robbing the rich and helping the poor. The year 1912, when Mexico and Arizona were admitted into the union, marks the end of this period.

Later Mexican American Period: 1912-1940

Between 1912 and 1930 more than 1.5 million Mexicans crossed into the United States, fleeing the turmoil in Mexico. Ernesto Galarza, the dean of Mexican American scholars and an early organizer in the farmworkers cause, called this phenomenon one of the greatest migrations in the history of the world. Although as many as one-third of this number (including bonafide American citizens) were "repatriated" to Mexico during the 1930s, it is from this reinforcement of the Mexican American community that the current Chicano population draws its numeric strength.

This period is also marked by Mexican American efforts to become Americans, shedding, if need be, their "Mexicanness," including their language to become part of the American mainstream. The League of United Latin American Citizens (LULAC) was organized in 1927 in Texas. The

---

*The *Penitentes* (Brothers of Our Father Jesus of Nazareth), carryovers from the original Spanish settlers, began organizing in the late 1700s in what is now New Mexico and Colorado. Mutual aid societies like the *Alianza* were radical organizations. One such organization, El Guante Negro Mutualista, was a secret organization dedicated to robbing the rich and helping the poor. The year 1912, when New Mexico and Arizona were admitted into the union, marks the end of this period.

organization's pledge to promote English and help its members become good American citizens led the effort.*

Modern Mexican American Period: 1940–1960

This was the period when Mexican Americans searched for America and discovered two Americas—White America and the Other America as Michael Harrington described it.[†] Although some 500,000 Mexican Americans served in the Armed Forces during World War II and emerged with a significant number of Medals of Honor, Mexican Americans learned painfully that "color" was still the way White America defined good Americans. In the apartheid system of the United States, Mexican Americans could not cross the color line.

In South Texas in 1947, a Mexican American soldier who died in battle during World War II but whose body had only then been recovered was denied burial in a municipal cemetery. This galvanized Mexican American Veterans into forming the American G.I. Forum, a powerful militant organization.

Two important court cases enjoined by LULAC had a profound effect on the Civil Rights Movement of the 1960s. In 1945 Gonzalo Mendez of Orange County, California brought suit against the public schools of Westminster, enjoining them from segregating Mexican American students. Judge McCormick ruled for Mendez, and the ruling was affirmed on April 14, 1947 by the Ninth Circuit Court. In 1948 a similar case was affirmed against the Bastrop School District in Texas. Both cases were important precedents in the 1954 Supreme Court ruling on Brown v. the Board of Education. With this action, the Alianza moved boldly into the forefront of the civil rights struggle of Mexican Americans. In 1955, the Alianza—then more than 60 years in existence—established a Civil Rights department. In 1955 the Alianza movement joined with the American Civil Liberties Union (ACLU) and the NAACP to further the civil rights of minorities. In 1957, for example, the *Alianza Magazine* informed Mexican Americans that Charlotte C. Rush, Patriotic Education Chairperson of the Denver Chapter of the Daughters of the American Revolution, didn't "want a Mexican to carry old Glory" in a parade at the State Industrial School for Boys. She believed that only "American boys" should carry the flag despite the fact that the boy originally chosen was an American of Mexican descent.

---

*LULAC, with a membership consisting of more than 380 councils and approximately 100,000 members, has a long list of civil rights, labor, and educational accomplishments.

[†]*New York Times*, January 17, 1978.

The Sixties and Beyond

A taxonomy for "Chicanos, Community and Change" since 1960 does not evolve neatly by decades. The patterns seem to fall from mid-decade to mid-decade. The momentum of the 1950s carries well into the 1960s and the consciousness of the Chicano Movement, faint though stirring, begins well before 1966. While the beginning of the Chicano Movement is not the beginning of the Civil Rights struggle for Mexican Americans, it begins a time of self-determination and a disruption of the traditional Americanization process. It is out of this resolve that the plethora of Chicano organizations emerged, dedicated to "going it alone" (at least for a while) rather than trying to "satisfy the man."

We have identified three organizational epochs since the sixties: (1) the epoch of the Chicano Renaissance, (2) the epoch of economic development, and (3) the epoch of Hispanicity.*

The Chicano Renaissance

In the late 1950s and 1960s organizations in Texas and California began aggressive organizing activities in state and national politics. The Mexican American Political Association (MAPA), under the leadership of Bert Corona for example, gained incorporation of East Los Angeles and the election of Edward Roybal to the U.S. House of Representatives. Roybal has been instrumental in the formation of several national organizations and elevating Hispanic issues to national significance.

Cesar Chavez, the quiet, unassuming son of migrant workers, in spite of strong opposition from growers, the Teamsters Union, and a history of abortive attempts at organizing farm workers, managed to organize farm workers into what is today known as the United Farm Workers' Organizing Committee. Chavez' organizing genius is one of networking diverse groups within the farmworkers by utilizing powerful religious symbols like fasting and the Virgin de Guadalupe; appealing to the outside liberal community that included students, elites, and a Ghandian nonviolence which has maintained the peace and made it difficult for the growers to retaliate. This approach has served to maintain a loyal following for nearly three decades.

---

*The information on organizations and their leaders comes from Gonzales' and Meier's dictionaries (refer to endnotes) and from the collective experiences of the authors who have witnessed many of the organizational developments over the last thirty years. Hispanic directories are incomplete because many organizations spring into being from the time they are submitted and the time the directories are published; they include only a fraction of Hispanic organizations.

Chavez, Roybal, and Corona as well as other Mexican American organizers were influenced by the Industrial Areas Foundation (IAF), first introduced to the Mexican American community via the Community Service Organization (CSO), a post war organization founded on the values of the mutual aid societies of past years.

In the mid-sixties many radically oriented organizations led by charismatic leaders sprang up in different parts of the Southwest. Most important were Reyes Lopez Tijerina's Alianza Federal de Pueblos Libres in New Mexico, Rodolfo "Corky" Gonzales' Crusade for Justice in Colorado, and Jose Angel Gutierrez' Raza Unida Party in Texas. Chavez' nonviolent posture stands in stark contrast to the militant tactics of the flamboyant protestant minister Reyes Lopez Tijerina, the leader of the Alianza, who fought to have the Spanish land grants restored to the original Mexican settlers in New Mexico, Colorado, and Texas. The Alianza lost its base when violence erupted in the infamous court house raid in Rio Arriba County in northern New Mexico which eventually resulted in Tijerina's imprisonment. Exhibiting similarly strong nationalistic orientation, Rodolfo "Corky" Gonzales, a former boxer and powerful charismatic leader inspired the passions of Chicano youth through his Crusade for Justice. The yearly Youth Liberation Conference sponsored by the Crusade of the 1970s had a powerful long-lasting effect on the more radical elements of the Chicano Movement. It is from these conferences that El Plan Espiritual de Aztlan emerged, which outlined a "declaration of self-determination" for Chicanos in the Southwest. "Nationalism," Gonzales claimed ". . . is a tool for organization, not a weapon for hatred." Under the leadership of the fiery Jose Angel Gutierrez, the Raza Unida party managed to gain victories in several communities in Texas where Mexican Americans held electoral majorities. Several prominent Chicano leaders have accused the Raza Unida Party of reverse racism. Important during this period also were the organizing activities of the Chicano students under the MECHA banner which led to the formation of numerous Chicano studies programs.

The mid-sixties were times of turmoil, confusion, and opportunity. It was a time when the stage was set for entry by Chicanos into the American system on Chicano terms. It was a time when the emerging Chicano intelligencia, some based at fledgling Chicano studies departments, began defining the Chicano community. Until this time, the social sciences depicted Chicanos as deficient and policy was aimed at transforming Mexicans into a narrow middle class success model. Padilla claims that because of its diversity and insignificant community participation, however, Chicano studies advocates created an idealized vision of the Chicano community. Focus on community, Padilla argues, reflected a desire on the part of Chicano intellectuals to participate in the struggle for equality.[16, 18, 20, 25]

Chicanos proposed bold visions of a bilingual/bicultural society to be maintained by Hispanic institutions during the 1960s and early 1970s; only a handful have survived. The most ambitious was the Hispanic University of America in Denver in 1972. Though headed by New Mexican Senator Joseph Montoya, the drive to secure funding comparable to that of congressional funding for Black colleges did not materialize. The Chicano Movement did not create bilingualism nor biculturalism in American society since both were there from the beginning of Anglo American society on the Atlantic frontier. The Chicano Movement, however, did raise the discussion to a national policy level, culminating in the Bilingual Education Act of 1968.

In the late sixties, Chicanos began to organize caucuses within various professional organizations. In social work, for example, the Trabajadores de la Raza, led by Paul Sanchez, organized chapters in cities in the South and Midwest. Chicano-oriented schools of social work were established at San Jose State University (where Sanchez became the first dean) and New Mexico Highlands. The Trabajadores de la Raza also had a part in curriculum changes and redirecting social service delivery systems. Many Chicano agencies that began as advocacy agencies converted into as social services agencies and in many cases unwittingly took the pressure off the traditional social services agencies. The reason for the conversion often was because funds were more readily available for drugs than for organizing communities. Many professional groups organized during this period have become institutionalized in the 1980s. And while blatant negative interpretations about Chicanos have gone by the wayside and institutions give lip service to Chicano concerns by establishing bilingual programs, there is no bilingual/bicultural society.

The Economic Development Period

The "economic development" era that took hold in the mid-seventies and continues to the present focused much of its efforts on gaining economic and political advantage requiring attention to administrative details rather than to the global aspirations of the sixties. Enhanced activity in Washington D.C. created, at least for the moment, a paucity of leadership at the local level. In the seventies, a more systematic approach toward solving problems appeared to be taking place. The tactics of the radicals were rejected; government and foundations began to encourage the establishment of Chicano agencies that would work within the system. There is little question that the rejection of many charismatic leaders at the hands of American society led to greater opportunities for the more moderate leaders that followed.

Activists (as opposed to agency heads) continued to confront established institutions on many of the same issues of the sixties. Invariably the confrontations lead to concessions, usually not for those who confront but for those who wait in the wings. The sixties are filled with examples to support this phenomenon. The Raza Unida Party enhanced the opportunities for Mexican Americans in the democratic party; MECHA opened the universities for newly graduated Ph.D's; demonstrations and disturbances in the inner cities created opportunities for Economic Development Corporations; and the Tierrra Amarilla raids in New Mexico brought massive funding for the Health Education Leadership Program (HELP) in New Mexico. In more recent times the Hispanic Community Forum in Arizona confronts issues and another set of people benefit. The relationship is never direct; accommodationist institutions never admit that the changes result from pressure. The prize goes to those who are "acceptable to the establishment," to quote a university administrator.

The most prominent organizational phenomena of the seventies was the formation of Community Development Corporations (CDC's) that emerged in the late 1960s and early 1970s in poor minority neighborhoods. CDC's goal was to develop "sources of strength and confidence in those neighborhoods" and alleviate "the economic and social distress caused by the malfunctioning of the private sector and the shortcomings of the public sector." The more than 100 CDC's (some controlled by Chicanos) are supported largely by federal programs and private foundations (especially the Ford Foundation) although the ultimate goal is to be self-supporting through profit-making ventures.[27]

The Mexican American Legal Defense and Education Fund (MALDEF), spearheaded by the LULAC network with monies from Ford and the Marshall Field Foundation, came into its own during this period. MALDEF's civil rights activities have touched every area of Mexican American life, from education to women's rights. The Ford Foundation has figured prominently in the organization and funding of these organizations, including the Hispanic Policy Development Institute and the Inter-Agency Consortium for Hispanic Research, two National Hispanic organizations, interestingly enough, headed up by non-Hispanics.

One of the most recent effective organizing efforts in the Mexican American community have been spearheaded by the Industrial Areas Foundation (IAF), a training network established by Saul Alinski in 1940. It was IAF trained organizers who built the Community Services Organization and the Farm Workers Union in the late fifties and early sixties. Their influence on the Mexican American community is again felt in the mid-seventies, first in Texas, later in California, and more recently in Albuquerque, New Mexico and Phoenix, Arizona. Ernesto Cortez Jr., who was the lead organizer of COPS (Communities Organized for Public Services) in San Antonio is critical of the more prominent Mexican American civil rights activities in the late sixties and early seventies because of their "ethnic exclusivity." In San

Antonio, Houston, and El Paso people were concerned with flooding and deterioration, education, and utility bills. "As a result, the initial flurry of 1960s success left many Mexicanos exhausted about public life and cynical about politics in general."[7]

Cortez' method of organizing is based on building relationships. "No organizer ever organizes a community." Power, he says, is based on broad-based organizing that requires money and organized people, not single individuals. What is needed is strategy and vision. "And our vision" Cortez concludes "comes out of our institutions and . . . Judeo-Christian tradition and democractic values." IAF's goal is to establish self-governing institutions and a political culture that can hold institutions accountable. It is not surprising that IAF organizing depends on linkages with religious organizations, particularly the Catholic church.

The link betwen the Industrial Areas Foundation led by Fred Ross and the formation of various Mexican American organizations such as CSO, MAPA, the Farm Workers Union, and subsequent organizations such as the Hispanic Caucus and The National Association of Latino Elected and Appointed Officials (NALEO), is a pattern manifested in the formation of other Hispanic organizations.

Union organizing efforts by Barraza and Lacayo, two prominent union leaders, brought about ideas for the development of the National Council of La Raza and a string of Community Development Corporations such as Chicanos Por La Causa in Phoenix and TELACU in Los Angeles, as well as several offshoots of the Council. Similar threads can be traced in the development of such organizations as LULAC, the American G.I. Forum, La Alianza Hispanoamerican, and most recently El Concilio de America.

The resources provided by the War on Poverty and the unions helped develop networks that remain to this day. The National Council of La Raza, at their annual meeting in Kansas City in 1989, for example, hosted 125 affiliates. It is not surprising, therefore, that organizational life in the Mexican American community is dominated by relatively few individuals connected through a national network. A network, however, that touches a relatively small part of the Chicano and Mexican communities in the United States.

The Age of Hispanicity

In the 1980s, many of the concerns of the 1960s were institutionalized. It was the epoch of Hispanicity. This was a period when many important Chicano leaders of the sixties became outcasts and when national Hispanic organizations gained prominence. It was also a period when corporations and political leaders at the highest levels saw the convenience of aggregating Spanish-speaking groups. The Spanish language television network, for example, owned by Hallmark, targeted groups in the U.S. and Latin America via the Hispanic rubric.

In the 1980s, leadership became important in Hispanic communities. MALDEF, LULAC, and the United Way of America initiated leadership programs to help Hispanics develop skills to enable them to serve on boards. In 1988, representatives from various Hispanic leadership programs established the National Network of Hispanic Leadership Programs. The program's goal is the formation of a national leadership training agenda.

Vigil reminds us that because of the ineffectiveness of elected officials many of the advances in education, employment, housing, affirmative action, and voting rights have "resulted from pressure groups activity in the courts, legislatures, and the executive branches of government."[29]

While still important, community-based organizations are giving way to profession-centered organizations. Local and national organizations have sprung up in business, education, and the arts. In the professions there are Hispanic organizations for accountants, executives, personnel managers, psychologists, and nurses. To commemorate the 500th anniversary of the Hispanic presence of the Americas, the National Hispanic Quincentennial Commission was organized to plan a national Hispanic commemoration program. IMAGE (The National Association of Hispanics in Government) established a commission to assess the status of Hispanics in the Department of Defense. Hispanic Corporate executives organized the National Hispanic Corporate Council, a Fortune 500 group, whose aim is to create opportunities within corporations. Just recently a similar organization headed by former New Mexico governor Jerry Apodaca established the Hispanic Association for Corporate Responsibility. The development of professional groups tied to their mainstream professional organization points to the kind of "moling" activities and to new tactics for change in the 1990s and beyond. In many places Chicano, Latino, and Hispanic organizations are being formed to tackle specific areas of the Hispanic agenda.

While general membership organizations like LULAC still "cover the waterfront" in their concerns for Chicanos, more and more of the specific issues of the Hispanic agenda are taken up by organizations with specific rather than general membership. The organizations of the 80s operate more like pressure groups galvanized by narrow goals and objectives rather than the more broad-based advocacy groups of the past.

Organizations oriented toward promoting individual or professional interests are a recent phenomenon in the Chicano community. They are indicative of the growing diversity (and fragmentation) of the Chicano community and of the emergence of a professional and merchant class. It is a source of great tension between the pragmatism of the 80s and the idealism of the 60s, between the poor, the working class, and the middle class.

There has been some dissatisfaction with national efforts of organizations like the National Council of La Raza because some critics claim they are removed from the pulse of the local communities, that they are influenced far too much by non-Hispanics, and their advocacy is geared more toward individual interests rather than to that of their affiliates. In many instances national agencies are becoming more involved in running programs rather than advocating for local efforts. These concerns have spurred organizing efforts such as those of Miguel Barragan, a longtime activist who organized El Concilio de America, an organization in Northern California with over 185 affiliates, some of which belong to both the National Council of La Raza and El Concilio. El Concilio's goal is to establish an Hispanic development fund for Hispanic self-determination, thus avoiding the control agencies like United Way have exerted on Hispanic Organizations. It is not surprising that these maverick efforts have angered Hispanic groups and individuals who have finally managed to maneuver themselves into the mainstream.

Most Hispanic organizing efforts are staff dominated and there is little attention paid toward developing leadership within the communities where the organizing takes place. Organizers and agency heads in many Hispanic communities do not live in the communities in which they work and rarely endure the indignities tolerated by residents of those communities. The dilemma facing the professional organizer is one of credibility; people must believe him or her when he or she speaks about dropouts, segregation, and housing. This is not to derogate the role of community agency organizers but to highlight the inevitable conclusion that while the individual circumstances of many Mexican Americans have changed, the social circumstances of communities—the targets of community organizers—have not changed dramatically.

Dissatisfied also are many Hispanic women, particularly with their level of participation in organizations of the Mexican American community. Numerous parallel groups for women like the Chicana Forum, MUJER, and the Mexican American Women's National Association, to name just three, have emerged in the last few years. Gonzales was one of the first women to raise this issue. Interstate Research Associates (IRA), an important nonprofit research and consulting firm founded on the idea of self-determination, she claimed, was out of touch with the women's movement.

> Most notable was the lack of female representation in its leadership hierarchy. Mexican American women . . . questioned the lack of women in IRA's decision-making process. More and more they felt that IRA's problem solving excluded the problem of women.[13]

What can be said of the 80s is that it was a time of institutionalization of Hispanics and the demise of the charismatic leaders of the 60s. In this period we witnessed the increased visibility of Mexican Americans within the broader community; the seriousness with which they are taken as consumers; dissatisfaction with the status quo among Hispanic women; the amnesty bill which at once legalizes illegal immigrants and makes it more difficult for illegal "aliens" to live in the United States; and the "English only" movement which attempts to restrict the use of Spanish in the United States. It was the period when the ideological and the materialistic divisions became apparent.

Assessments and Revaluations

In the new science of "Chaos," consideration of data focuses on the sensitivity to initial conditions. This is an appropriate consideration in assessing and revaluating Chicanos, community, and change from the perspective of 30 years (1960–1990).

The initial conditions that engendered the tumult of the 60s—poverty, employment, housing, foreign and domestic policy—are still with us, exacerbated by demographic imperatives that augur the realizations of all past apocalyptic visions, especially those of Malthus.

Have things changed for the better since the 1960s? The individual circumstances of many Mexican Americans have changed dramatically. Many make more money; live in better homes than their parents; are better educated, and generally have a higher standard of living than they had when they were children. Dramatic changes have also occurred at the national level. National organizations like MALDEF and National Council have fulfilled one of the most important goals of the 60s: to get into the national agenda. In spite of these efforts, however, for most Chicanos things have not changed appreciably. The Chicano population is young, rapidly growing, poor, and beset with problems—crime, drugs, teenage pregnancy, and dropouts—and its level of participation in electoral politics is low, although improving. Chicano communities have become more segregated; income distribution more lopsided; and indicators of family life increasingly more pathological. Chicanos are living in a society not equipped to deal with these problems.[10]

Is the relative lack of progress the fault of leadership or of organizations? Both, perhaps. Though the fault may lie, as Mark Antony intoned, not in the stars but in ourselves. We expected the miraculous from our ordained leaders and perhaps the impossible from our organizations. We expected a larger response from mainstream America. When Sanchez wrote *Forgotten People*, he hoped that the U.S. Government would redeem its pledge to his people—the pledge imbedded in the Treaty of Guadalupe Hidalgo— that it would help his people lift themselves up by their bootstraps; instead, Sanchez wrote, "it took away our boots." The Chicano Movement, unlike previous Mexican American movements, made a clarion call that change would have to come from Mexican Americans themselves, not externally nor benevolently from government. This did not mean that government has no role to play. On the contrary, government has a large role to play because it was, after all, government that made Chicanos an internal colony—in the same way it made Puerto Rico an internal colony.[26]

Chicano organizations did not spring into being sui generis. Though most often in opposition to historical oppression, Chicano organizations nevertheless modeled their structures on organizations they had experience with. This was in keeping with Franz Fanon's observation in *Black Faces/White Masks*: having experience with few other models, invariably the liberated turn to models with which they are familiar.

Still, the objectives of Chicano leaders and organizations were sufficiently radical to alarm mainstream America and even some Mexican Americans. That's why the term "Chicano" describes a generation whose socio-political directions veered sharply from the historical trajectory of the Mexican American experience.

Organizations are oftentimes ephemeral and evanescent entities of the moment, chimeras of a hopeful vision. The perduring "artifacts" of change are most often the ideas which give birth to change, ideas written down on clay tablets, or parchment, or codices, or books for future generations to ponder and by which to judge the efficacy of the past.

The most fertile and perhaps the most dynamic period of the Chicano Movement was the Chicano Renaissance. Its most enduring manifestations are found in education and the cultural arts. Loosely, the decade of the Chicano Renaissance can be likened to an Iliad of Chicano assaults on mainstream America; and by extension, the decade from 1976 to 1985 can be regarded as the odyssey of Chicanos navigating through the rocks and shoals of mainstream America on the "final lap home," as Ricardo Sanchez, the Chicano poet laureate of Aztlan, put it.

Unfortunately that meaning is becoming blurred and obscured by the mindset of Chicanos since 1986 as they grapple with the notion of Hispanicity: are they Chicanos or Hispanics? Constituting more than three-fifths of the Hispanics in the United States, many Chicanos are wary that by subsuming themselves under the rubric of Hispanics they will lose their edge in numbers to Cuban Americans, who make up less than 5 percent of the U.S. Hispanic population but, like Jewish Americans, are influential beyond their numbers in the population.

The decade from 1986 to 1995 and to the close of the 20th century seems to be a period during which Chicanos are receding into the backdrop of American culture as an ethnic group being culturally if not economically assimilated into the mainstream. High school textbooks still do not reflect the ethnic mosaic that is the American experience, and Chicano high school students do not inquire why that is so, nor do their parents. In the 90s we will see national organizations like G.I. Forum and S.E.R. move their headquarters from the southwest to Washington, D.C. providing further testimony to the prominence of Chicanos in the national scene. The Chicanos of this generation are busy professionalizing their lives, fashioning them on the templates of the dominant culture.

Forgotten now seem to be the Mexican American heteroclites who fashioned and shaped the various canons of the Chicano Movement. Here and there, chispas of those thoughts flow and fan the flame for a flickering moment. The Chicano Movement was a distant mirror to time denigrated by mainstream thought. Chicano intellectuals fashioned a heuristic tradition for the proper study of Chicano life and culture. Has it all been for naught?

No. We do not think so. The Chicano Movement and its cultural renaissance stand as a metaphor to the integrated vision of past and present. This renewed sense of pride in their bicultural heritage has helped Mexican Americans understand better the socio-political context of their lives in the United States. More and more, national and local Chicano organizations (in concert with other Hispanic organizations) are impacting the national education agenda. This is particularly evident in the appointments of the Texan Lauro Cavazos and the New Mexican Manuel Lujan as the first Mexican Americans to cabinet rank. This is an acknowledgement of the importance of the demographics and of the emergence of a Chicano middle class, a factor that surely inspired President Bush to appoint them.

Summary

The problems that confront Chicanos and Hispanics are the problems of most Americans—environment, war and peace, poverty, the population explosion, and most recently unbridled government and corporate corruption. These problems, according to Hans Morgenthau result from deliberate policies from powerful interests. Noam Chomsky points to a "system of ideological control which aims to make the issues seem remote from the general population and to persuade them of their incapacity to organize their own affairs or to understand the social world in which they live without the tutelage of intermediaries.[21, 5]

Chicano organizations have been influenced by the same forces—perhaps to a greater extent—that influence mainstream culture and its leaders; they are vulnerable to the real power brokers—interests that set the broad direction of economic and government policy. It is not only the powerful interests, however, that prevent Chicanos from forging a better life for themselves—strong families, strong friendships, viable communities, and strong vocations. The fragmentation in the Chicano community mirrors the larger society. The distorted concept of democracy that sets up a competitive system for the resources of the society with little concern for the common good makes it difficult to organize around a common purpose. Chicano organizations often work at cross-purposes with one another and they often miscommunicate one another's motives. Within these circumstances it is difficult to lay out a strategy or a set of strategies on how to organize. The only way to approach an organizing strategy with Chicano communities is to openly and honestly recognize its problems; identify the institutions that can address these problems—family, schools, government, and churches; and work to see that they do not deviate from their institutional and moral mission. Ernesto Galarza once referred to this as "institutional deviance." At bottom, it is Chicanos that have to set the example to behave justly and democratically; it is only in this fashion that a true idea of community can be developed.

Realistically, given the existing power arrangements and the strategies available to counter them, it is difficult to expect anything other than token changes from American institutions.

In the end, however, it may be the demographic imperative that will promote the Hispanic agenda. And in the end it will be the demogrpahic imperative that will be the demise of the Hispanic agenda. At the moment there appears to be some planning for that eventuality and until then, we suspect, Hispanics will proceed with their agenda tuned to that eventuality. But when that moment comes, Hispanics will not need an ethnic-specific agenda because the eventuality makes the public agenda their agenda. If this does not happen, internecine conflict will surely follow.*

There are no quick fixes and there are no Chicano messiahs. There must be an understanding of the disjunctures between democratic and Judeo-Christian values and the reality facing not only Mexican Americans or Hispanics but all segments of American society: black or white, rich or poor. Practice must be based on engaging dialogue where there is no dialogue, organizing where there is no organization, and creating jobs where there are no jobs. It is a slow, gradual process that will require a vision and perhaps more than anything else courage, the courage to assume responsibility for their own problems and to face the future.

We conclude by citing Chomsky in his lecture on Russell "On Changing the World:"

> Yet it would be tragic if those who are fortunate enough to live in the advanced societies of the West were to forget or abandon the hope that

---

*There are many explanations for the state of affairs in American society: liberal secularism and the loss of religious values; individualism and the loss of civic virtue[2]; capitalism and the loss of morality; the loss of moral content[23]; the absence of a shared vision of the public good[4]; and the narcissism of American culture.[14]

our world can be transformed to "a world in which the creative spirit is alive, in which life is an adventure full of hope and joy, based rather upon the impulse to construct than upon the desire to retain what we possess or to seize what is possessed by others."[6]

Endnotes

1. F. D. Bean, E. H. Stephen and W. Ortiz, "The Mexican origin population in the United States: A demographic overview." In R. O. de la Garza, F. D. Bean, C. M. Bonjean, R. Romo and R. Alvarez (Eds.), *The Mexican American experience: An interdisciplinary anthology* (Austin: University of Texas, 1985), 57–75.
2. R. N. Bellah *et al.*, *Habits of the heart* (Berkeley: University of California Press, 1985).
3. William Blake, "London," in *Songs of Experience* (London: R. Brinley Johnson, 1901).
4. A. Bloom, *The Closing of the American Mind* (New York: Simon & Schuster Inc., 1987).
5. N. Chomsky, *Language and Responsibility* (New York: Pantheon Books, 1977), 4, 5.
6. N. Chomsky, *Problems of Knowledge and Freedom: The Russell Lectures* (New York: Vintage Books, 1971).
7. E. Cortez Jr., "Changing the Locus of Political Decision Making." In the Gospel in the World: Community Organizing, *Christianity and Crisis* 47 [(February 1987)]: 18–22.
8. F. M. Cox, J. L. Erlich, J. Rothman and J. E. Tropman, *Strategies of Community Organizing: A Book of Readings* (Itasca, Ill.: F. E. Peacock Publishers, 1979), 3.
9. F. M. Cox, J. L. Erlich, J. Rothman and J. E. Tropman, *Tactics of Community Practice* (Itasca, Ill.: F. E. Peacock Publishers, 1977), 1–11.
10. R. O. de la Garza, F. D. Bean, C. M. Bonjean, R. Romo and R. Alvarez, *The Mexican American Experience: An Interdisciplinary Anthology* (Austin: University of Texas, 1985).
11. Franz Fanon, *Black Skin White Masks* (New York: Grove Press, 1982), 100.
12. M. Ginsberg, *The Idea of Progress: A Revaluation* (London: Methvens, 1953), 68.
13. S. A. Gonzales, *Hispanic American Voluntary Organizations* (Westport, Connecticut: Greenwood Press, 1985), 106, 107.
14. C. Lasch, *Haven in a Heartless World: The Family Besieged* (New York: Basic Books, Inc., 1979).
15. R. W. Ludomyr, *Encyclopedic Directory of Ethnic Organizations in the United States* (Littletoy Colorado: Libraries Unlimited Inc., 1975).
16. C. Marin, Rodolfo "Corky" Gonzales: The Mexican-American Movement Spokesman," *Journal of the West* 14 (April, 1975): 107–120.
17. C. McWilliams, *North from Mexico: The Spanish-Speaking People of the United States* (New York: J. B. Lippincott Co., 1949).
18. M. S. Meier and F. Rivera, *The Chicanos: A History of Mexican Americans* (New York: Hill and Wang, 1972).
19. B. E. Mercer, *The American Community* (New York: Random House, 1956), 27.

20. M. Montiel, *Hispanic Families: Critical Issues for Policy and Programs in Human Services* (Washington, D.C.: National Coalition of Hispanic Mental Health and Human Service Organizations, 1978).

21. H. Morgenthau, "The end of the republic?" *New York Review of Books* (September 1970): 39, 40.

22. R. Nisbet, *The Social Philosophers, Community and Conflift in Western Thought* (New York: Thomas Y. Cromwell Co., 1973), 446.

23. M. Novak, *The Spirit of Democratic Capitalism* (New York: Simon and Schuster, 1982).

24. F. D. Ortego y Gasca, *Backgrounds of Mexican American Literature* (Austin, Texas: Caravel Press, 1981).

25. R. V. Padilla, "Chicano Studies Revisited" *Occasional Paper #6*, (University of Texas, El Paso: Chicano Studies Program, 1987), 9, 10.

26. G. I. Sanchez, *Forgotten People: A Study of New Mexicans* (Albuquerque: University of New Mexico Press, 1940).

27. Search, *A Report from the Urban Institute 5* (5–6).

28. R. Sennett and J. Cobb, *The Hidden Injuries of Class* (New York: Vintage Books, 1972), 17, 18.

29. M. Vigil, *Chicano Politics* (Washington: University Press of America, 1977), 134.

30. R. L. Warren, *The Community in America* 2 ed., (Chicano: Rand McNally & Co., 1972), 53.

31. L. Wirth, *The Ghetto* (Chicago: University of Chicago Press, 1928).

References

R. Brischetto and R. O. de la Garza, "The Mexican American Electorate: Political Participation and Ideology." Occasional Paper No. 3. In *The Mexican American electorate series* (San Antonio: Southwest Voter Registration and Education Project).

J. L. Erlich and F. G. Rivera, "The challenges of Minorities and Students." In F. M. Cox, J. L. Erlich, J. Rothman and J. E. Tropman, *Strategies of Community Organizing: A Book of Readings* (Itasca, Ill.: F. E. Peacock Publishers, 1979), 491–496.

C. D. Garvin and F. M. Cox, "A History of Community Organizing Since the Civil War with Special Reference to Oppressed Communities." In F. M. Cox, J. L. Erlich, J. Rothman and J. E. Tropman, *Strategies of Community Organizing: A Book of Readings* (Itasca, Ill.: F. E. Peacock Publishers, 1979), 45–75.

M. Harrington, *New York Times* (January 1978): 17.

J. Limon, "El Primer Congreso Mexicanista de 1911: A Prescursor to Contemporary Chicanismo," *Aztlan* 5 (January and February 1979).

M. S. Meier, *Mexican American Biographies: A Historical Dictionary, 1836–1987* (New York: Greenwood Press, 1987).

F. D. Ortego y Gasca, *American Hispanics: A Contemporary Perspective* (Austin, Texas: Caravel Press, 1986).

O. I. Romano, "The Historical and Intellectual Presence of Mexican Americans," *El Grito: A Journal of Contemporary Mexican Thought* (Fall 1969).

M. G. Ross, *Community Organization: Theory and Principles* (New York: Harper & Bros., 1955).

The Tomas Rivera Center: A national Institute for Policy Studies. (October 1985). *The Changing Profile of Mexican America, A Sourcebook for Policy Making* (Claremont, California).

U.S. Bureau of the Census. (September 1983). *Condition of Hispanics in American Today* (Washington, D.C.).

R. L. Warren, *The Community in American* (Chicago: Rand McNally & Co., 1963).

CHAPTER FOUR

The African-American Community in 1990: The Search For a Practice Method

WYNETTA DEVORE

The author wishes to thank Chester H. Jones, MSW, Ed.D, of the School of Social Work at Rutgers, the State University of New Jersey, for his consultation and comments and his commitment to the work. Thanks also to William Pollard, Dean of Syracuse University School of Social Work for his comments and suggestions.

It was the best of times, it was the worst of times, it was the age of wisdom, it was the age of foolishness, it was the epoch of belief, it was the epoch of incredulity, it was the season of light, it was the season of darkness, it was the spring of hope, it was the winter of despair . . .*

Dicken's classic work involves a spectacular revolution, where the fortunes of the politically powerful social elite decline drastically, and where, for many, there was death at public executions. For the poverty stricken and the impotent, there was a stimulating sense of power, of hope for change that would indeed bring light into the dreariness of their lives.

This dramatic change in the political fortunes of France occurred in times that seemed to be the very best and the most oppressive at the same

---

*C. Dickens, A Tale of Two Cities (New York, Dodd, Mead & Company, 1942).

time. Although Dickens's work is fiction, it holds truths related to consequences growing out of the gross misuse of power and the possibility for
change when the oppressed join together in activities designed to free themselves from tyranny.

The dichotomy of best and worst, wisdom and foolishness, belief and
incredulity, light and dark, is presented in this chapter about the African-
American experience, to suggest that this is the reality of experiences in the
past and the present as well.

I would suggest that for social work a "war" is not the solution. Rather, I
would suggest a serious reconsideration of familiar interventions related to
community work. Social planning, community development and social
action, and systematic change processes, while successful in the past in
ethnic minority and mainstream communities, seem no longer viable in
African-American urban communities. A reassessment is essential if we are
to be effective in these communities of oppression in the 1990s.

The Montgomery Bus Boycott
December 5, 1955 to December 21, 1956

Community action such as the Montgomery bus boycott does not "just happen." The narrow view of this historical event suggests that one day Mrs.
Rosa Parks, an African-American woman living and working in Montgomery, Alabama decided on December 1, 1955, that she would no longer be
ordered from her seat on a public bus to accommodate a white passenger
who was standing.

A more diligent search would reveal that the African-American community had activists with a framework for change in place. Earlier attempts to
challenge the segregation policy of the state of Alabama, enforced by the
Montgomery City Lines bus company, had failed.

The principal participants early in this episode were E. D. Nixon, a Pull-
man porter and past president of the NAACP (National Association for the
Advancement of Colored People), Fred Grey, an African-American lawyer,
and Clifford Durr, a white lawyer and former member of the Federal Communications Commission. Each played a part in releasing Mrs. Parks from
jail and the events that were to unfold.

Charged only with violating the state bus segregation laws, Mrs. Parks
was released from jail. She was still in a precarious position, however, E. D.
Nixon asked if she would be willing to fight the case according to plans that
had already been laid-out by the NAACP. Her decision was yes, she would
continue the fight. Branch quotes her as saying, "If you think it will mean
something to Montgomery and do some good, I'll be happy to go along with
it." Mrs. Parks also displayed the personal characteristics that would make

her the best defendant in this case. She was "humble enough to be claimed by the common folk, and yet dignified enough in manner, speech, and dress to command the respect of the leading classes."[3]

The NAACP was not the only group active in the community. The Women's Political Council had been founded in 1946 responding to the continual arrest of African-American bus passengers. A leader of the Council, Jo Ann Robinson, was also a member of the women's group that was a part of Rev. Martin Luther King's new political affairs committee at Dexter Avenue Baptist Church. These women were ready when their help was requested.[3, 36]

The Council membership of middle class professional women met last in the evening at Jo Ann Robinson's office at Alabama State College. They composed and mimeographed a letter and recruited students to help them circulate it to the community. The letter began:

> Another Negro woman has been arrested and thrown into jail because she refused to get out of her seat on the bus and give it to a white person.

It concluded asking:

> . . . every Negro to stay off the buses on Monday in protest of the arrest and trial.

A second letter prepared by a group of community leaders supported the Council request and added another request.

> Come to a mass meeting Monday at 7:00 P.M. at the Holt Street Baptist Church for further instruction.

The local press reported that a "top secret" meeting of Montgomery Negroes who planned a boycott on city buses was planned for Monday, December 5. The press announcement that the meeting was open to people of all races gave leaders assurance that white people would not attend and would get the word of the meeting to more community people. The white press in its disdain of the challenge would continue to be used by the boycott leaders to inform the African-American community. The press was among the community institutions that could be placed on the list of oppressors. "Negro" news was of little consequence unless related to crime. This news story was placed only at the behest of E. D. Nixon.

The community did not ride the buses on Monday as the leaders requested. At the very least, 5,000 persons attended the mass meeting. Dr. Martin Luther King Jr., the new pastor of the Dexter Avenue Baptist Church, was presented as the chairperson of the newly formed Montgomery Improvement Association, which would lead the efforts for change in bus policy. The list of demands set forth by the MIA leaders was approved and those in attendance agreed to continue the boycott of the buses. Much to the amazement of bus company officials, city and state officials, the nation, and themselves, they continued to walk, use taxis, or drive or ride cars supplied by neighbors or the Association.

The Supreme Court decision on November 13, 1956 affirmed a decision of a special three-judge panel in declaring Alabama state and local laws requiring segregated buses unconstitutional. The boycott ended officially on December 21, 1956.

The success of the Montgomery Boycott provided a framework for change in oppressed African-American communities throughout the nation. The components of success were the organized groups: the NAACP, the Women's Political Council, the Montgomery Improvement Association, the churches, members and clergy, and a community willing to follow trusted leaders of this revolution. While we may identify elements of community organization in the process this was an entirely new phenomenon, perhaps even a revolution of sorts.

In a December 1956 review of the boycott, King suggested that the experience had presented six lessons:

1. We can stick together for a common cause.
2. Our leaders do not have to sell out.
3. Threats and violence do not intimidate those who are sufficiently aroused and nonviolent.
4. Our church is becoming militant, adding a social gospel.
5. We have gained a new sense of dignity and destiny.
6. We have discovered a new and powerful weapon, nonviolent resistance.

These lessons were to be used by youthful leaders as they began the implementation of the social gospel. The church, already the center of social life, added a political activist role. Pastors became political leaders and were often candidates for political office as the movement proceeded.

The new sense of dignity and pride was heard in the proclamation that "black is beautiful." It was seen in the use of African patterns and materials used in the clothing of men and women. Women no longer attempted to emulate white women as they pressed their hair. The natural was seen as beautiful and closer to the African heritage than straight hair, achieved through a torturing procedure. The colors Green, Black, and Red in banners, flags, and clothing were reminders of the dignity to be claimed in an African heritage.

The call for dignity and destiny was heard in the call for "Black Power" which proclaimed that: "We blacks must respond in our own way, on our own terms, in a manner which fits our temperaments. The definitions of ourselves, the roles we pursue, the goals we seek are *our* responsibility."[5]

Nonviolence was the only viable weapon available. The courts could not be depended upon, individuals and communities had no ability to influence poltical institutions, the vote was withheld in many jurisdictions, and social welfare systems were callous in their responses. Nonviolence provided strength and was a weapon that was unfamiliar to the oppressor. It was thereby their undoing, destroying their myth of a violent, volatile African-American community.

Entering the 1960s: The Way It Was

Employment and Income

African-American communities entered the 1960s greatly influenced by the repercussions of World War II. As in other communities, the war had brought about some relief from the Depression and provided employment for skilled and nonskilled workers alike. Prior to World War I there had been movement from rural areas in the South to cities where there was a demand for labor created by the building of railroads and the growth of industrial and commercial enterprise.

Unskilled farmers moved from their rural homes to the cities. The more noted movement was to the North, but many persons moved to other southern cities searching for opportunities. In the north and the south they were unprepared for the increasingly technological work place. As department stores, hotels, and office buildings installed self-service elevators there were few jobs as elevator starters, a prime position for persons with few skills.

Experiences in the military provided young people with their first integrated work and social experience. Antidiscriminatory and desegregation policies and practices of the federal government and the military had changed to a great degree the earlier personnel practices of the armed forces. A new perspective on segregation was developing; the way in which African-Americans viewed the future began to differ from that of their family and community. Their life chances were enhanced by the G.I. Bill, which provided for higher education or vocational training.

Federal and state Fair Employment Practice Commissions gave greater assurance of nondiscrimination in the defense industries and government employment. The Civil Rights Acts of 1957 and 1960, the 1954 Supreme Court decision to desegregate the public schools, along with other favorable legal decisions, provided support for movement into the American mainstream. There was a light from this positive legislation. But at the same time there was the darkness of the continued struggle for employment and a decent education.

Buses were desegregated; it was no longer necessary for an African-American to give up his or her seat for a white person who was standing. These desegregated buses carried their African-American passengers to a variety of positions, some marginal, others offering the promise of advancement.

A million workers, mostly women, were identified as domestics and employed as servants for white families. African-American men with an elementary school education were able to fill service positions vacated by white men who had high school educations.[26]

Social Class

The level of formal education received in the 1960s as well as the present had a direct relationship to one's place in or out of the labor force. The median income for the jobs listed above was less than $4,000. Those at the lower end of the continuum had little or no income resulting in reliance on the public welfare system. There are varying notions as to the range of social classes. For discussion here, the work of Myrdal, Drake, and Frazier supply the perspective.[27, 12, 16]

Drake and Cayton present the class structure as a pyramid with a large lower class at the base, a moderate-size middle class in the middle, and a small upper class at the apex. At some points the middle and upper classes seem to merge.[13]

No matter what the delineation may have been, a distinct social class system existed and was important to daily life and the potential for community action related to the oppression felt by persons at each level.

Middle class persons with college degrees, often unable to find employment in their fields, became lower echelon government employees. Very often this employment was found in the United States Postal Service.

The large lower class contained unskilled or semiskilled laborers and domestic workers in the north and the south. Jobs held by agricultural day laborers, tenant farmers, and household servants paid poorly and lacked stability. The lack of education only compounded job insecurity.

Many older persons were illiterate. Their standards of industry and honesty were rated as low. They were accused of gambling, excessive drinking, narcotics use, as well as interpersonal violence. Drake (1965) defined these families as "unorganized".[27, 12]

At a higher level were the "organized" families who had ambitions to do better than their own or their children's status. They had memberships in social clubs, lodges, and churches. They were charged to "get ready for the Judgment Day" and were extolled "to be in the world but not of the world." A social gospel was not a priority on Sunday morning. Rather, the social gospel and social justice was the weekday task of the clergy.

The smaller middle class, referred to by Frazier as the Black Bourgeoisie, had more secure positions than did the lower class. Few, except teachers, had college educations. The majority had a primary or secondary education. Attainment of either level was high on the list of family values. Education helped their children to "get ahead," or "make something of themselves." Thrift, independence, honesty, industry, appropriate public behavior, and respectability were included in their standards.[16]

Family goals of home ownership or going into business were not easily met as banks refused funding for either. Frazier (1957) describes the black middle class as seeking acceptance, through hard work and achievement, by a white society that continued to reject them.[16]

Like the "organized" lower class, much of their social life centered around Baptist or Methodist churches. In addition, there was an array for men and women of social clubs and voluntary activities. Only on rare occasions were they to be included in social cliques and voluntary activity along with white persons.[12]

The life style of the small African-American upper class was similar to that of the white middle class. This status could be held by successful farmers, persons with training or employment in banking or insurance, contractors, real estate agents, or the delivery of personal services. Employment in public agencies, particularly the postal service, coupled with home ownership and a high school education, carried great esteem and membership in the upper class.

Education was a substitute for inherited wealth and therefore carried great prestige despite the level of employment. Upper-class African-American children were protected from the lower-class African-American and the humiliation of discrimination.

Members of this upper class were the "race leaders" who found positions in public administration. They were participants on local civic boards and interracial councils, members of the NAACP, and other defense organizations such as the Montgomery Women's Political Council, but these men and women were absent from the boards of local or national political operations or the boards of foundations and professional organizations.

The upper-class social world was maintained through interaction on the national and local level through membership in fraternities and sororities, college alumni and professional associations, as well as civic and social clubs.

Their churches, Episcopal, Congregational or Presbyterian, were more subdued than churches mentioned earlier. Their leaders "had some education and refinement."[27]

Members of this social class, essential to the movement for social change, were the victims of oppression as were members of the lower class that they wished to avoid. The lower class was clearly out, the upper class was half in—half out. This marginal position denied them access to the persons with influence who could serve as their contacts in the larger society. Personal contacts provided advancement in social, political, and professional life for the white middle and upper class. This limitation hampered the ability of African-Americans to make significant contributions to their own communities and to society as a whole.

Community Movement

The struggles presented here did not occur in a vacuum but rather in the context of communities. In a review of community movement in the 1960s Tidwell proposes a partial list of "Happenings" beginning with urban revolts. These "riots" began in 1963 and continued throughout the decade in cities such as Tampa, Florida; Cincinnati, Ohio; Atlanta, Georgia; Newark, New Brunswick, and Plainfield, New Jersey; and Detroit, Michigan.[35]

The Report of the National Advisory Commission on Civil Disorders placed the responsibility for the disorders on "White racism . . . which has been accumulating in our cities since the end of World War II." A combination of white attitudes and behaviors including pervasive discrimination and segregation, flight from the cities as African-Americans arrived, and the growth of poverty in the resulting ghettos were seen as the base for disorder. Added to these were frustrated hopes and the sense of powerlessness.[7]

Other "happenings" were the change in behavior of African-American college students who began to challenge public policy by "sitting-in." Middle and upper class young people became restless as they questioned the status quo. The Student Nonviolent Coordinating Committee (SNCC) was founded in 1960. The actions of radical groups such as the Black Panthers prompted the Congress of Racial Equality (CORE), which was founded earlier in 1942, to reconsider their ideology and programmatic orientation.

Demands for community control, particularly in New York City, were based on the conviction that such power was a necessary precondition for the welfare of the community. This demand was particularly evident in the area of education.

Crowded schools were without sufficient educational supplies. The curriculum, designed for middle class white suburban children, did not consider the needs of urban children who were captive audiences in a hostile environment. Their teachers had less professional experience and lower verbal skills than those assigned to predominantly white schools.

Charged by the Supreme Court decision of 1954, schools began the move toward integration. This change in the public school policy was seen as the solution to the educational problems of African-American students. In this redesign of the educational system, African-American students lost a core of their own teachers who were committed to them and had "expectations of excellence and instilled a sense of pride in achievement in their students."[11]

The final "happening" on the Tidwell list was the popularity of a new set of verbal symbols indicating the depth and direction of the ideological change that was occurring. An emerging vocabulary used by the entire community included words such as imperialism, oppression, exploitation, liberation, and revolution. The new rhetoric was reinforced by public figures such as Malcolm X.[35]

The Politics of the 1960s

Andrew Billingsley suggests that the political system was even more oppressive than the educational system. At no level, national, state, or local was there any indication of a reasonable consideration of the African-American perspective. Nor was there meaningful representation at any level.[4]

In 1968 there were six African-American representatives in Congress, 1 percent of that body. At the same time, African-Americans were 12 percent of the population. Without adequate political representation, social justice was impossible. An increasing electorate was unable to make inroads. In large cities, where the bulk of these voters were found, there were few political organizations.

Prominent among the organizations that did exist was the Mississippi Freedom Democratic Party, founded in 1966. This legally constituted political party challenged the regular democratic party of Mississippi which excluded African-American voters from membership. During Freedom Summer 1964 thousands of volunteers, both white and African-American, registered voters for the new party and taught in freedom schools. These volunteers established health clinics and freedom theaters which contributed to the renewal of pride and self-worth in distressed communities.[36]

In 1961 Atlanta voters were encouraged as they were able to influence the mayoralty race through the defeat of Lester Maddox, an avowed segregationist. The developing political leadership, often based in the church and in the business community, was able to organize a campaign and "get out the vote."

The success in the Atlanta effort and in other cities and towns throughout the country encouraged greater participation in political processes. As organizations developed there was a recognition that if success was to continue, coalitions were essential. Alliances were formed in the south with upper-class business and professional groups who supported voting rights and the end of police abuse.

Vital contributions were made by white liberals and the white business community as they encouraged voting and exerted political pressure on their colleagues. It was dangerous for northern politicans to show anti-Negro sentiments. Cooperation enabled them to "look good" in the community and retain the respect of white peers. These alliances were fragile, to say the very least. The need was to strengthen community political organizations where they existed and to develop them in cities where they were needed. A new corps of leaders who were youthful, and who had vision, vitality and plans for action was needed.[37]

An Emerging Leadership

Pfautz suggested that a "New Negro" was emerging. These Negroes began to carve out their own self-image of self assurance and pride in race. They were the educated children of World War II veterans, encouraged by the changes that their parents had witnessed, but they were impatient. Their education provided them with motivation, capacity, and the skills to bring about significant change. These young leaders enabled their communities to initiate independent action and make demands on the white power structure for equality. The Montgomery Improvement Association was their organizational model, the Montgomery Bus Boycott, their measure of success.[31]

The 1960s Sit-Movement was initially the activity of young college students who did not always receive the support of elderly members of southern communities who were accepting of life as they found it at the moment. They wondered why it was necessary to picket in demand for a seat at a Woolworth lunch counter, asking a young picket sign holder, "Lady, ain't you got a table at home"?[8]

In addition to sit-ins, there was a wave of protests that used a new tool, nonviolence, which provided a message of hope. Participants began to sense a new kind of power in themselves and in the race. Nonviolence mandated that one love oneself, seeking to win opponents to a just cause rather than destroying them.

This new tool provided a method and the philosophy and strategies needed to confront the social order of the time. It was used in "wade-ins," "kneel-ins," and on picket lines. Other activities of challenge were economic boycotts, selective buying campaigns, coalitions, and litigation.[30, 8] This leadership and its followers were supported by the major organizations such as the Urban League and the NAACP. Although their agendas and methods differed, the goals were congruent. The older organizations, initially working toward the integration of middle class facilities, placed better housing, decent schools, quality education, and better jobs higher on their list of efforts; an urban agenda was developing.

Approaching the 1990s: A Dilemma

Two articles are highlighted on the cover of *Ebony* magazine's August 1989 issue. The first banner proclaims, "War! The Drug Crisis," the second, "A Special Report: 25 Years after the Civil Rights Act of 1964." An advertisement with a very brown-skinned woman follows inside the cover. On the first page there is a photograph of Toni Morrison, the novelist, and an essay by Maya Angelou entitled, "The Divining Ms. Morrison" which celebrates her as a recipient of an award honoring women of outstanding achievement. These three pages and the following articles represent the best and the worst of times for African-Americans at the end of the 1980s.

Political Developments

The best of the 1980s included progress in the state of Mississippi which experienced success and failure during Freedom Summer 1964. The segregated classroom no longer exists; African-Americans attend and graduate from the University of Mississippi. 600 African-Americans are presently serving in elected positions including mayors, city council members, and county commissioners.

Light and darkness are seen in major cities where there is political and social success while success in the economy remains illusive. In Richmond, Virginia, 51 percent of the total population is African-American, with a median family income of $12,643 in relation to the overall median of $16,820.

In the midst of public acclaim, noting breakthroughs in the city of Atlanta, there remains the reality of increased poverty, as well as an increase in crime and drug traffic. Despite economic progress there continues to be an economic gap, estimated to be about $600 billion plus between African-Americans and the mainstream of American society.[32]

The light of accomplishment may be seen in the judicial system. There are presently eleven African-Americans sitting on the United States Court of Appeals, once there was no representation. Persons who hold these positions were the emerging leaders of the 1960s. These men and women are also strategically placed in the Congress of the United States in growing numbers, enough to form a recognized Caucus.

The number of African-Americans serving in the legislative bodies of towns and cities increases, as do the number of mayors and other local and state officials, elected and appointed. There has been a viable candidate for president. The candidacy of Jesse Jackson, the election of Ron Brown as Chairperson of the National Democratic Party and Ed Cole as Chairperson of the Mississippi State Democratic Party are all markers of movement.

Social Class

Ebony, Essence, and *Black Enterprise* are magazines designed for a general audience, white and/or African-American. Their message is clear: it is possible to "make something of yourself." Each month there are stories of current political and academic success achieved by men, women, and children. There are regular glimpses into the palatial homes of those who have achieved celebrity status in the world of sports and entertainment.

The advertisements are for products that are associated with middle-class status: credit cards, banks, jewelry, automobiles, airlines, and designer clothing. Items that make for finer living find a place as well: vacation resorts, fine wines and liquors, and household appliances. The expectation is that readers will be able to afford these items. The difficulty here, as with much of the media, is that only a portion of the story is told.

Stories of those found in the lower class may be seen daily in newspapers and on television newscasts. The stories relate to welfare reform legislation which seeks a method of moving clients into the work force into marginal, low-level positions; to high rates of teenage pregnancy among the poor; to underemployment and unemployment; to homeless families; and to special programs designed to alleviate poverty and the stress that accompanies it.

While the lines between the social classes remain unclear in many instances, there is a small upper class, a growing middle class, a working class that may be similar to Drake's "organized" poor and a group of persistent poor.[12]

John E. Jacob, president of the Urban League, suggests that twenty years after the Kerner Commission report, which noted two societies—one Black, one white—"but also two societies within the African-American community—one middle class and aspiring, the other desperately poor and increasingly without hope," Douglas Glasgow's concept of a black underclass encompasses the persistent poor and Jacob's description.[22, 18]

The underclass cuts across race as do other social stratifications, yet there are particular qualities to the minority experience. Glasgow explains that not only must this group contend with structural factors which limit opportunity but with continuing racial discrimination as well. The African-American underclass finds itself in "double jeopardy."[18]

Technology has taken the place of men and women in industry. The minority underclass lacks the educational experiences that prepare them to compete in this new technological work place. Like their grandparents, they have been displaced by technology.

It is urgent that attention be given to the future of African-American families and communities. Reassessment must take place and agendas and strategies must be formulated to ensure individual, family, and community growth.

Agenda and Strategies for the 1990s

Issues that confronted African-American families and communities in the 1950s, the point at which this narrative begins, remain at the forefront as the last decade of the 20th century begins. Teenage pregnancy, unemployment, underemployment, and homelessness have been cited. To these may be added alcoholism, abuse of illegal drugs and the resulting health crisis related to HIV+ and AIDS, dropouts from unresponsive educational systems and low scholastic achievement for those who remain. A most pressing issue is the status of young males who have been called "an endangered species." These young people have been "miseducated by the criminal justice system, mislabeled by the mental health system, and mistreated by the social welfare system".[17]

An agenda and strategies that respond to these and other issues will gain greater success if they are supported by a perspective which recognizes the "two-ness" of the African-American experience. This two-ness is felt as one claims an African heritage and membership in American society. It is the reality of life in the America at present. The historical review presented earlier in this chapter has emphasized the continuing two-ness of the African-American experience.[14]

In the same vein Norton speaks of the need for social workers to have a dual perspective acknowledging the two-ness of minority status in America. Chestang finds it to be a force in individual development as African-Americans combat hostile environments. Recognizing the reality of two-ness or a dual perspective Edelin (1990) declares that if African-Americans are to respond to new community agenda items they "must want and decide to make the most of being an African in America."[28, 6, 15]

In the 1990 issue of the National Urban League's annual publication, *The State of Black America*, Ramona H. Edelin of the National Urban Coalition proposes that a new model for group development be considered with agenda items evolving from an inward look that concentrates on "what we ourselves can and must do." The new community model would build upon ancient and traditional values and customs of respect and independence, the family as a haven of love and protection, the development of institutions for the common good, mastery in learning, encouragement and development of creative genius, and deep spirituality.

Strategies for development would coordinate or merge the work of organizations, businesses, and institutions into one effective cultural entity that would propel personal and group development. Goals and timetables would be developed in the light of Du Bois' concept of the two-ness of the African-American experience.[14]

This new model may be examined in the light of Roland Warren's (1963) concept of the community as a social system which is based on the idea of structured interaction of two more units. He suggests that a variety of processes take place within systems and identified them as communication, boundary maintenance, systemic linkage, socialization, social control, and institutionalization. In this instance they are examined as essential processes in African-America communities as they seek a new model for growth.

As traditional values and customs provide a foundation for community development, boundary maintenance and socialization processes take place. The need is to reclaim those traits that are a part of the two-ness of life. To claim an African heritage goes beyond the incorporation of hair and clothing styles. Rather its goal is to claim and incorporate the traditions of family and community pride along with a lasting cohesiveness.

Boundaries are maintained as communities define themselves as African-American with connections to the Africa of today rather than a mythical past. Definitions of community presented by the media and social welfare systems can not be accepted in that they interrupt the community boundary maintenance processes which preserve and maintain self-definition.

Social control and systems linkage processes take place as educational and religious institutions and businesses merge to foster personal and group development through a deep spirituality, mastery in learning, and the support of creative genius. These empowering activities replace those elements of deviance that have been identified earlier as continuing community issues.

The new model requires communication processes through which information, decisions, and directives may be transmitted. Edelin recalls the "magic of the movement" when goals were set and there was no doubt or fear that they would be reached if everyone worked on them together. Reviewing the success of the Montgomery Bus Boycott, Martin Luther King cited the ability of the community to stick together and the new sense of dignity and destiny that ensued. Communication skills and techniques that provided information, encouraged sound decision-making processes, and encouraged communities to follow the directions of community leaders in earlier social action are still useful. They are essential in the search for new leaders in developing new models for group and community growth.[15, 3]

The Social Work Dilemma

As social work educators, administrators, and practitioners examine the urban community today there is a dilemma which lies in our current lack of success. While we may understand Warren's (1963) concept fo the community as a social system we are not sure that the traditional definitions of community hold true when urban centers are considered. We know that there is strength in African-American communities but it is illusive knowing that the income of some welfare recipient families is supplemented by their children, who sell drugs to suburban middle-class customers entering urban neighborhoods searching for dealers. We know that parents warn their children of the physical danger that is to be found in the streets where the buying and selling of drugs is ordinary activity. Too often the elderly remain in their homes, fearful of the real danger that they have found in the street.

Even though there is empirical evidence that the African-American middle class does not always abandon their lower income kin, our practice experience tells us that many in the middle class have indeed abandoned their relatives as they moved to other cities for greater employment opportunities, or moved to the suburbs for comfort. This flight to the suburbs is facilitated by highways, parkways, and special transportation plans for commuters of all races working in the city.[25]

Social workers know that the quality of education available for suburban children, as compared to education available for urban children, supports the decision to move away from the city. Families may have greater assurance that services will be received in return for taxes paid. Such is not the experience in the city, where there are few services and high taxes.

We have available theory and practice models that have served the social work professional in the African-American community well in the 1960s, 1970s, and perhaps into the early 1980s. Their usefulness in the 1990s and into the twenty-first century, however, must be reconsidered.[29, 34, 24]

A Framework for Community Work in the 21st Century

As the new model of group growth is considered, a perspective for practice presented by Devore and Schlesinger should be considered as a guide to practice. The framework continually takes into consideration the experiences of African-American individuals, families, and communities and consists of six components which have been termed the "layers of understanding." These layers are comprised of the knowledge, values, and skills that are essential in all fields and approaches to practice. They will be used here as we search for a new, effective model for community organization in the 1990s and into the 21st century.[11]

Layer 1: Social Work Values

As students begin their social work education and practitioners begin their work with the various client populations, their attention is called to the values held by the profession. These values undergrid relationships with clients, colleagues, and various entities in the social welfare system.

These values are related to (1) our conceptions about people, who they are and their ability to cope with their environment; (2) the outcomes we wish for people, the quality of their lives, and the belief held about provisions and policies designed to improve that quality; and (3) the means that we use for dealing with people. How should people be treated?[23]

Brager, Specht, and Torczyner speak about the competing values in community organization, noting the changes that took place in the 1960s when participation by the social welfare consumer was encouraged in planning, policy making and programming, and new notions about organizing low-income people were developed. By the 1980s it appeared that people were less valuable and their participation became less important as "structured unemployment" became accepted and allocations for human resources were reduced. Our social values appear to be askew. Our social work values are at risk in such an environment.[2]

Layer 2: Basic Knowledge about Community

Throughout this chapter, community has been used as a term related to neighborhoods in which African-Americans live, raise their families, and attend church and a variety of social activities. A review of the social work and sociological literature would reveal the number of definitions suggesting that the concept is an evolving one.

Ross in 1955 defined community as a geographical area, or an association of ideas. In 1987, Brager, Specht, and Torczyner chose to offer the characteristics of a community, which includes community relationships that are systematic, interactive and interdependent and "based on shared history, mutual expectations, predictable roles, values, norms, and patterns of status differential".

Rivera and Erlich ask that we reconsider our definition of community as it relates to minority communities, including the African-American community. Their notion of neogemeinshaft grows out of the concept of gemeinshaft as relations based on how we feel about people;

our intimate relationships, which would be personal and informal based on sentiment. The Rivera-Erlich model assumes that community "life experiences take place within a causal, deterministic reality based on racism and economic exploitation." Neogemeinshaft communities are seen as examples of communities becoming and evolving within a hostile environment. Their survival skills, which often relate to their ethnic history, add to their uniqueness thereby requiring a reconsideration of the concept of community.[33, 21]

Warren's idea of the community as a social system has been examined here in relation to Edelin's model for community growth. The definitions of community provided by Ross, Pfautz, Cox and Brager, Specht, and Torczyner all have value as they call attention to geography, systems, problem generation and solution, history, roles, and expectations. They are less helpful if they are used in defining and understanding the complexities that are the reality of the African-American family and community of the late 1980s and early 1990s. It is difficult for families to feel a sense of community that defines shared history, mutual expectations, roles, values or norms. The city as a community is no longer a haven for families. They appear to be trapped in a dangerous environment, at significant risk in the economic and social areas of their lives.[15, 34, 31, 9, 2]

Glasgow laments a literature that claims that positive family and community values are on the wane. However, a cursory search of the literature suggests that, at present, we do not have available, empirical work that provides a clear profile of African-American families and their values in the 1980s. Empirical work such as this is needed in order have a clear view of the diversity to be found in African-American families and communities, and to dispel the negative views of each held by many.[18]

While social workers may hold to the values that respect the uniqueness of client groups, they find that the inner-city community may be a frightening place. Our practice experience tells us that families live in the inner city where the streets are unsafe for young and old; where housing is inadequate and neglected by landlords who exploit tenants; where the sale and use of illegal drugs is rampant; where children drop out of schools that lack quality and pay them scant attention.

Layer 3: Knowledge and Skill in Social Welfare Policies and Services

To accomplish the expectations of this layer of understanding an understanding of legislation and policy development is important. Not only must one have an understanding of and access to health and welfare resources, there is a need to have welfare rights information, legal information regarding evictions, and some knowledge of housing codes. In addition one must have knowledge of the indigenous African-American resources that are available.

The church stands out as a center of community life providing spiritual, social, and economic resources. The tendency is to look to the mainstream denominations such as Baptist, Methodist, and Episcopal. Often overlooked are small storefront congregations with self-appointed charismatic leaders. Although out of the mainstream, they are a significant resource for community action.

The work of Greek fraternities and sororities has been mentioned earlier in relation to work with individuals. They have the ability to expand their efforts to include communities. Add to these national groups, local social clubs with no national affiliation, lodges and their auxiliaries, self-help groups focused on particular problems, for example, the AIDS crisis in urban African-American communities, alcoholism and substance abuse, and union-sponsored health and welfare programs. The number of these resources that are in place and active will be related to the vitality of the community.

Layer 4: Self-Awareness, Including Insights Into One's Own Ethnicity and an Understanding of How that May Influence Practice

The essential task of this layer of understanding is to come to grips with one's own ethnicity. This undertaking requires a movement beyond race, beyond white or black, to much finer designations of ethnic heritage. The personal inquiry may well be for white practitioners: (1) How has my group related to African-American historically?, (2) Was there a family/community message about the value or worthlessness of African-Americans?, (3) Did I or do I believe it?, (4) What is my community like in relation to the African-American community in which I practice?, and (5) Does it make a difference?

For African-American practitioners there are another set of questions that reach for self-awareness. (1) Although we may have the same history in America are we really all the same?, (2) How different/similar have our life experiences been in relation to family, education, employment experiences, and church experiences?, (3) Does social class make a difference?, (4) Will it make a difference in our expectations of each other?

Gordon Hamilton identified self-awareness as attendant learning; when pursued as an object in itself it becomes more elusive. It must then be "caught." The dilemma then is how does one catch it? Finally, for each practitioner there is the concern for how well heightened ethnic sensitivity will influence practice.[20]

Layer 5: The Impact of the Ethnic Reality Upon the Daily Life of the Community

The concept of the ethnic reality is related to ethnicity and social class. Milton Gordon has identified the point at which ethnic group membership and social class meet as "ethclass". This concept is used to explain the role that social class membership plays in defining the basic conditions of life and at the same time account for differences between groups at the same social class level. We have seen that the life style of middle-class African-American families is different from whites at the same level. We realize that life for the low-income white family is stressful, yet the experience of the African American is compounded by racism.[19]

As the African-American community is reconsidered as "neogemeinshaft" the argument is that the primary cultural, social, political, and economic interrelationships are of fundamental importance for they are the major determinant of daily life. This is an extension of the ethnic reality related to community. African-American cultural, social, and economic position will determine the quality of life. Communities with little means may sense structural oppression to a greater extent than those who have achieved middle- or upper-class status.

A most particular task for the practitioner is to recognize the impact of deprivation on a community. There are few jobs within the community, few businesses owned by community members, and schools provide few skills. The public welfare system and its social workers have the ability to determine the extent of available income. Such disheartened, distressed communities have little ability to act on their own behalf. Their ethnic reality as low-income African Americans has a significant impact on the quality of their daily lives.

Layer 6: Adaptation and Modification of Skills and Techniques in Response to the Ethnic Reality

An awareness of the theories of community organization; organizational processes and procedures, both administrative and political, at all governmental levels; and the nature of the work of existing community groups are essential areas of knowledge. It is within this context that community organization traditionally occurs.[1]

There are familiar strategies: locality development, social planning, and social action assumes that some residents have the ability for community participation. The Alinsky model for intervention poses that groups are moved by self-interest, poor and affluent alike, and as soon as the poor understand this they will be able to get power and thereby gain control over their own destiny, again assuming the community has the ability to participate.[9, 2]

Practice experience tells us that many communities have no sense of cohesion. The traditional community pattern of "watching out" for the neighborhood children is considered to be an intrusion and encouragement to become active in the church or other groups is termed intrusive as well.

Neighborhood activist groups invite uncaring city officials to their neighborhoods to show them the inner-city impoverished environment. In truth many of our cities are dying. How can officials, citizens, and social workers be convinced that it is possible, given a strategic plan, to bring about change?

The social work practice and education dilemma poses that we are no longer sure that available models provide the skills and techniques needed for intervention in particular African-American communities. Ethnic-sensitive practice asked that social workers consider the significant impact of social class. Such an assessment is urgent in African-American communities where there is little or no economic base. In these communities residents are stuck in the underclass. The ethnic-sensitive framework for practice requires a consideration of the historical base for the present problem and an assumption that while the community may generate many of its own problems, it may at the same time hold the means for a solution.[10]

An important aspect of the framework is that it calls for simultaneous attention to individual, community, and systemic concerns as they grow out of community need and professional assessment. Often our clinical concerns are such that we attempt to "fix" individuals without a clear consideration of the community context in which the personal problem exists.

In asking for a consideration of the neogemeinshaft community, Rivera and Erlich examine the familiar variables of ethnicity, social structure, power structure, leadership patterns, economics, physical appearance, and social networks; the light of redefinition paying particular concern for the practice implications that evolve from this analysis. Neogemeinshaft implications require a greater knowledge of the ethnic reality of a community than might have been considered essential in the past. As community profiles are developed, attention must be given to the impact of social class, race, and ethnicity in the life of the community.[33]

Implications for Social Work Education

Social work education holds no immediate solutions to the practice dilemmas presented here. However, there are beginning steps that may be taken. Those responsible for curriculum development must be truly committed to mandates that require that attention be paid to racial and ethnic diversity. How much of the human behavior curriculum is devoted to community content? How often are African-American communities examined in relation to their strengths as well as the poverty, deprivation, and crime that may be found there? How often are the strategies of the Civil Rights Movement of the 1960s, including nonviolence, used as models for change? How much of the history of the struggle for equality may be found in our curriculum? What was the role of social work, if any, in the struggle? Who are the major African-American social work educators and practitioners? What have been their contributions to the profession?

Positive answers to these questions need not burden an already crowded curriculum. The question and answer process calls attention to a significant void in our education for the social work profession. The absence of such content leaves much of the African-American family and community story untold and therefore an area for practice remains unexamined.

As students search for the clinical, wishing to intervene with individuals and families, field offices search for field placements that will fulfill their educational needs. Scant attention is given to the possibility of field instruction in the at-large and the African-American community in particular. Perhaps it is through these well-designed experiences that we may be able to find a viable method for community intervention in the present. It is our belief, and our practice wisdom has taught us, that problems as well as solutions lie within the client system.

Endnotes

1. A. Barr, "Placements in Neighborhood Community Work: Evaluation of student performance," *Community Development Journal* 16 (January 1991):11–20.

2. G. Brager, H. Specht, and J. L. Torczyner, *Community Organizing*, 2nd ed. (New York: Columbia University Press, 1987), 36.

3. T. Branch, *Parting of the Waters: America in the King Years* (New York: Simon and Schuster, 1988), 130.

4. A. Billingsley, *Black Families in White America* (Englewood Cliffs, N.J.: Prentice Hall, 1968), 3–33.

5. S. Carmichael and C. V. Hamilton, *Black Power: The Politics of Liberation in America* (New York: Vintage Books, 1967), ix.

6. Leon Chestang, "Character Development in a Hostel Environment," *Social Work* 17 (May 1972): 100–105.

7. Commission on Civil Disorders, *Report of the National Advisory Commission on Civil Disorders* (New York: The New York Times, 1968), 10.

8. D. Cotton, "Reflections on an Experience in Social Change," *The Legacy* 1 (February 1989):4–6.

9. F. M. Cox, Communities: Alternative Conceptions of Community: Implications for Community Organization Practice. In F. M. Cox, J. L. Erlich, J. Rothman,

and J. E. Tropman, (Eds.), *Strategies of Community Organization Macro Practice* (Itasca, Ill. F.E. Peacock Publishers, Inc., 1987), 232–242.

10. W. Devore, *The Education of Black in New Jersey, 1900–1930: An Exploration in Oral History*, Unpublished doctoral dissertation, (Rutgers University, New Brunswick, N.J. University Microfilms No. 81055216, 1980).

11. W. Devore and E. G. Schlesinger, *Ethnic Sensitive Social Work Practice*, 2nd ed. (Columbus, Merrill Publishing Company, 1987), 23–32.

12. St. Clair Drake, "The Social and Economic Status of the Negro in the United States, *Daedalus*," 94 (February 1965):771–814.

13. St. Clair Drake and H. R. Cayton, *Black Metropolis: Study of Negro Life in a Northern City*, Rev. ed. (New York, Harcourt, Brace & World, Inc., 1962), 526–715.

14. W. E. B. Du Bois, *The Souls of Black Folks* (Chicago, A.C. McClurg, 1903), 20.

15. R. H. Edelin, Toward an African-American Agenda: An Inward Look, In J. Dewart, ed., *The Status of Black America 1990* (New York, National Urban League 1990), 173–183.

16. E. F. Frazier, "Urbanization of the Negro Population. In Introduction to *Afro-American Studies*," 4th ed. (Chicago, Peoples Collective Press, 1978), 214–219.

17. J. T. Gibbs, *Young, Black and Male in America: An Endangered Species* (Dover, Mass., Auburn House Publishing Company, 1988), 1, 2.

18. D. Glasgow, "The Black Underclass in Perspective," In J. Dewart, ed. *The State of Black America 1987* (New York, National Urban League, 1987), 129–144.

19. M. Gordon, *Assimilation in American Life* (New York, Oxford University Press, 1964), 51–54.

20. G. Hamilton, Self-awareness in Professional Education, *Social Casework* 35 (September 1954): 371–379.

21. J. B. Holland, "Contrasting Types of Group Relations," In P. I. Rose, ed. *The Study of Society: An Integrated Anthology* (New York, Random House, 1977), 372–375.

22. J. E. Jacob, "Choosing As Past and Future Converge," *American Visions*, 3 (Fall 1988):6–11.

23. C. S. Levy, "The Value Base for Social Work," *Journal of Education for Social Work*, 9 (1973):34–42.

24. T. M. Meenaghan, R. O. Washington and R. M. Ryan, *Macro Practice in the Human Services* (New York, The Free Press, 1982), 74–91.

25. H. P. McAdoo, ed. *Black Families* (Beverly Hills, Sage Publications, 1981).

26. D. P. Moynihan, "Employment, Income, and the Ordeal of the Negro Family," *Daedalus* 94 (April 1965):745–770.

27. G. Myrdal, *An American Dilemma: The Negro Problem and Modern Democracy* (New York, Harper & Row, 1962), 702.

28. D. G. Norton, *The Dual Perspective: Inclusion of Minority Content in the Social Work Curriculum* (New York, Council on Social Work Education, 1978), 3–10.

29. R. Perlman and A. Gruin, *Community Organization and Social Planning* (New York, John Wiley, 1972), 52–89.

30. H. W. Pfautz, "The Black Community, the Community School, and the Socialization Process: Some Caveats." In H. M. Levin, ed. *Community Control of Schools* (New York, Simon and Schuster, 1979).

31. H. W. Pfautz, "The New "New Negro": Emerging American," *Phylon* 24 (April 1963):360–368.

32. A. Pointsett and A. Russell, "Black Churches: Can They Strengthen the Black Family?" *American Visions* (October 1988):9–11.

33. F. G. Rivera and J. L. Erlich, "Neogemeinshaft Minority Communities: Implications for Community Organization in the United States," *Community Development Journal* 16 (March 1981):189–200.

34. M. G. Ross, *Community Organization: Theory and Principles* (New York, Harper & Brothers Publishers, 1955), 155–199.

35. B. J. Tidwell, "The Black Community's Challenge to Social Work," In J. A. Goodman, ed. *Dynamics of Racism in the Social Work Profession* (Washington, DC: National Association of Social Workers, 1973), 247–255.

36. J. Williams, *Eyes on the Prize: America's Civil Rights Years—1954–1965* (New York: Viking Penguin Inc., 1987).

37. J. Q. Wilson, "The Negro in Politics" *Daedalus* 94 (April 1965):949–973.

References

F. Cox, J. L. Erlich, J. Tropman and J. Rothman, "Models of Community Organization and Macro Practice," in *Strategies of Community Organization*, 4th ed. (Itasca, Ill. Peacock, 1987), 3–26.

R. Fein, "An Economic and Social Profile of the Negro American," *Daedalus* 94 (February 1965):815–846.

CHAPTER FIVE

Community Social Work with Puerto Rican Communities in the United States: One Organizer's Perspective

JULIO MORALES, PH.D.

Ideology, Values, and Social Change

In the late 1950s and early 1960s the Puerto Rican Association for Community Affairs (PRACA) sponsored youth conferences for Puerto Rican high school and college students. The theme of the conferences was "Aspire and Attain" and the organizers contributed their time to reach young Puerto Ricans and involve them in community work. PRACA's efforts served a backdrop to the creation (in 1962) of ASPIRA, the first Puerto Rican controlled private social service agency in the United States. Both groups had ideologies which stressed the importance of a college education, a positive sense of identity, knowledge of Puerto Rican history and culture, and a commitment to making a contribution to the Puerto Rican community.

In the late 1960s and early 1970s, as Puerto Rican Studies programs began to take root in New York and New Jersey colleges, a more progressive ideology developed. This ideology urged a rejection of traditional learning and teaching. It encouraged more collective methods of working, defined new sources of knowledge, discarded ideologies which condoned colonialism, and designed theoretical constructs which look at the power of macro forces on poor and powerless people.[1, 2]

Community social workers must confront the traditional "victim-blaming explanations" in themselves and others and must look to new historic, economic, and political interpretations that empower the poor and the oppressed and validate their contributions and struggles. As part of the community organization process, organizers must also consciously plan (formally and informally) discussions around how people are oppressed. This, however, must be done in a way that is meaningful to the everyday reality of peoples' lives.

For example, Puerto Rican elderly can be encouraged to talk about their days in Puerto Rico and their migration to the United States and why they left Puerto Rico. "We had to try elsewhere" is a frequent reply. "Why?" is the next logical question. "There were no jobs for us in Puerto Rico" is almost a universal refrain. "You mean you did not come here to get on welfare? That's what a lot of people think," the organizer can add. Such discussions with Puerto Rican elderly yield interesting anecdotes that underscore much hard work and high aspirations for themselves and their families. The sharing is emotional and empowering and can act as a springboard for addressing other stereotypes. After such discussions, the participants are more prepared for a victim's perspective on Puerto Rican powerlessness. Groups of elderly Puerto Ricans can become more assertive about their rights and inspired to duplicate the discussions with other elderly and with members of their own families.

An ideology which empowers client systems must also question societal priorities and forces that have led to huge differences in income and wealth distribution among Americans. For example, a recent congressional study[3] documents a 9.8 percent decrease in income for the nation's poorest and a 15.6 percent increase for the wealthiest. Similar studies also document that 35 percent of this nation's wealth is owned by .5 percent of its people, while 44 percent of the people share only 2 percent of the wealth.[4] Fifty-two percent of Puerto Rican families who live in New York City have incomes that fall below the poverty level.[5]

The community social worker must be able to project genuine caring for people and must strive to continuously enhance, integrate, and interpret knowledge, skills, and values when working with Puerto Rican and other oppressed groups. To some extent this departs from the social work ethos of impartiality, neutrality, and objectivity. It means placing the problems of a specific individual or community within the context of larger social, economic, and political problems and generously sharing such knowledge with the client and action systems.

On The History of the Americas and Puerto Rico

Many history lessons and books on Puerto Rico, other Latino American nations, and the United States start with Columbus' discovery of a new world in 1492. It is an arbitrary historical continuation of a European perspective and a good example of institutionalized ethnocentric and racist thinking which dismisses the fact that Native Americans preceded Columbus by thousands of years.

Columbus did not know that the Americas and the Caribbean were between Europe and Asia when he stumbled into the Caribbean. When the white people, with superior weapons of destruction, realized that Columbus had opened up a different land—rich and sparsely populated—they took the land through the use of violence, killing the vast majority of its red, bronze, or copper skinned inhabitants.

The Europeans brought to the Americas and the Caribbean millions of black people from Africa to use as slaves, selling them as they would any other property. In the United States and elsewhere, whites justified the killing of the people they called Indians and the enslavement of Africans by viewing them as subhumans, heathens, barbarians, stupid, lazy, and inferior. Later, the descendants of Africans and Indians would be viewed as inferior races. Today they are considered culturally deprived people and are still treated as inferior.

Puerto Ricans are a racially mixed people of Taino Indian, European, and African heritage. Puerto Rico became part of the United States in 1898 following the Spanish-American War as a result of the United States long-standing interest in its economic and geographic value.

The Foraker Act of 1900 established an American-controlled government in Puerto Rico. The president of the United States appointed the Island's governor and the upper chamber of the legislature. Economic control followed and a diversified agricultural society was turned into a sugar cane economy dominated by absentee businesses. The poorly paid and seasonal nature of work in the cane fields, shipping monopolies, and an unjust tax system helped to create a poverty so severe that by 1940 Puerto Rico became known as the "Poor House of the Caribbean."

> Operation Bootstrap, the industrialization of Puerto Rico's economy, was seen as a remedy. American capital quickly moved in to enhance a factory system that guaranteed owners seven years of tax exemptions, a cheap labor force, and political stability not associated with other Third World countries. . . Operation Bootstrap did not provide enough of the labor-intensive work it had promised. Instead, it has favored pharmaceutical, computer, and other capital-intensive industries. Factory owners often leave Puerto Rico when their tax exemptions expire and find a cheaper work force in other Third World countries. . .[6]

In Puerto Rico, unskilled workers often compete with each other and with undocumented workers from neighboring Caribbean nations. In the United States, Puerto Ricans compete for jobs as the manufacturing and farm work which they were recruited to do after the 1940s has dramatically decreased. Ironically, Puerto Rican migrants generally have more formal education than past immigrants, but jobs available today require more education and technical skills than those of yesterday's newcomers. In 1910, 90 percent of Americans did not finish high school but they could drop out of school and into jobs. That is no longer possible.

On Culture and Practice Issues

The Indian, European, and African mixture; the geography and topography of the Island; and a history of oppression and colonization by both Spain and the United States have combined to create a culture that is different from American, Spanish, and other Latin cultures. Community social workers must understand cultural nuances that could either enhance or limit their effectiveness.

In Puerto Rico, the Spanish rulers imposed their language, religion, values, family patterns, and culture onto the people. However, these were altered by the vocabulary, values, family patterns, diet, and religions of the Africans and Indians. Spain held on to Puerto Rico until the American invasion; thus Puerto Ricans as a people have always been a colonized and oppressed nation.

Out of this historical reality Puerto Ricans developed powerful survival mechanisms which are reflected in their culture. Much of that culture has survived even in an urban, highly technical world. Nevertheless, culture is not stagnant. Puerto Rican culture is in transition and often either adapts to or clashes with American culture and dominance in the United States and in Puerto Rico. It is important to stress that Puerto Rican communities and individuals differ from each other. Urbanization, social class, levels of formal education, length of time residing in the United States, and many other variables affect how Puerto Ricans in both the United States and Puerto Rico relate to traditional cultural patterns. For this reason, caution is essential in avoiding the possibility of acquiring or reinforcing stereotypes.

Respect, Honor, Dignity, and Hospitality

Traditionally, the Puerto Rican feelings of pride and esteem are rooted in community and are culturally related to being respectful to others and obtaining respect from others. Respect is: shown by politeness and good manners; being cordial; addressing neighbors and acquaintances, even very vulnerable ones such as clients or patients; using Don or Doña (Sir or Madam) followed by their first name (for example, Doña Juana and Don José); using the formal you (Usted); not joking or "jiving" unless all the people involved feel comfortable; calling adult strangers Mr., Miss, or Mrs.; avoiding eye contact when culturally appropriate; respecting specific dating rituals; and showing concern and consideration for other peoples' opinions, contributions, and feelings.

The cultural concept of honor goes beyond respect. Many demonstrate honor for parents, grandparents, aunts, uncles, and godparents by asking for their blessing (bendición) when entering or departing from their presence. Family honor is shown by: avoiding situations that would dishonor or shame one's family or community; bringing honor to one's family and community through work and accomplishments; being responsible for one another. A sense of obligation for the family is culturally expected and hospitality is captured in the phrase "mi casa es su casa" (my house is your house).

Honor and respect affects one's sense of dignity, or inner importance and value. One is entitled to his or her dignity because one is a person, uninfluenced by the accident of birth or the privileges and/or burdens of economic status. Such concepts, along with the race mixing, are partially responsible for relative harmony among Puerto Ricans regardless of color. This does not mean that racism is completely absent in Puerto Rican society but that American-style racism is unusual.[7]

Extended Family, Espiritismo

The mixing of the races has also enabled a mixing of Indian and African religions with Catholicism. American Protestantism on the Island and in the United States has also added a unique flavor to spirituality and religion in Puerto Rican communities. While most Puerto Ricans identify themselves as Catholic, Pentecostalism, an evangelical form of Protestantism has gained much support and acceptance, particularly among the poor. Congregrations of "brothers and sisters" may act as an extended family system, which has been "giving way" to the nuclear family in recent times.

The influence of African and Indian religion and dieties is obvious in most Puerto Rican communities. Botanicas, shops that deal in herbs and magic charms, are common and sell candles, statues, incense, perfumes, and other paraphernalia needed to practice rituals to ward off evil; heal the body, mind, and soul; or do harm to one's enemies. Such practices are part of "espiritismo," and "espiritistas" are forces to be recognized in community social work.[8]

Until recenlty, the extended family system overshadowed the nuclear family, even in Puerto Rican communities in the United States. "Compadres," "comadres," "padrinos," and close friends are also seen as part of the family, and most Puerto Rican families will include "jijos de crianza."[9] The traditional extended family or the new combination of extended and nuclear family is for the most part patriarchal and often hampered by traditional male/female roles which are also tied to concepts of dignity, honor, and respect.[10]

Personalismo—Confianza

"Confianza" means trust and culturally established acceptable boundaries for interpersonal behavior. Confianza evolves and allows for relajo (joking around) and for bonding. Confianza is given. To take it is disrespectful and culturally unacceptable. Establishing trust, an essential component of social work practice, requires approaches that may be new to social workers who are inexperienced in their work with Puerto Ricans as individuals, families, groups, or communities.

"Personalismo" is a culturally supported expectation of "personalizing" individual contact in important relationships. Puerto Rican youngsters often complain that teachers, guidance counselors, or social workers do not show that they care about them as people, as individuals. "They are just doing their job, they really don't care" is a statement often expressed by Puerto Rican youngsters in education systems of large urban centers. No matter how much a social service system says it is concerned about people, the Puerto Rican must feel it at the personal level. Community workers need to understand this pattern because getting Puerto Ricans to become involved in community work may depend on their feeling connected, in a personal way, to the organizer and others involved in community organization activities. A face-to-face contact is important in all community organization but may be especially crucial in organizing Puerto Ricans.

On Self-Oppression

As a result of centuries of oppression and colonization under Spain and the United States, many Puerto Ricans have internalized stereotypes and developed personalities comparable to that described by Paulo Freire in his discussion of the oppressed and by Franz Fanon when he writes of the colonized mentality.[11] Many Puerto Ricans blame themselves for their fate, not understanding that their poverty is responsible for their alienation and feelings of helplessness or that their poverty is a function of a macro process over which they have little, if any, control.

Community organizers and other social workers need to consider the implications of certain behaviors and beliefs that are best understood within the context of religious, linguistic, social, political, and economic colonization and oppression. Among them are the following potential patterns:

1. A dependency or often unwarranted respect for authority and

authority figures, making it difficult, at times, to organize Puerto Ricans against school, police, hospital personnel, and policies.
2. An expectation that leaders and "experts" will solve their problems.
3. A fatalistic approach to life and a reliance on saints, God, the Virgin Mary, and spirits.
4. A belief that "pala" (influence, connections, or political pull) is crucial in self-advancement and that confrontations are to be avoided. Doing things "a la buena" (without conflict), and if necessary using "la pelea monga" (fighting, but passively), may mean telling people what they want to hear but not necessarily meaning it.[12] This may include giving the impression that they will come to a meeting when in actuality they may have no such intention. It is possible for some people to confuse culturally sanctioned behavior for what appears to be acceptance of injustice.

Machismo, Marianismo and Other Isms

Puerto Rican society, like all others, oppresses certain members within its own group. For example, all else being constant, adult males have more privileges than women, and homophobia and heterosexuality may be stronger in some Puerto Rican communities than in most non-Puerto Rican communities in the United States. Machismo sanctions male privilege. It also strongly emphasizes adult male financial responsibility and protection of the wife and other women and children in the family. Husbands and fathers, particularly poor men, often feel a sense of shame and dishonor if they cannot be good providers, even when it is a function of unemployment or underemployment. This may be one explanation for some pathological behavior in Puerto Rican and other Latino males. Desertion, abuse, or neglect may stem from a perceived lack of masculinity due, for example, to women obtaining welfare payments. However, sometimes the male "disappears" so that his family will become eligible for government support. Organizing these men to channel their anger and frustrations constructively is a challenge that very few organizers have undertaken.

"Marianismo" is a cultural institution which (like the whore-madonna counterpart in other societies) divide women into two mutually exclusive categories—the saintly, sacrificing, wife, mother, sister, virgin (until marriage) female and the sinful, cold hearted, unlady-like, promiscuous "other." Although these values are less dominant than in the past, like the more global malady of sexism, marianismo and machismo persist. Although sexual taboos are less prevalent and some young females are also becoming sexually active, strict gender roles and close supervision of female children may still lead to young marriages, early common-law marriages, or early consensual living arrangements.

Strengths

As a society, Puerto Ricans value hospitality, cooperation, and sharing, characteristics that can enhance organizing efforts. Because of the racial mixing that has formed Puerto Rican culture, racism is less of an issue than in other client groups.[13] The collective humanism of Puerto Rican society is also a culturally sanctioned pattern that enhances community organizing. It appears to a sense of justice and fairness, an important guiding principle for community social work practice.

The tradition of close knit extended families is a source of community strength and stability. Involving the entire family in various community organization activities (youth in tutoring programs and adults in tenants organizing, for example) can be an effective method of tapping into this strength. Organizing projects that address housing, jobs, education, and other tangible improvements for the entire family, and especially its children, have a greater chance of attracting Puerto Rican participation. Respect for the organizer is more likely if the organizer can "win over" the people by demonstrating that he or she cares. One way of showing you care is by socializing in the Puerto Rican community and spending time with the action group involved in the organizing efforts. This may mean drinking coffee, chatting about each other's families, attending block parties, going to a church service, and shopping at the local stores.

Unquestionably, centuries of exploitation and colonization have led many Puerto Ricans to economic and other forms of dependency. Nevertheless, it has also led to a spirit of survival, a strong sense of peoplehood, and a readiness for assertiveness when organizers tap the leadership and the resourcefulness of Puerto Ricans.

Problems and Programs—Strategies and Tactics

Puerto Ricans, as a community and as individuals, confront myriad problems which are often a result of the causes and the effects of poverty. If, for example, most Puerto Ricans were middle class, housing problems could diminish as could the related problems of neighborhood and school segregation. Middle-class people tend to hold jobs which pay enough money to cover essential needs and provide job-related benefits such as health care insurance, paid vacations, sick leave, and job protection. Poverty is associated with political powerlessness that, in turn, minimizes the ability to compete for resources. The traditional American values of individualism, competition, and ethnic and racial rivalry clash with the Puerto Rican values of cooperation and collectivity.

More importantly, competition in the United States is less than perfect. . . . politicians and bureaucrats often side with those having greater access to power, not those having greater needs. . .

A society needing less unskilled work, stressing profit and middle-class comfort, and generally accepting cuts in social programs and services will have little empathy for Puerto Ricans and other oppressed populations. The high price of housing and necessities; national trends of unskilled jobs moving out of large cities where Puerto Ricans are concentrated; gentrification and continued automation add to Puerto Rican poverty.[14]

Homelessness, lack of low-income housing, higher levels of school dropouts than all other groups, AIDS, unemployment and underemployment, substance abuse, racism, discrimination, teen pregnancy, violence, crime, political powerlessness, underrepresentation in professional and technical occupations, unequal access to the judicial system, lack of day-care, insufficient culturally and liniguistically sensitive services and an endless list of problems confront Puerto Rican communities in the United States and are issues that continuously lend themselves to community organization intervention. Attacks on bilingual programs and affirmative action, and the English First/Only movement further threaten Puerto Ricans. Mobilization of Puerto Rican communities is a challenge that social workers must consciously undertake.

Mobilizing in the 90s must capitalize on the efforts of past struggles; competition with other oppressed groups must be avoided; and coalition building must become a conscious effort. The political process must be targeted for attack because it is in that arena that decisions affecting Puerto Ricans and other poor people are made. The organizer must challenge prejudices, such as sexism, that exist within oppressed communities although these must be confronted with sensitivity and only after a relationship of trust and confianza have been established.[15]

Specific Strategies

The ideal community social worker in the Puerto Rican community is a progressive, bilingual, and bicultural advocate who is rooted in the community, makes community empowerment a primary goal, has a repertoire of community organization skills, and a theoretical understanding of macro forces and dynamics. Such a person should be able to access values that impact specific problems and possible solutions. Included in the analysis should be his or her own values, the values of the community, the values of the action group he or she is working with, values reflected by the agency that sponsors the organizer, the values of the target group which he or she wishes to impact, and the values of the client group which is to benefit from the organizing effort.

How a problem is defined "hooks" one into a solution and often reflects a value judgment. For example, teen pregnancy can be viewed from many perspectives. It can be seen as a crisis in morality, a health-care issue, or a reflection of the hopelessness of young people who do not relate to the future privileges middle-class youngsters envision for themselves. Some people, of course, do not see teen pregnancy as a problem at all.

Solutions to the problem of teen pregnancy can range from pastoral counseling programs to birth control information, from prenatal health programs to organizing for more accessible abortion services and advocacy for the most progressive abortion policies possible. Conflicts about the definition of the problem, based on emotional responses flowing from value differences, are difficult to address and may lead the organizer to work on less emotionally charged issues or, conversely, to taking on a controversial position and accepting the consequences and difficult challenges that it presents. The latter is certainly essential in pioneering a much needed revolution of values that will move us all to a more just nation.

Obviously, it is equally important to assess the potential resources available to the organizer and to increase them, while being conscious of the resistance she or he will face from various constituent groups at the local, regional, or national levels.

Organizers with the characteristics and skills outlined above are hardly plentiful. Therefore, schools of social work must teach community organization skills that will enable social workers to be more effective with Puerto Rican client systems regardless of their ethnic/racial backgrounds, job titles, or specialization. Social workers must be prepared to use community organization approaches to problem solving when appropriate and to seek, enlist, support, train, and validate potential organizers from the community at large, from their own collegial network, and from their client roster. Social workers trained in community organization and working with Puerto Rican communities have a special responsibility to enhance their practice by becoming more and more like the ideal organizer described above.

Case Studies—From a Puerto Rican Studies Project*

Poverty, powerlessness, racism, and the social ills stemming from the combination of those forces have led to the "full-plate syndrome" facing many Puerto Ricans and other poor communities of color. Racism, violence, AIDS,

---

*The Puerto Rican Studies Project at the University of Connecticut School of Social Work was by this author to address the need for culturally sensitive social work practitioners in the Puerto

drugs, crime, homelessness, alienation from the judicial system, massive underemployment or unemployment, high levels of school dropouts, rivalry among adult leadership, etc. are common ingredients on that crowded plate. Insufficient services to families, inappropriate foster care for Puerto Rican children, lack of school curriculum on the Puerto Rican experience, lack of curriculum aimed at building the self-esteem of Puerto Rican youngsters, and the competing and clashing of cultural values within the larger society further add to the full plate. The needs leading to the migration to and from Puerto Rico, of many families, the different perspectives and levels of acclimation to U.S. society that first, second, or third generation experience, and intra-community issues such as competition for resources, struggles related to gender, color, sexual preference, etc., at times fragmentize community efforts. Organizers must decide on which of these and other issues to concentrate.

In selecting on what issues to work, the organizer in the Puerto Rican community will often be restricted by the agency which employs her or him. The saliency of issues in the specific community obviously will also influence this work. At times, catastrophes will lead to decisions surrounding short-term organizinig projects. Such projects can be used as springboards for other work. Clearly, an agency employing community social workers can relate to a specific tragedy by encouraging a community to collectively express pain or anger and harness the energy such emotions release to call attention to injustices and challenge policies. For example, the killing of a young girl in Hartford by a hit-and-run driver who held an influential job created outrage in the Puerto Rican community and led to planned forums on racism, classism and to organized marches and vigils. In that process, new community leaders emerged and the criminal justice system was bombarded with complaints. Although immediate changes were not made, the unified and organized voice of a people was empowering. Community social workers must not miss such opportunities.

The recent arrests and trials in Hartford surrounding the "Wells Fargo robbery" and alleged conspiracy of the Macheteros to use the money to overthrow the American government in Puerto Rico was used as a good consciousness raising tool by some organizers addressing Puerto Rican concerns. Newspaper headlines were used to generate discussions about Puerto Rico's colonial status. Such discussions are becoming easier due to an upcoming referendum on the Island's future political status through which Puerto Ricans will select between independence, statehood, or an "enhanced"

Rican community, to recruit, retain, and graduate Puerto Rican and other Latino graduate social work students, and to train social work providers throughout Connecticut and South Western Massachusetts. Prior to the Project, initiated in 1980, the University of Connecticut School of Social Work had graduated 25 Latino students (1946–1979). From 1980 to 1990 it has graduated 140.

commonwealth status. The United Nations Committee on Decolonization has ruled that under the present commonwealth arrangement, Puerto Rico is a U.S. colony. A plebiscite originally scheduled to take place in 1991 may be delayed due to Louisiana Senator J. Bennett Johnston Jr.'s version of a bill that differs from the one approved by the House. Unlike the House version, the Johnston bill is more detailed in defining conditions and implications of the independence, statehood, and commonwealth alternatives. It also calls for a single and binding referendum. Note that President Bush has joined former Presidents Reagan, Carter, and Ford in urging statehood for Puerto Rico in spite of America's failure to provide economic and political justice for Puerto Ricans in Puerto Rico or the United States. Statehood would permanently guarantee America's economic control of the Island and the military bases that currently appropriate 13 percent of Puerto Rico's soil. Puerto Ricans are divided on the status alternatives and discussion on the issue is often emotional. Generally, however, organizing in favor of one or another alternative has not been a major focus in grassroot community work in the U.S. However, Puerto Rican studies programs discussed earlier tend to address the colonial relationship between Puerto Rico and Spain and between Puerto Rico and the U.S. Many organizers link Puerto Rican poverty in the Island and in the U.S. to the colonial reality.

The tragedy of Hurricane Hugo led many community organizers to help raise money for grassroot agencies wishing to contribute to the hurricane victims. Such efforts make agencies and organizers more human and caring in the eyes of a community of people whose friends and relatives may have suffered from the violence of the storm.

Obviously, organizers cannot rely on trials, hurricanes, or other tragedies to facilitate community cohesion or to demonstrate personal caring to a group that values "personalismo." Fortunately, there are other ways of doing that. The following cases suggest possible problem areas and strategies that may facilitate trust. They also emphasize specific skills and highlight essential coalition building.

Organizing Church Constituents— A Pentecostal Example

"I knew that I needed to get people to trust and like me and my singing and playing my guitar at the services helped a lot," said Ms. Ada Suarez, a young and dedicated second year community organization student at the University of Connecticut School of Social Work who wanted to harness the potential strength of the members of a large Puerto Rican Pentecostal Church in Connecticut. Ada had been raised as a Pentecostal in Puerto Rico and was convinced that organizers can tap into the spiritual mandate that Pentecostals have to do "God's work" and enable the "brothers" and "sisters" to be more effective with their own goals for church and community improvements.

The church was not a traditional social service agency and obviously had no social workers as staff. Therefore, a member of the Puerto Rican Studies faculty accepted the role of supervisor to Ms. Suarez. The possibility of having access to a college professor to help the church was seen as positive. Culturally, college professors are respected as "experts" and the church's pastor welcomed Ada's help, seeing her as a nonpaid staff member who also brought University resources.

In addition to singing and helping the pastor with clerical duties, Ada visited the homes of people she identified as having leadership potential, met with the church's elders, and played big sister to some of the church's youth. She also distributed questionnaires to members, asking them to provide information about what they felt their needs were. She did this data gathering at youth meetings, meetings of the women volunteers, prison visiting committee meetings, etc. She then shared with the congregation what they had identified as problems and recommendations for addressing them. "Some brothers and sisters want to read and write better in Spanish, some want to learn English, and others want help in finding work or better jobs. . . Some committees want help in functioning better at meetings and others want to know more about how to help people. . . The youth want to discuss school issues and some church elders wish to learn how to be better leaders in and out of the church."

Ada brought the public school system into the church to teach literacy (in Spanish) and English classes for non-English speakers. She organized leadership training workshops and called on Puerto Rican Studies faculty, community organization students, and community leaders for help. Wherever possible, church members themselves introduced speakers and planned gatherings. Workshops on job training, resume writing, interviewing skills, and on eligibility for food stamps were conducted at least twice in one year.

Ms. Suarez also chose to work on some more controversial projects. For example, she organized workshops on AIDS. Some members expressed problems with the language that the speakers used in their church. Ada encouraged young people to talk about their feelings of isolation in school and in the community due to the strict moral codes of the church (no hard rock music, makeup, movies, smoking, etc.) and some parents were less than comfortable with that. In addition, she facilitated and encouraged the women of the congregation to become more assertive and to be more represented on the Board of Elders.

With sensitivity, she explained to the church members that since they welcomed drug addicts and worked with prisoners, some had expressed interest in knowing more about the AIDS epidemic. She led a discussion on why certain language might not be appropriate for the subject and asked them to suggest less-offensive words. She also promised to convey the group's thoughts to the speakers. Women did join the board of elders and the youth group continues meeting. Ms. Suarez used culturally relevant strategies, maximized participation of groups of people that had not been previously involved, and, while being very respectful, also tackled controversial issues. She imparted community organization skills to elders and had them prepare flyers, lead discussions on setting agendas, form committees, and select strategies. She utilized videos, films, and other visual effects when talking about conserving energy, applying for a job, presenting information on AIDS, etc.

Electing a Puerto Rican to State Office

In September of 1988, Juan Figueroa, a progressive Puerto Rican lawyer, unseated a four-term incumbent, a white male from Hartford's Third Assembly district, in a Democratic Party primary. Mr. Figueroa hired Jorge Chevres, who had completed his first year as a C.O. major at the University of Connecticut School of Social Work, to help with the campaign. Jorge analyzed the strategies used in Puerto Rico to get people to vote. He surmised that since 90 percent of Puerto Ricans eligible to vote in Puerto Rico are registered to vote, and since 78 percent of those registered actually do vote, the small voter turnout in the United States is something other than apathy. Candidates, he reasoned, did not inspire Puerto Ricans or did not work hard enough to get Puerto Ricans to vote. He modeled his efforts on campaigns on the Island. Strategies included block-by-block analysis of the potential voters, engaging residents in charlas (chats) about issues, and the need for accessible political figures who would represent local interests. He also highlighted Figueroa's ethnic ties and made sure that Figueroa was involved in the charlas. Bars, stores, churches, beauty shops, botánicas, etc. were visited and literature in Spanish and English (usually with a Puerto Rican map, flag, or other Puerto Rican motif) were distributed. Teams of volunteers, one of whom had to speak Spanish, visited and registered as many eligible voters as possible. Childcare and transportation to voting sites were guaranteed.

Equally important, Figueroa hired John Bonelli, another C.O. student actively involved in the lesbian and gay community, to do similar work in the general community, but especially in the lesbian and gay community in the district. Fund-raisers in all the communities were organized but the efforts were on getting potential voters to attend "fun" fund-raisers as much as on raising money. Getting voters to spread the word and committing them to register and vote was the key goal. Another important goal was recruiting and training Puerto Rican volunteers to make phone calls to Spanish speaking homes in the district in pursuit of their vote and a commitment to register and mobilize their families, friends, and neighbors in their own building or block.

Puerto Ricans comprise the largest ethnic group in the third Assembly district. 95 percent of Puerto Ricans and 41 percent of the "others" who voted, voted for Juan Figueroa. His victory was resounding. It is an excellent example of good community organization in a Puerto Rican community. It is also an excellent example of two oppressed groups coalescing around one candidate. Neither Figueroa nor Chevres are members of the gay community but their support of lesbian and gay issues elicited enthusiastic response from the lesbian and gay community interested in forging alliances in its struggle to have Connecticut prohibit discrimination on the basis of sexual orientation or preference. John Bonelli became Connecticut's first openly gay candidate. He ran for the Hartford City Council in the slate of a new progressive political party called People for Change. John had the active support of most of the Puerto Rican volunteers who worked in Figueroa's campaign.

English First/Only

Few issues have mobilized Puerto Ricans as much as fighting against the English First/Only bill in Connecticut. In February of 1989 a massive organizing effort duplicated and amplified strategies used two years earlier to defeat the English First bill in Connecticut. Opposers of the bill acknowledge that initially the bill sounds like a good idea, because learning English is essential. However, English is already first, and the bill has ethnocentric and racist overtones. Furthermore, it would curtail civil rights and could eliminate or severely limit essential bilingual services, including emergency health and police responses. Organizers spoke at schools, colleges, Latino agencies, etc. They mobilized Spanish language media, wrote letters and editorial responses to local and state media, organized debates, and created a coalition of Latino leaders who had access to the community and to resources. The emphasis was on a multiplicity of community organization strategies which included calling attention to the adverse effects of what appeared to be a good bill. Getting people to attend and testify at hearings on the bill and bombarding neutral members of the legislative committee with calls, letters, and telegrams proved effective. Rallies were organized before and during the hearings to further call attention to the Puerto Rican community's outrage. Never in Connecticut have so many Puerto Ricans walked, car pooled, or chartered buses to be present at any state hearing. The bill was defeated, but will probably be brought back in the near future. Continued mobilization against the English First/Only movement in Connecticut, and elsewhere, is essential.

Research, Consultation, and Evaluation as C.O. Tools for Action

Two years ago this author was hired by the Bridgeport school system as a consultant/researcher to study why Puerto Rican youngsters drop out of school. As an organizer I knew that if the research was to lead to changes, a strong and diversified community team, to which I would be accountable, had to be organized. Fortunately, the Ford Foundation, sponsor of the study, insisted on broad community participation. A collaborative team, with heavy Puerto Rican representation, was formulated. Reporting directly to them and actively seeking their involvement in all aspects of the research process empowered the team. They were encouraged to help develop all research instruments and trained to interview Puerto Rican youngsters who had dropped out, Puerto Rican youngsters that were at-risk of dropping out, and youngsters who were achieving. Parents, teachers, administrators, counselors, social workers, and other staff were also interviewed in order to get the broadest level of participation, as well as raise awareness and obtain support. All questionnaires addressed community and school factors contributing to the dropout problem in addition to addressing factors attributed to students and their families. Numerous community forums were organized to share findings and obtain more input on problems and solutions. The collaborative "owns" the study, continues meeting, advocates for programs flowing from the study's recommendations, and monitors them. Programs addressing school policies, teacher training, and a Puerto Rican studies curriculum have been initiated as a direct result of the study.

Make Something Happen

A year ago this author became a volunteer consultant to Project MASH (Make Something Happen), sponsored by the Hartford Office of the Puerto Rican Forum and the Greater Hartford Urban League. The Project is staffed by two Puerto Ricans and two African American community organizers. The organizers work with residents of Stowe Village, a low-income housing project considered the most troublesome of Hartford's public housing communities. Specific goals and strategies to avoid ethnic/racial competition between staff or clients were identified and enhanced by the collaboration of the two sponsoring groups.

The on-site staff managers focus on family, community, and institutions. They have secured Stowe Village-based job placement, career development, day-care, and educational and other job-related training programs. Door knocking and socializing in a personal manner were utilized as strategies and meetings were held at different times of the day for different groups of people. Issues such as the drug epidemic and the violence in the project were tackled. As organizers, the staff has developed a network of support from city and regional leaders in the political, religious, social service, and corporate sectors, facilitating their ability to utilize a variety of resources for their "hard to motivate" client systems. The power, influence, status, and connection of the corporate leadership has greatly enhanced the program's success. As part of my services I organized a conference for personnel directors of the largest private sector employers, including banks and insurance companies, in the area. The conference focused on issues that need to be considered when recruiting and maintaining low-income Puerto Ricans and African Americans who are often on welfare and in families headed by young women, into entry level positions within the firms. The one-day conference utilized films stressing the importance of diversity; performances by the organizers which highlighted the barriers that young women from Stowe Village entering the work force often encounter; and professionally led discussions on the policies, attitudes, and behaviors that could result in such barriers. The conference will be duplicated for lower-echelon staff. A current evaluation continues to address barriers to employment, the strengths of the residents, and potential advocacy strategies for enhancing the success of this project.

Project MASH organizers have often systematically acted as catalysts, forcing public and private systems to examine their ideology, policies, and practices. Their success in reaching and "winning over" Stowe Village residents, who many agencies have given up on, is evidence of the organizers' skills and the motivation of people labeled as "hopeless." The most tangible proof of MASH's success is that some of the families have begun to move out of Stowe Village and off MASH's rosters. As they move out, these once "unmotivated" and now successful families make space available for others to also succeed.

Addressing AIDS

In Hartford, the largest number of children with AIDS are Puerto Ricans, and Puerto Ricans in Connecticut and elsewhere are almost four times more likely to be AIDS patients than are whites. The need for organized involvement in AIDS prevention and services in Puerto Rican communities cannot be overstated.

Puerto Rican Studies faculty and students at the University of Connecticut School of Social Work have been working on a four-part study on AIDS and the Puerto Rican community. The first part elicits responses from Puerto Ricans with AIDS concerning their illness and their perception of the type of services they receive, need, or recommend. The second seeks a similar assessment from social service providers working with Puerto Ricans with AIDS. The third is being administered to families of Puerto Ricans with AIDS to assess the traditional Puerto Rican family pattern of supporting its members. Does the family withhold its support in cases of AIDS? The fourth component seeks to assess current attitudes and knowledge in Hartford's Puerto Rican community by interviewing Puerto Rican owners or employees of Puerto Rican bodegas (grocery stores), beauty shops, and other small businesses in Puerto Rican neighborhoods. Furthermore, Puerto Rican churchgoers are being interviewed after Sunday services. The results will be used to better understand Puerto Ricans with AIDS, to advocate for them and others suffering from the epidemic, and to recommend more effective AIDS prevention and education programs.

Former Puerto Rican community organization students have coordinated AIDS services for Puerto Ricans and other Latinos and their families;* utilized Puerto Rican Studies faculty and students in their work; and organized AIDS advocates to secure state support for grassroot organizing in AIDS-related work. They have also coordinated a network for sharing problems, ideas, and success stories. Strategies for "reaching" the drug addict, for targeting male and female prostitutes, and gay latinos were developed and organizing "charlas" in peoples' homes are being implemented. Latinos Contra SIDA (Latinos Against AIDS) was organized out of the homes of these Puerto Rican organizers.

In the Fall of 1987, Puerto Rican community organization students actively raised funds and consciousness in the Puerto Rican community around apartheid. Five years earlier both African American and Puerto Rican students and faculty at the University of Connecticut School of Social Work coalesced, demanded, and obtained additional financial aid for minority students at the school. These are also important examples of coalition building between African Americans and Puerto Ricans.

Summary of Strategies and Conclusions

The above are some examples of good social work practice concentrating on community organization in the church, in the political arena, in housing projects, and in academia. All have stressed coalition building, conscious-

---

*In Connecticut, 70 to 75 percent of all Latinos are of Puerto Rican heritage.

ness raising, educating client systems to their own oppression and the oppression of others, political awareness, and empowerment. The importance of cultural sensitivity, knowledge of specific communities, good research skills, and alternative explanation of history and political power have been highlighted. Advocacy tools, including "educating" funding sources, boards of directors, and agency personnel; becoming familiar with "model" programs; planning pilot projects' the use of consultants; the testimony of experts and grassroot people; administrative redress; demonstrations; and developing community leadership have been incorporated in the examples.[16] The Figueroa victory and recent victories of progressive Black mayors in key cities offer much hope for future political coalitions. Personal involvement and involving friends, relatives, neighbors, and client systems in the political arena must be part of community organization in the 1990s.

Certainly not all of the C.O. endeavors associated with Puerto Rican Studies at the University of Connecticut have been successful. For example, much work on a needs assessment of the Puerto Rican community in New Britain, Connecticut was stymied by political forces in that city, even though it was initiated through much collaboration between Puerto Rican faculty, students, and community groups. Organizing is political. At times, personnel in Puerto Rican and non-Puerto Rican agencies will choose not to initiate or participate in organizing efforts if the organizing is perceived as potentially risky to their programs, their own agendas, or agency funding. Furthermore, most churches can be a tool for either supporting victim-blaming ideology, dependency, sexism, and heterosexuality or for helping to liberate Puerto Ricans. Many institutions may never mobilize to directly confront employers, politicians, landlords, schools, or other powerful systems that may discriminate or oppress Puerto Ricans. Nevertheless, it may be easier for most agencies or churches to show some support for affirmative action, for greater access to employment, education, business opportunity, for bilingual, bicultural education, more equitable welfare benefits, stricter health and sanitary housing codes, and other such programs and policies. Although such support may be inadequate, given the needs of most Puerto Rican communities, organizers must accept such support. More importantly, they must also continue to raise questions about a system that seems to need poor people at the bottom of the social and economic ladder and consciously and continuously address short- and long-range goals for human liberation for all oppressed populations.

Future C.O. work must also include organizing for a national health insurance, for guaranteed childcare, jobs, income, housing, and quality education. Organizing the unemployed, the "disappearing male" referred to earlier, the homeless, and the uninsured is a challenge community organizers must undertake. Day-care, health care, and housing must be a right, and homelessness must end.

Schools of social work have a special responsibility to hire Puerto Rican faculty and administrators and to provide social service agencies with trained Puerto Rican staff by graduating Puerto Rican students. Puerto Rican content in social work curriculum must be visible. Social work schools must also bring back community organization as a prominent and more visible social work method. C.O. has not been given enough attention in the late 70s and 80s. The 90s must make up for it, and organizers in the 90s must project confidence, appreciate diversity, and demonstrate that they are comfortable in and with that diversity. Furthermore, just as caseworkers often must more consciously address macro forces, organizers must more consciously address the importance of organizing style and the culture, class, and values of the client systems worked with. This implies learning how to address victim-blaming ideology at all levels, including that of client systems. Liberating the minds of oppressed people is as challenging and important as attacking the problems that oppressed people confront.

Endnotes

1. Julio Morales, "Puerto Rican Studies and Social Service Careers," and Josephine Nieves et al., "Puerto Rican Studies: Roots and Challenges," in *Toward A Renaissance of Puerto Rican Studies* Maria Sanchez and Antonio M. Stevens–Arroyo, eds. (Highland Lakes, New Jersey: Columbia University Press, 1987), 93–107.
2. Julio Morales, "Puerto Rican Studies: An Example of Social Movements as a Force Towards Social and Economic Justice," in *Towards Social and Economic Justice* David Gil and Eva Gil, eds. (Cambridge, Mass: Schenkman Publishing co., 1985), 203–223.
3. *New York Times* Thursday, March 2, 1989.
4. Bob Kaplan, "Who's Worth More—America's Richest 400 Families or Its Poorest 40 Million," *New England Prout Journal* (December 1986), 10.
5. Centro De Estudios Puertorriqueños, 2 (Spring 1989), 5.
6. *Hartford Courant*, Sunday, August 10, 1986. Julio Morales, *Puerto Rican Poverty and Migration* (New York, New York: Praeger, 1986).
7. Emelicia Mizio, "Puerto Rican Culture," and Sally Romero, "Counseling Puerto Rican Families," in *Training for Service Delivery to Minority Clients*, Emelicia Mizio and Anita J. Delaney, eds. (New York, New York: Family Service Association of America, 1981), 109–120, 158–171.
8. Espiritistas are either male or female and some Puerto Ricans may "consult" them when seeking a cure for health (or mental health) problems or advice on other problems. See Melvin Delgado, "Puerto Rican Spiritualism and the Social Work Profession" *Social Casework*, 58 (October 1977):451–458.
9. Compadres and comadres are close relations among the adults, established as a result of the baptism of a child. Padrino means godfather and madrina means godmother (of the baptized child). Padrinos de boda are the best man and the maid of honor at a wedding. Hijos de crianza means "children by raising" and is usually translated as "stepchildren."
10. See Mizio and Delaney, op. cit.
11. Frantz Fanon, *Black Skin, White Mask* (New York: Grove Press, 1967), Frantz

Fanon, *The Wretched of the Earth* (New York: Grove Press, 1968), and Paulo Freire, *Pedogogy of the Oppressed* (New York: Herder and Herder, 1970).

12. See Mitzio, op. cit. and Karl Wagenheim, *Puerto Rico: A Profile* 2nd ed. (San Francisco: Holt, Rinehart, and Winston, 1975).

13. Please note that Puerto Ricans in the Island, and in the United States, are not totally free from racism. For example, in his autobiography, *Down These Mean Streets*, Piri Thomas describes the pain he experienced because he was the darkest child in his family. John Longres' article "Racism and Its Effects on Puerto Rican Continentals," *Social Casework*, 55 (February 1975), 67–75, discusses a preference among many Puerto Ricans for lighter skin. Nevertheless, it is next to impossible to be racist in the American sense when there is so much variation of skin color (and hair texture) within Puerto Rican families. Puerto Ricans will often call someone negro or negra (black) as a sign of affection and love, therefore referring to someone as "negro(a)" has nothing to do with color. Furthermore, to be "jincho" (too white) is perceived as unattractive.

14. Competition for resources (jobs, housing, scholarships, etc.) can lead to conflict between oppressed groups, and organizers must be conscious of such possibilities. See "Black Puerto Rican conflict: The Inevitable Systemic Outcome," Chapter II, in Morales's *Puerto Rican Poverty and Migration, op. cit.*

15. Julio Morales, "The Elusive American Dream," *Op. cit.*

16. For other advocacy strategies, see Julio Morales, "The Clinician as Advocate: A Puerto Rican Perspective," in Mitzio and Delaney, *op. cit.*

CHAPTER SIX

A Feminist Perspective on Organizing with Women of Color

LORRAINE M. GUTIERREZ   EDITH A. LEWIS

Women of color—black, Latina, Asian, and Native American—make up 20 percent of the total female population of the United States. However, the distinctive perspectives, problems, and potentials of women of color have rarely been addressed within the field of community organizing. Ways in which oppression based on both race and gender can be a point of intervention have not been fully developed. As educators, activists, and practitioners in community practice and ethnic-sensitive social work, we feel that this oversight can have negative effects on women of color themselves and those who wish to work within their communities. In this chapter we present one approach to organizing with women of color which suggests a way in which race and gender issues can be worked on simultaneously. The issues and practice principles we present here are relevant for both women of color and white woman organizing in communities of color.[24]

Women of Color: Who Are We?

The term "women of color" has been adopted by African American, Latina, Asian, and Native American women in the United States as a way of unifying what we have seen as commonalties between us, especially in contrast to the experiences of white women in our society. However, the acceptance of this umbrella term does not mean that we do not recognize the differences between and within racial and ethnic groups in our society. Understanding the specific historical experiences and cultural expressions of different groups of women of color is as important as understanding ways in which we are similar. All women of color have been affected by the domination of white America, but this has taken different forms with different groups. The experience of reservation life, for example, creates a different social context from that of slavery or forced deportation. Women of color have tended to draw strength from their ethnic minority communities, but this can be expressed quite differently within each group. Therefore, although this chapter is written about women of color in general, it is important to keep in mind that differences exist between these groups which must be recognized and used when working within specific communities.* Understanding differences and similarities is particularly important in the development of multiethnic coalitions or when the organizer is from a different background than the majority of the women involved.

Although the specific ethnic and racial groups encompassed by this umbrella term differ in many respects, together we share similarities in terms of our strengths, low status, and power. Women of color experience the "double jeopardy" of racism and sexism in our society. We are hampered by average earnings lower than that of white women, by overrepresentation in low-status occupations, and by a low average level of education. Correspondingly, women of color are underrepresented in positions of power within our government, corporations, and nonprofit institutions.

These statistics suggest ways in which our powerlessness as a group has very direct and concrete effects on our daily experiences. Lack of access to many social resources is both a cause and effect of the powerlessness of this group. The poverty rate of women of color is double that of white women: 49.4 percent of all black women and 51 percent of all Latins live below the poverty line, in contrast to 25.7 percent of all white women. Therefore, women of color are more likely than white women to suffer from conditions of poor or no housing, insufficient food and clothing, inadequate access to health and mental health services, and to be located within low-income and physically deteriorating communities.[13, 22, 24, 47]

Women of color also share similarities in terms of strengths and coping strategies. Within our own communities we have developed values and behaviors which have allowed us to survive in the face of oppression. Economic necessity has led women of color to participate in the labor market at higher rates than white women. Although this role has not always been chosen, it has helped us to develop ties and a sense of self outside of the

---

*It is beyond the scope of this chapter to detail the specific historical and cultural conditions particular to the experience of women within each ethnic minority group. The references at the end of the chapter include resources organizers can use in order to learn about specific populations and communities of women of color.

family and has reduced our economic dependency on men. Women of color are also likely to have strong family ties and ties with other women in our community to whom they can go for concrete and emotional support. These informal ties can be a form of strength. Another commonality is a strong connection to spirituality, through formal or informal religion, which has helped us to survive. This history of coping and surviving within a hostile world has led many women of color to perceive themselves as strong and capable of dealing with adversity.[10, 45]

Existing models of community practice need to recognize the ways in which women of color differ from white women and from men of color. Organizers have most often recognized the impact of powerlessness on women of color from the perspective of institutional racism while overlooking the role of gender inequity in influencing the life chances of women of color. Similarly, the strengths of women of color are also often ignored in community work. When women of color are viewed solely as members of their racial or ethnic group and gender is not taken in account, community organizers may alienate women of color and reinforce ways in which sexism, both in the larger society and within ethnic minority communities, is a form of oppression.[1, 44, 48]

A feminist perspective, which assumes that issues of power and powerlessness are integral to the experience of women of color, is one way to address this oversight. It proposed concrete and specific ways in which community organizers can work with women of color by increasing their power on a number of different levels and by drawing upon their strengths. The goal of this approach is to eliminate the social conditions which are oppressive to women of color by increasing their influence in our society. However, the historical tension between white feminists and communities of color has led some to reject this method without looking closely at ways in which differences can be dealt with and used constructively to the benefit of women of color. In this chapter we attempt to bridge this gap by outlining the assumptions of the feminist perspective and the practice principles it involves, describing ways in which feminist organizing has excluded women of color, and present a reformulation of feminist organizing for use with women of color. Although we anticipate that our ideas may be controversial, it is our belief that feminist methods provide one useful framework for ensuring that attention be given to both sexism and racism when organizing with women of color.

Defining Feminist Organizing

Feminist organizing developed from efforts by feminists to improve the lives of women. Community work has always played an important role within the feminist movement in this country. Nineteenth century feminists were leaders in the abolitionist movement, the suffrage movement, in community settlements, and in the progressive movement. Community organizing has been equally important in more recent feminist movements, especially those coming from a radical rather than liberal perspective.[31, 44] It has focused primarily on work for improving womens' health, for ending violence against women, and for increasing economic opportunities for all women.[30, 36, 46]

The overarching goal of feminist organizing is the elimination of permanent power hierarchies between all people which can prevent them from realizing their human potential. The objective of feminist methods is to reduce sexism, racism, and other forms of oppression through the process of empowerment which ". . . seeks individual liberation through collective activity, embracing both personal and social change."[30]

Recent research on feminist organizing has begun to identify ways in which it differs from mainstream models of community practice. Most often this research has taken the method of "participant observation" to come up with the values and practice principles upon which feminist organizing is based. The following have been found to be common to most feminist organizing:

1. *A "gender lens" is used to analyze the causes and solution of community problems.* Sexism is assumed to be an important force in the experiences of all women and at the root of many problems. All women are thought to be a part of a "community" of women, as well as members of their own specific community.[4, 14, 18, 22, 30, 48] Although it is critical to understand the impact of sexism on women of color, this perspective has sometimes prevented feminist organizers from perceiving the importance of racism and ethnocentrism when analyzing community issues and developing tactics.

2. *Attention is paid to the "process of practice"* in an effort to create organizations based on feminist principles.[19] As described by the Women Organizers Project.[20]: "Feminist organizing is based on values and actions carried out in a democratic, humanistic framework . . . [it] must affect the conditions of women while empowering them. Efforts are made to make feminist movement organizations safe spaces where women can escape the larger and more oppressive external social environment. This has most often involved developing feminist organizations based on principles of collectivity and gender equality in which women can support and develop the confidence and skills necessary to increase their political power.[4, 19]

3. *Empowerment through consciousness raising* is characteristic of feminist organizing efforts. Empowerment is a process of increasing personal,

interpersonal, or political power so individuals can take action to improve their lives.[4, 14, 16, 21, 26, 30, 32, 33, 37, 39] Empowerment theory assumes that society consists of separate groups possessing different levels of power and control over resources.[14] Recognizing the way in which power relationships affect daily reality and understanding how individuals can contribute to social change is the process through which empowerment takes place.[8, 16, 26]

Consciousness raising contributes to empowerment by helping individuals to make this connection between personal problems and political issues. By examining the nature of their lives, women can begin to understand the commonality of their experience and its connection to community and social issues. Consciousness raising can be carried out in one of two formats: group discussion or praxis and the integration of action and reflection. An important outcome of consciousness raising is an understanding of ways in which women, individually and in groups, can begin to change the social order.[4, 8, 16, 35]

4. A major assumption is that *the personal is political,* therefore organizing often takes a *grassroots, bottom up approach.* Organizing efforts must often grow out of issues which are impinging on womens' daily lives. Therefore, the development of alternative services for women is integral to this method. As described by Withorn ". . . for the past 15 years, to be a feminist has meant to engage in service work as much as it has meant to do the things which are normally defined as political. . . ." Alternative services such as support networks, health clinics, shelters, and hotlines are important elements of feminist organizing.[9, 46]

5. Efforts are made to bridge differences between women based on such factors as race, class, physical ability, and sexual orientation with the guiding principle that *diversity is strength.* According to this model ". . . feminist practitioners will not only strive to eliminate racism, classism, heterosexism, anti-semitism, ableism, and other systems of oppression and exploitation, but will affirm the need for diversity by actively reaching out to achieve it." As described in the following section this principle has often been difficult to put into practice.[4]

6. *Organizing is holistic.* It involves both the rational and nonrational elements of human experiences. Emotions, spirituality, and artistic expression are used as tactics for unifying women and expressing issues. Involvement in social change is considered organic, not an adjunct, to womens' lives. The use of puppets and street theater in the womens' disarmament movement is one example of this tactic.[25]

The brief discussion of feminist organizing indicates some of the ways it can be an effective strategy when working with women of color. Feminist theory provides a means for understanding ways in which racism, sexism, and classism have an interactive impact on the lives of women of color. In addition, it suggests a method for directly addressing how we are affected by conditions of powerlessness. By placing a value on multiethnic and racial coalitions, it assumes that women of color should play an important role in the movement. However, as discussed in the following section, this coalition has historically been the exception rather than the rule.

Issues for Feminist Organizing with Women of Color

Problems and Issues

It is no surprise that the feminist movement of the United States has had relatively little participation of women of color. The growth of this movement has historically excluded women of color in three ways. First, there has been an inability within the ranks of the movement to acknowledge its racist tenets and foundations. Second, issues affecting women of color have not been a focus of the feminist movement. Third, there has been a difficulty within the feminist movement in the United States to integrate other "voices" into the formulation of feminist theory and practice. Lack of attention to these three problem areas relegates the feminist movement in the United States to providing a platform for a minority of women on issues that have been addressed by women of color in other arenas.

The historical inability to address racism in the feminist movement has been documented by numerous scholars.[6, 9, 17, 40, 42] While the movement has advocated paying critical attention to the domination of women in their historical and political contexts, only recently has it done so when examining its own formation. Hooks notes two instances of this historical racism.[17] Elizabeth Cady Stanton, a leader of the Suffragist movement at the turn of the century, identified the rights of white women to vote as being distinct from those of other men or women of color:

> "If Saxon men have legislated thus for their own mothers, wives and daughters, what can we hope for at the hands of Chinese, Indians and Africans?. . . I protest against the enfranchisement of another man of any race or clime until the daughters of Jefferson, Hancock are crowned with their rights."

In the early 1900s, during a meeting of the General Federation of Women's Clubs, the President, Mrs. Lowe, stated her own reluctance for the integration of black women into the clubs:

> "Mrs. Ruffin belongs among her own people. Among them she would be a leader and could do much good, but among us, she can create nothing but trouble."

It is curious that during this time, black male scholars and activists such as Fredrick Douglass and Henry Garnett were welcome in white womens' social circles as speakers.

Recent feminist scholarship demonstrates how racist tendencies in the contemporary womens' movement have also interfered with the involvement of women of color. Although many white leaders of the womens' liberation movement gained an awareness of gender inequity through their involvement in the Civil Rights movement, they were unsuccessful in working collaboratively with women of color.[7] Because feminist movements have often presented gender as the sole form of oppression, how women of color perceive their experiences with racism or ethnocentrism has been ignored.[34, 15] Only recently have efforts been made to incorporate issues of racism and other forms of oppression into the womens' movement.[15, 44]

A second impediment to the involvement of women of color has been the nature of the issues selected for mobilization. Because the majority of the leaders of the movement emerged from the white, middle class, their life experiences have influenced the direction of the movement.[22] Women of color, who have traditionally had high rates of labor force participation, often could not identify with the emphasis placed by feminists on the right of women to enter the workplace. Many of these women attributed their low wages to racism rather than the issues involved in reproductive rights would involve both access to contraception and abortion *and* the ability to exercise one's reproductive capacity.

The third general problem faced by the women's movement in organizing women of color is one of willingness to acknowledge the other "lenses" or "voices" through which the experiences of women can be analyzed. The emergence of a number of theories about the status of women in the United States have been criticized for their lack of application to those other than white women.[42, 9, 17, 40] Contemporary theories of the womens' movement are only now acknowledging the existence of an ethnic labor market structure, as in the case of Chinatown women.[27] They further fail to fully acknowledge the oppression of men of color, or differences in family or gender roles in some ethnic communities.[29, 40, 38]

Community Organizing by Women of Color

Organizing by women within ethnic communities in the United States has a rich and diverse history. An example of this involvement is the organization of black Womens' Clubs in the United States one hundred years ago. At the time when the Charity Organization Society and Settlement House movements were born, a parallel movement which focused on the concerns of women of color was initiated by women such as Ida B. Wells Barnett. In this movement, African-American women took leadership roles in the organization of their communities. Black womens' clubs during the 1880s organized nursing homes, day-care centers, and orphanages because the need for assistance with the care of children and the aging were of critical concern to African-American women in families during this period. These clubs organized around the challenges facing African-American families long before these same concerns were raised by white women. While the settlement houses focused on the needs of new immigrants, Wells-Barnett focused on antilynching and rape campaigns. The National Urban League, in which women had an important founding role, was another example of a community of color organizing nationally to address the problems and concerns of people of color in the United States.

More importantly, the organizations supported and developed by women of color had goals of benefitting all society, not just their own target ethnic group. Macht and Quam note:

> "But the contributions of these groups did not stop with the Black community. They also played a vital role in World War I. The Committee on Womens' Defense Work of the Council for National Defense consisted mainly of black women. It helped care for families of absent soldiers, gave comfort kits to the soldiers, helped conserve and enlarge the food supply, and formed canning clubs. The Committee also brought attention to the high infant mortality rate in this country. It discovered a need for better community health services. To correct these problems, the Council set up programs to weigh and measure infants and provide them with milk. In addition, the Committee sought to improve recreational facilities available to youth and pushed for nurses' training for black women. Medical personnel for black people had always been woefully inadequate; the committee compiled and circulated a list of hospitals where black women could be trained."[28]

Women of color in these and other organizations did not view their work as affecting only their constituencies. Their work allowed for the incorporation of additional perspectives which would assist all families.

Organizing by women of color has been based upon existing networks of family, friends, or informal and formal *ethnic community* institutions. Gilkes notes in her research on African-American women community organizers that these women were embedded in black communities and became active because of their commitment to their communities.[11, 12] Barrera describes the extra activities willingly taken on by Latina professionals and para-professionals. These individuals, he notes, have developed organizations and political interest groups and have served as interpreters of the wider society to those Latinos with limited access to it.[2]

Other examples of community organization in long-standing ethnic communities are the mutual aid societies. The Hui, among the Chinese, the Ko among the Japanese, and the Tribal Councils among the Native Americans have all served as vehicles for assisting individual ethnic group members, families, and entire communities through the establishment of business loans, funerals, and community programs. Organizing with women of color from a feminist perspective must acknowledge and build upon these rich traditions.

Case Examples

Feminist organizing methods place a high value on experience-based knowledge. Effective feminist organizing with women of color builds upon this base by drawing upon two sources: techniques based in feminist efforts and those from the tradition of women of color organizing within their own communities. The following examples indicate ways in which these traditions have been integrated.

The Network Utilization Project (NUP)

NUP project was developed by one of the authors in her work with women in a small midwestern city. The purpose of the project was to use the strength of African-American families as an intervention for empowerment. This was done in a variety of ways. First, the project was designed to be community-based. All participants lived in the same geographic promixity and had freuqent interaction. Secondly, the project focused on the small group as a primary form of interaction. In this way, women had an opportunity to meet with each other on a weekly basis in a small group which did not require that they either physically or psychologically remove themselves from their community of origin.

A third principle underlying the NUP project was that women of color in communities of color were a part of both those communities as well as extended family networks. It was necessary for these networks to be acknowledged in any change effort undertaken by the women, either individually or in groups. Each decision for change was met with an analysis of its possible consequences for the participants, their families, and the host community.

Lastly, it was assumed that experiences with individual problem resolution could be expanded to community problem resolution. It was in this effort that the program was most effective in its pilot.[23] NUP participants, through the group meetings, organized a Tenant's Council in one of the city's low-income communities; were instrumental in closing down a city-funded agency which had not provided service to the community although it was being paid to do so; and participated in organizing a city-wide organization for low-income womens' rights in the city. The Network Utilization Project activities moved participants from developing a sense of personal empowerment to bring about change in their communities as well.

Project Oasis

Safe Home networks were created early in the battered womens' movement to provide short-term emergency shelter to victims of abuse and their children. The core of such a program is volunteers who agree to shelter battered women and their families within their homes for a limited period of time.[36] Safe Homes programs have most often been used in white middle-class and rural areas and have rarely been developed within low income, minority, or urban settings.

Project Oasis was an attempt to bring this form of feminist organizing into multiracial and multiethnic urban communities. The goal of Project Oasis was to end violence against women in these communities through the provisions of advocacy, counseling, and shelter services, and through community education, legal advocacy, and the development of self-help networks. The program was initiated by one of the authors while working with a larger organization which offered counseling and community organization programs for all victims of crime in a large northeastern city.

Developing a Safe Homes network for women of color involved modifying the structure it had taken in other localities. The organizer was able to draw upon the natural support networks of women of color within each community. She found that it was not unusual for women of color to shelter sisters in need, but that this sheltering was often done with expectations of reciprocity. Few low-income families could afford to provide financial support for a woman and her children. Therefore, this program gained funding which allowed them to reimburse volunteers for room and board so women who had the desire to help others were given the financial means to do so.

The program was ethnically and racially integrated in terms of staff on all levels, and attempts were made to administer it collaboratively. The director and 50 percent of the staff were women of color. Personal attributes and a commitment to using a feminist perspective in working with women of color were considered more important qualities for staff and volunteers than actual academic training. Staff and volunteers were involved in all aspects of administration, particularly in the area of program planning and outreach. The goal was to develop a structure in which the women on the staff could grow and learn from each other.

Working within this multiethnic environment was a challenge for all of those involved in the program. Many of the white staff and volunteers had never worked in an environment in which women of color had the leadership roles and many of the women of color had never been in a position in which they were allowed to take a major role in the development of programs. In an effort to deal with these issues, and others which emerged in this kind of program, much attention was paid to staff development and training. Based on principles of feminist management, each month an all-day staff retreat was scheduled in which team building and organizational activities were carried out.[19] Responsibility for these meetings was rotated among the different staff and units. These efforts were successful and opened up lines of communication and provided a structure for shared responsibility and collaboration among staff and volunteers. However, they did not prevent or eliminate the emergence of conflicts or issues present in any multiethnic organizing effort.

The multiethnic and urban nature of this program also affected the location and development of Safe Homes. Many Safe Homes networks established within white middle-class settings have focused their efforts for volunteer recruitment within the feminist community. Project Oasis was most successful when focusing outreach to organizations within minority communities: churches, Asian merchant associations, schools, health clinics, Head Start centers, and multiservice community centers. These organizations saw Project Oasis as an asset to the community and provided us with support and assistance. As a method for feminist organizing, Project Oasis was most successful in educating the community regarding violence against women and providing shelter. It also was effective in empowering individual women to become involved in helping others, volunteering, and testifying at public hearings. In these ways, women of color became more directly involved in ending violence against women.

Future Directions for Feminist Organizing with Women of Color

The purpose of this chapter is to explore ways in which knowledge concerning feminist organizing methods and an understanding of the issues relevant to women of color can be integrated toward developing a new and more inclusive organizing strategy. What do these examples and the preceding discussion tell us about the use of feminist methods when organizing with women of color? We believe that the following practice principles can provide directions for future work:

1. *Organizers must have intricate knowledge of and willingness to be a part of the woman's ethnic community.*

This involved knowledge of its institutions and how they work for or against women. Churches, community centers, schools, and social clubs can be avenues for reaching women of color and affecting change within the community. Organizing requires an analysis of societal institutions, including the one represented by the organizer, and how they might ultimately benefit or hurt the women being organized. Gaining this knowledge could involved learning more about specific communities of color through reading and participation in community events.[22] Working with women of color requires an understanding of the cultural context.

In an effort to become involved in the community, one of the group facilitators of the NUP project participated in activities sponsored by the local community center. She worked weekly with the children of the community in enrichment programming for several months before proceeding to organize the women. During this time, she became aware of community members' patterns of interaction, their relationships with agencies in the city, and other potential issues in the community. Community members and group participants had the opportunity to meet and talk with the community worker and to watch her interact with their children. Many of the initial participants later mentioned that their decision to participate in the project was directly related to their approval of the facilitator's work with their children and presence in the community. Similar examples are found in Carol Stack's and Linda Burton's work.[5, 43]

2. *Effective feminist organizing with women of color requires that women of color be in leadership roles.*

Too often attempts to use these techniques with women of color have taken the unidirectional "outreach approach:" communities of color are targets of feminist efforts rather than active participants. When this method is used, women of color often resist these efforts or can undermine them.[36, 22] In both of the case examples described here, women of color acted as the organizer of the activity within the community and used "community expertise" to guide her work. Although she was an outsider, her presence as a woman of color assisted her entry into the community. As a woman of color, she was capable of assessing strategies of feminist organizing and making them more compatible with the minority community in which she worked.

Feminist organizations which would like to carry out more organizing with women of color will need to incorporate women of color as active participants and leaders *before* taking on this kind of work. This kind of collaboration may require redefining the kind of work they do and their attitudes toward institutions such as the church and family. The history of attempts at collaboration suggest that effective work involving white feminists and women of color requires identifying how racism and goal setting may exclude women of color from feminist efforts. Therefore successful collaboration will require that white women change their interactions with women of color. This kind of organizational work embraces the tenet of feminist organizing that "diversity is strength."*

Women of color around the world continue to organize. It is necessary to increase our ability to learn organizing strategies from each other. Wilma Mankiller, Chief of the Cherokee nation, models effective feminist organizing tenets, doing consciousness raising in the communities, and creating organizations in which women have leadership roles. She has also used the feminist organizing principle of taking a grassroots approach which allows organizing issues to be developed by the community. She worked to secure funding to finance the building of new homes, and a pipeline to bring water into many homes for the first time. The labor for these projects, however, came primarily from Cherokee national members. This is only one example of ways in which women of color continue to work as exceptional community leaders.

3. *The organizer must be willing to serve as a facilitator and to allow the problem to be studied through the "lens" or "vision" of women of color:*

This requires allowing this vision to alter the way the organizer herself views her work and sharing that new information with others hoping to organize and work within communities of color. An organizer who is from a different racial, ethnic, or class background than the women must recognize

---

*White feminists interested in working more effectively with women of color might find the books and articles in the bibliography and suggested readings particularly useful.

how her life experience has colored her perceptions. Her definitions and perceptions should not dominate the organizing effort.

In the Network Utilization Project described earlier, the initial design of the project was to separate individual from community concerns. We believed that group members would work on individual problem resolution for a period of eight weeks and then, having established a pattern of interaction within the group, be able to work cooperatively on analysis and resolution of community concerns. It became clear within the first two meetings that the project could not separate individual from community issues. As one participant put it: "My individual problems *are* the community's problems." The flexibility to alter the design based on the realities of the community allowed the group to continue to work toward resolution of its identified goals, not those of the facilitator/researcher.

4. *Utilizing the process of praxis to understand the historical, political, and social context of the organizing effort.*

This means that the organizing process will inform not only the organized community but the "community" of the organizer as well. Praxis involves an analysis of the process and outcome of organizing efforts. When this technique is used the outcome of a tactic is often less important than what the community and organizer learn about the nature of the problem being addressed. In this way community issues are often redefined.

The involvement of women of color in the battered women's movement provides an example of this principle. When many feminist shelters observed that they were unsuccessful in reaching women of color many defined the problem as that of inadequate outreach. When outreach was successful, women of color in some localities provided feedback to many shelter programs that their approach was alienating and foreign to communities of color. Those programs which have been most successful with women of color have been those that addressed their own racism, classism, and ethnocentrism in the development of alternative programs.[37]

5. *An effective strategy for organizing women of color is the small group.*

The literature on empowerment and feminist organizing suggest that small group interaction can play a critical role.[16, 32] The small group provides the ideal environment for exploring the social and political aspects of "personal" problems and for developing strategies for work toward social change.[37] Therefore, feminist organizing often begins with interactions between women in small groups.[18]

In working with women of color, it is preferable to gather small groups of individuals to work on specific or local problems, and later coordinate these small groups so that they can work together with others on joint issues. On a national level, women of color have been organizing movements to improve conditions in ghettos and barrios which are based on a "house meeting" strategy.* For example, Clementine Barfield's work with SOSAD (Save Our Sons and Daughters) in Detroit began with a small group of individual mothers who had experienced the loss of a child through a violent death in the inner city. This organization has grown and become an influential force in lobbying for gun control and related issues.

6. *Women of color who are involved in feminist organizing must anticipate the possible backlash from within their own community of origin, the wider society, and the feminist movement*:

These sources of conflict will affect the outcomes of the organizing effort. The extent to which the worker/organizer anticipates conflict related to group interaction; the possibility of internalized oppression; wider society strategies to destroy the community change effort; and similar issues will often determine whether the efforts are successful.

Women of color have often worked effectively as organizers, but often at great expense to their physical and emotional health.[11] Organizing around issues shared with white women may place the organizer in additional jeopardy within the ethnic community due to the notion that organizing groups of women can be divisive.[1] Creative strategies such as mapping out the benefits and drawbacks of sharing a community change effort are necessary when these linkages are desired. Efforts will often require dealing directly with incidents of homophobia or sexism within communities of color.

When the consequences outweigh the benefits, alternatives to the proposed organizing effort must be identified. In some cases, this may mean that organizers who are not community members must continue their work outside of the ethnic community and share strategies with organizers who are inside the ethnic community.[22]

Women of color inside the community can look to other women of color across the country who are involved in an organizing effort for support as well. Pat Collair's efforts at organizing rural southern poor women rely not only on work with these women but also with other women involved in similar grassroots change efforts. This continued communication is one way of dealing with the problem of the emotional drain related to issues of racism and sexism in community organization.

It continues to be necessary for women of color to voice the differences between community organizing in general, feminist community organizing, community organizing with people of color, and specifically, community

---

*"Fighting Back: Frances Sandoval and her mother's crusade take aim at gangs," *Chicago Tribune Magazine*, (Oct. 16, 1988):10–24.

organizing with women of color. To do this, however, we need more women of color trained in community organizing. The number of students majoring in community organization, in general, declined for much of the last decade and only now are beginning to increase. To complicate things further, it has been our experience that students of color in many Schools of Social Work are still treated as though they were not as capable as other students. In some schools, remedial programs are designed without attention to some of the rich undergraduate programs these students have attended. Sometimes, the discussion of the need for these programs is overtly racist, more often it is practiced covertly, such as giving extra admission points for "good undergraduate programs." Women of color in schools of social work, as teachers and students, are in the peculiar position of having to resist these efforts to stereotype and limit our sisters.

  7. *Feminist organizers must recognize ways in which women of color have worked effectively within their own communities.*

  Women of color have traditionally been involved in activities to benefit their community. Feminist organizers should work with these indigenous leaders and learn from them the most effective ways of working in particular communities. Working with existing leaders may involve feminist organizers in different types of activities than those in which they may usually engage. For example, existing community leaders may be active in church-related activities or in working with municipal agencies to provide necessary survival services.[3] Organizers can learn the ways these leaders have survived and exercised political leverage.

  It is more important than ever to recognize and facilitate effective organizing efforts among women in communities of color. Poverty levels in the U.S. that have always disproportionately affected families of color are at pre-1965 levels for women and children. Homelessness, originally theorized to be a problem of unemployed men, is now a serious problem for poor women and their families. Many of the reasons for the organizing efforts of the 1800s for people of color have been resolved (inability to vote, restricted access to banks and insurance companies, etc.). The mutual aid societies and African-American women's clubs, however, may still be used as entry-level points to women of color. Just as the early African-American Womens' Clubs of the 1880s began with a concentration on antilynching strategies and later expanded to problems facing the general society, so can the mutual aid societies form a basis for organizing on both the micro- and macro-levels for women of color.

Conclusion

A feminist perspective on organizing with women of color is one way to address the profound effects of sexism and racism on our lives. Knowledge based on feminist organizing suggests very specific ways in which organizers can move individual women from feelings of powerlessness and apathy to active change. However, this model of feminist organizing must be modified when working in communities of color. Feminist organizers must recognize how their life experiences might differ from that of community members and be willing to accept the problem definitions and strategies developed by women of color. Another critical technique requires recognizing how historical conflicts between feminist and antiracist movements may affect interactions between white women and women of color and point to ways of opening up a dialogue which will work toward creative resolution of these conflicts.

Traditionally, feminist organizing has usually moved in one direction only: from the organizers representing the white middle-class community to the community of color. For example, little of the literature on feminist organizing or community organizing describes the activist roles of women of color within our communities. As students, we learned of our contributions to social change only through reading the popular African-American press (*Ebony, Essence, Black Digest*), local ethnic press, or through oral tradition within our communities.

In this chapter we suggest that the flow of information about the best ways to engage in organizing activities with women of color is to adopt a multidirectional approach: from the individual women of color; through their families; informal institutions; and back to the feminists representing the wider society. In this way, feminist community organization techniques can contribute to the empowerment of individual women and to their involvement in solving the problems of all women of color.

Endnotes

1. T. Aragon de Valdez, "Organizing as a Political Tool for the Chicana," *Frontiers* (1980):7–13.

2. M. Barrera, "Chicano Class Structure." In R. Takaki, ed. *From Different Shores: Perspectives on Race and Ethnicity in America* (New York: Oxford University Press, 1987), 130–138.

3. A. Bookman and S. Morgan, *Women and the Politics of Empowerment* (Philadelphia: Temple University Press, 1986).

4. Bricker-Jenkins and N. Hooyman, *Not for Women Only: Social Work Practice for a Feminist Future* (Silver Spring: NASW, 1986).

5. L. Burton and V. Bengston, "Research in Minority Communities: Problems and Potentials," In R. Manual, ed. *Minority Aging: Sociological and Social Psychological Issues* (New York: Greenwood Press, 1982).

6. B. T. Dill, "Race, Class and Gender: Prospects for an All-Inclusive Sisterhood, In R. Takaki, ed. *From Different Shores: Perspectives on Race and Ethnicity in America* (New York: Oxford University Press, 1987), 204–214.

7. S. Evans, *Personal Politics* (New York: Vintage Books, 1980).

8. P. Friere, "Cultural Action for Freedom," *Harvard Educational Review* 40 (1970):205–225, 452–477.

9. P. Giddings, *Where and When I Enter: The Impact of Black Women on Race and Sex in America* (New York: William Morrow and Company, 1984).

10. C. Gilkes, "Building in Many Places: Multiple Commitments and Ideologies in Black Womens' Community Work," In A. Bookman and S. Morgan, eds. *Woman and the Politics of Empowerment* (Philadelphia: Temple University Press, 1986).

11. C. Gilkes, "Going Up for the Oppressed: The Career Mobility of Black Women Community Workers," *Journal of Social Issues* 39 (March 1983):115–139.

12. C. Gilkes, "Holding Back the Ocean with a Broom: Black Women and Community Work," In L. F. Rodgers-Rose, ed. *The Black Woman* (Beverly Hills: Sage, 1981), 217–233.

13. R. Gordon-Bradshaw, "A Social Essay on Special Issues Facing Poor Women of Color," *Women and Health* 12 (1987):243–59.

14. K. Gould, "Feminist Principals and Minority Concerns: Contributions, Problems, and Solutions, *Affila: Journal of Women and Social Work* 3 (1987):6–19.

15. K. Gould, "Life Model vs. Role Conflict Model: A Feminist Perspective, *Social Work* 32 (1987):346–351.

16. L. Gutiérrez, Working with Women of Color: An Empowerment Perspective, *Social Work* 35 (1990):149–154.

17. B. Hooks, *Ain't I a Woman: Black Women and Feminism* (Boston: South End Press, 1981).

18. C. Hyde, "Experiences of Women Activists: Implications for Community Organizing Theory and Practice," *Journal of Sociology and Social Welfare* 13 (1986): 545–562.

19. C. Hyde, "A Feminist Model for Macro Practice: Promises and Problems," *Administration in Social Work* 13 (1990):145–181.

20. B. Joseph, T. Mizrahi, J. Peterson, and F. Sugarman, *Women's Perspectives on Community Organizing: A Feminist Synthesis of Theory and Practice*, Paper presented at the Annual Program Meeting of the Council on Social Work Education, Chicago, IL March, 1989.

21. C. Kieffer, "Citizen Empowerment: A Developmental Perspective," In J. Rappaport, C. Swift, and R. Hess, eds. *Studies in Empowerment: Toward Understanding and Action* (New York: Hawthorn Press, 1984), 9–36.

22. R. Kopasci and A. Faulkner, "The Powers that Might Be: The Unity of White and Black Feminists." *Affila* 3 (1988):33–50.

23. E. Lewis, "Ethnicity, Race and Gender: Training and Supervision Issues in the Treatment of Women, In B. De Chant, J. Cunningham, J. Lazerson, and R. Perls, eds. *Women, Gender and Group Psychotherapy* (New York: American Group Psychotherapy Association Monograph, in press).

24. J. Lin Fu, "Special Health Concerns of Ethnic Minority Women. *Public Health Reports* 102 (1987):12–14.

25. R. Linten and M. Witham, With mourning, rage, empowerment and defiance: The 1981 Women's Pentagon Action. *Socialist Review, 63,* 11–36.

26. J. Longres and E. McLeod, Consciousness Raising and Social Work Practice, *Social Casework* 61 (1980):267–627.

27. C. Loo and P. Ong, "Slaying Demons with a Sewing Needle: Feminist Issues for Chinatown's Women, In R. Takaki, ed. *From Different Shores: Perspectives on Race and Ethnicity in America* (New York: Oxford, 1987), 186–191.

28. M. Macht and J. Quam, *Social Work: An Introduction* (Columbus, Ohio: Merrill, 1986), 96.

29. J. McAdoo, "Black Father and Child Interactions, In L. Gary, ed. *Black Men* (Beverly Hills: Sage, 1981), 115–130.

30. C. Morell, "Cause is Function: Toward a Feminist Model of Integration for Social Work, *Social Science Review* 61 (1987):144–155.

31. J. Nes and P. Iadicola, "Toward a Definition of Feminist Social Work: A Comparison of Liberal, Radical, and Socialist Models, *Social Work* 34 (1989):12–22.

32. R. Pernell, Empowerment and Social Group Work, In M. Parenes, ed. *Innovations in Social Group Work: Feedback from Practice to Theory* (New York: Hawthorn Press, 1985), 107–117.

33. E. Pinderhughes, Empowerment for Our Clients and for Ourselves, *Social Casework* 64 (1983):331–38.

34. P. Reid, Feminism vs. Minority Group Identity: Not for Black Women Only, *Sex Roles* 10 (Month 1984):247–255.

35. N. Rosenthal (1984). Consciousness raising: From revolution to re-evaluation. *Psychology of Women Quarterly,* 8, 309–326.

36. S. Schechter, *Women and Male Violence: The Visions and Struggles of the Battered Women's Movement* (Boston: South End Press, 1982).

37. S. Schechter, S. Szymanski, and M. Cahill, *Violence Against Women: A Curriculum for Empowerment.* Facilitator's Manual (New York: Women's Education Institute, 1985).

38. D. Segura, "Labor Market Stratification: The Chicana Experience, In R. Takaki, ed. *From Different Shores: Perspectives on Race and Ethnicity in America* (New York: Oxford, 1987), 175–185.

39. C. Simmons and R. Parsons, Empowerment for Role Alternatives in Adolescence, *Adolescence* 69:193–200.

40. B. Solomon, Alternative Social Services and the Black Woman, In N. Gottlieb, ed. *Alternative Services for Women* (New York: Columbia University Press, 1980), 333–345.

41. B. Solomon, Empowering Women: A Matter of Values, In A. Seick and S. Vandiver, eds. *Women, Power and Change* (Silver Springs: NASW, 1982), 206–214.

42. E. Spelman, *Inessential Woman: Problems of Exclusion in Feminist Thought* (Boston: Beacon Press, 1989).

43. C. B. Stack, *All Our Kin* (New York: Harper and Row, 1974).

44. M. Weil, "Women, Community and Organizing," In N. Van DenBergh and L. Cooper, eds. *Feminist Visions for Social Work* (Silver Springs: NASW, 1987), 187–210.

45. B. White, "Black Women: The Resilient Victims, In A. Weick and S. Vandiver, eds. *Women, Power and Change* (Washington, DC: NASW, 1981), 69–77.

46. A. Withorn, *Serving the People: Social Services and Social Change* (New York: Columbia, 1984).

47. R. Zambrana, "A Research Agenda on Issues Affecting Poor and Minority Women: A Model for Understanding Their Health Needs," *Women and Health* 12 (1987):137–60.

48. P. Zavella, The Politics of Race and Gender: Organizing Chicana Cannery Workers in Northern California, In A. Bookman and S. Morgan, eds. *Women and the Politics of Empowerment* (Philadelphia: Temple University Press, 1986).

References

A. Bookman and S. Morgan, *Women and the Politics of Empowerment* (Philadelphia: Temple University Press, 1986).

P. Friere, *Education for Critical Consciousness* (New York: Seabury Press, 1973).

G. Joseph and J. Lewis, *Common Differences* (Boston: South End Press, 1981).

R. Kopasci and A. Faulkner, "The Powers That Might Be: The Unity of White and Black Feminists," *Affilia* 3 (1988):33–50.

C. Moraga and G. Anzaldua, *The Bridge Called My Back: Writings of Radical Women of Color* (New York: Kitchen Table Press, 1981).

R. Sarri and V. du Rivage, *Strategies for Self-Help and Empowerment of Working Low-Income Women who are Heads of Families* (Unpublished Manuscript, Ann Arbor, University of Michigan, School of Social Work).

B. Solomon, *Black Empowerment* (New York: Columbia University Press, 1976).

N. Van DenBergh and L. Cooper, ed. *Feminist Visions for Social Work* (Silver Spring: NASW, 1986).

P. J. Williams, "On Being the Object of Property," *Signs: Journal of Women and Culture* 14 (January 1988).

J. Wilson, Women and Poverty: A Demographic Overview, *Women and Health* 12 (1987):21–40.

T. Wolverton, "Unlearning Complicity, Remembering Resistance: White Women's Antiracism Education," In C. Bunch and S. Pollack, eds. *Learning Our Way: Essays in Feminist Education* (Trumansberg: The Crossing Press, 1983).

CHAPTER SEVEN

The Chinese Americans— Community Organizing Strategies and Tactics

ISAIAH C. LEE

Introduction

The purpose of this chapter is to present an analysis of Chinese Americans as a minority ethnic group in America and to discuss the historical, socio-cultural, and political-economic dynamics related to their psychological and social adaptation and adjustment problems, social services needs, community organization, and leadership development in this country. The first part of this chapter will attempt to define who the Chinese Americans are, since there is no official or unified definition of Chinese Americans available for the purpose of academic and intellectual discussion related to community organization and social services for this particular ethnic group.

The second part of this chapter will present a brief historical background of Chinese-American immigrants and explain their motivations for immigrating to this country. The characteristics of their political-economic development, psycho-social adaptation, self-images, and the way of preserving their ethnic identity will be discussed.

The third part of this chapter will discuss the socio-economic and socio-cultural adjustment problems encountered by the new and old Chinese-American immigrants in this country, their impact upon community agencies, social work, and other professional schools, and to explore the possible solutions to these problems.

The final part of this chapter will conclude with recommendations and proposals for providing new community planning, community organization, and human care services to the new and old immigrants of Chinese-American communities in the United States.

Who Are the Chinese Americans?

The term Chinese American can be defined as an ethnic group of people who originally immigrated from China and shared the same socio-cultural traits, values, and common psychological identity as Chinese. This may include the first generation of immigrants and all subsequent generations. For Chinese, the term Chinese American covers several categories of Chinese people in America; the first one is called "American Born Chinese" (A.B.C.), individuals who are generally the second or third generation Chinese brought up and educated in this country, the second one, "Fresh Off the Boat" (F.O.B.), describes the newly arrived immigrants who brought with them the old traditional cultures and different languages that are strange to the American, and the third one, "Overseas Chinese" (O.S.C.), are the first generation old Chinese who generally involved themselves in the political-economic affairs of Chinatown in all major cities in the United States, and the fourth one, "Made In Taiwan" (M.I.T.), describes the group of business people and students from Taiwan.

Each category carries a different identity and consciousness. As a group of ethnic Chinese in this country, A.B.C.s, who had the opportunity to get an American education, tended to accept America as their homeland and rejected some of their parents cultural values. But many of them might eventually develop a "banana personality" that is used by the first generation Asian immigrants to mean yellow skin outside and white mentality inside. The F.O.B.s have always regarded themselves as Chinese people and treated whites as foreigners even though they are living in white society. They carry a mentality of "permanent guest" in this country. Almost one-half of their mind and heart is left behind in their native land of Taiwan, mainland China, or Hong Kong. Except for earning a living in the United States, they are mostly concerned about the political-economic issues and socio-cultural affairs of their native country instead of the local community in which they are living now. The O.S.C.s are usually established old Chinese immigrants who came from mainland China before the communist takeover. They are usually linked with the political-economic systems of the native land—either Taipei, Peking, or Hong Kong. They have become the extended arms of the Chinese government in American communities. For better or for worse, many of these O.S.C. leaders can be classified as "opportunists" who use American citizenship as protection to engage in foreign politics and to promote their business interests. The M.I.T.s, who originally described the American markets as being filled with a large volume of goods and commercial items made in Taiwan, became a popular joke, describing the business people and students who came from Taiwan as M.I.T.s. Many of the M.I.T.s separate their political-economic identity from the rest of the Chinese groups. They even refuse to be classified as Chinese in the U.S. Census.

The Formosan Association for Public Affairs and many Taiwanese social groups have asked the U.S. Bureau of Census to list Taiwanese as a separate category from Chinese. If we attempt to define Chinese Americans as Chinese who live in America or a group of people who have immigrated to America from China, while logical, is not really satisfactory for a discussion of community organization or for the planning of social services.

There are many Chinese business people and students in America who do not intend to make America their permanent home; therefore, they can not be considered Chinese American. Also, among the immigrants from China there are few groups of Chinese people who do not identify themselves psychologically, ideologically, or linguistically as Chinese American even though they might have been born in China and grew up there. This includes people from Tibet, Inner Mongolia, and many overseas Chinese student associations that are currently fighting for a democratic China in this country. They intend to return to mainland China when the political current is favorable to their political interest. Therefore, the new definition of Chinese Americans is necessary to clarify these confusions. For non-Chinese people, the term Chinese American is a subgroup of the larger Asian-American or Pacific-Asian group in this country. Geographically, China is as big as the United States. The socio-economic conditions of northern China is comparatively poorer than southern China, but for thousands of years the invaders, warlords, and revolutionaries have always surged from northern China and pushed millions of refugees to southern China and even forced the refugees to escape to Southeast Asia and the United States. The political and socio-cultural traits and values of northern China are usually the main force that shapes the ruling mentality in China. People in southern China have usually resisted the ruling force from northern China by such dialects as Cantonese, Amoy, Fukien, and Taiwanese. They maintain separate psychological identities and mistrust people from other groups.

In order to understand the socio-political and community infrastructure of Chinese Americans in this country, one must grasp the brief historical dynamics of Chinese immigrants.

Each stage of the history reflects certain political-economic and socio-cultural characteristics of Chinese and American societies.

The Stage of Oppression (1751–1965)

In 1751, Chinese shipbuilders started to appear in California.[1] In 1785, documented records indicate that three Chinese crewmen were stranded in Baltimore for almost a year where they lived on public funds. In 1786,

George Washington appointed Major Samuel Shaw the first American consul to China. His primary function was to promote trade and he was responsible for the great boom in Chinese labor immigration. In 1820, one Chinese immigrant entered America.[5] The first census notation of Chinese in America listed 3 persons in 1830, 8 in 1840, and 758 people in 1850.

After the Opium Wars, from 1839 to 1842, and the Anglo-French War against China, from 1848 to 1865, China was forced to become an international colony for all big powers, not only providing raw materials and goods, but also cheap human labor. The Taipin Rebellion of 1848 also brought chaos to China for seventeen years, and millions of lives were lost to wars and famine. These miserable political and social conditions motivated the Chinese peasants to risk their lives and venture abroad to Southeast Asia and finally, in the 1850s, across the Pacific Ocean to the United States. From 1848 to 1852, Chinese arrived here as indentured servants during the California Gold Rush. The bulk of Chinese immigrants came soon after as a cheap source of labor to work on the railroads, mines, fisheries, farms, orchards, canneries, garment industries, manufacturing, etc. As a result, a total of 41,397 Chinese entered California during the period from 1851 to 1860.[7]

These Chinese immigrants and the ones who followed had to endure both hardships and indignities. The Chinese handled the racial hostility and discrimination by dispersion to different cities as far away as the east coast and by adopting the jobs of cooks, barbers, laundry men, and grocers—jobs that were usually performed by women—to avoid competition with white men. In 1859, the exclusion of the Chinese from public schools in San Francisco pushed all Chinese students into home teaching in Chinatown. This was the way that the early Chinese immigrants preserved their own ethnic identity and cultural values for their children. In 1868, the U.S. Treaty with China, which recognized the right of immigration of Chinese for "purposes of curiosity, trade, or permanent residence," expressly restricted the right of naturalization. In fact, the 1870 Naturalization Act excluded Chinese from citizenship and forbade the entry of wives of laborers. In 1876, when the national economy collapsed, the Chinese became the ready victims of riots and daily bloodshed in San Francisco. In 1877, a gang descended on Los Angeles' Chinatown in the midst of a Tong war and hung fifteen Chinese, including women and children, from lamp posts and killed six more by other means.[7] What had motivated these public outrages? Listen to the words of one of the most outspoken of the Sinophobes, Frank M. Pixley, explaining his attitude to the U.S. Senate in 1877:

> The burden of our accusations against them is that they come in conflict with our labor interests; that they can never assimilate with us; by that they are a perpetual unchanging and unchangeable alien element that

can never become homogeneous; that their civilization is demoralizing and degrading to our people; that they degrade and dishonor labor;
that they never become citizens; and that an alien, degrades labor class,
without desire of citizenship, without education and without interest in
the country it inhabits is an element both demoralizing and dangerous
to the community within which it exists.[5]

Did it justify the inhumane treatment of the Chinese immigrants? The
white vigilantes staged pigtail-cutting parties in which they not only hacked
off Chinamens' queues but ripped off their scalps as well. In one of the most
extreme and gruesome atrocities on record, a mob served a Chinaman's
genitals in a saloon, where they were roasted and eaten as prairie oysters.[9]

In 1882, The Chinese Exclusion Act, which prohibited the entrance of
Chinese laborers and continued the denial of citizenship to the Chinese,
was intended to last for ten years but was later extended to 1902 at the insis-
tence of Californian Denis Kearney of the Knights of Labor and the Working Man's Party, who cried, "The Chinese must go!" Chinese merchants,
particularly laundries and miners, were excessively taxed, and the following occupations were restricted: medicine, teaching, dentistry, mining,
railroading, and manufacturing. In 1906, California's antimiscegenation
laws were amended to bar marriages between whites and "Mongolians",
or Asian persons. In 1921, California legislated a special act directed
against Chinese women so that those who married American citizens
could not automatically become citizens.[8] These negative social and political trends against Chinese immigrants went totally unchanged until after
the Pearl Harbor Incident of 1941; the Magnuson Act of 1943 finally
repealed the Chinese Exclusion Act of 1882. However, not until 1952 did
the McCarran-Walter Act grant the right of naturalization to foreign-born
Asians, but it set a token quota of 105 persons per year for Asian countries.
The legal oppression against the Chinese continued in the United States
until 1965, when the National Origins Act under the Kennedy Administration raised all Asian immigration to 20,000 per year for each nation. This
law gave a fair and equal immigration opportunity to the Chinese in the
United States. Then, in 1967, the antimiscegenation laws were ruled
unconstitutional by the U.S. Supreme Court, reflecting a period of positive
change in social attitudes toward Chinese and other Asian immigrants.

During the 145 years from 1820 to 1965, an estimated 320,000 Chinese
immigrants entered into the United States. Their impact upon the national
and local politics was negative except for the recognized fact that thousands
of Chinese laborers had sacrificed their lives for the completion of the
railroads across the country and for cutting the forests for the white people to
rush for the gold in California. During World War II, many young Chinese
Americans who fought the Imperial Japanese Army in the Pacific Theater

and the German Army in Europe, had earned some friendly treatment. For the development of community and political infrastructure during this period, the Chinese Americans were forced to organize themselves through the Tongs, which were the associations of kinship and extended family groups as well as the clubs of people who came from the same native village. These organizations, plus many secret clubs engaging in either political or economic affairs, exerted their authority and influence upon all facets of life for Chinese living in the United States. They could settle civil disputes, criminal cases, or group conflicts when local courts or governments could or would not handle them. Also, the Catholic and Protestant missionary churches in the heart of Chinatown, and in many of the metropolitan areas, had served as the bridge of communication between the socio-political structures of Chinese Americans and the American society at large. Instead of the local government agencies, the missionary churches and various voluntary agencies had delivered many social services and community organization projects for the Chinese American. The community-based leadership emerged from the approval of Tong associations and the support of the missionary churches.

What had kept these early Chinese immigrants together in this strange land? What had made them develop their identity as a minority ethnic group? Based upon sociological theories and cultural analysis, two basic socio-cultural values of Filial Piety and Family System have kept these Chinese immigrants together as a minority ethnic group in this country. The concept of filial piety, one of the great cultural values and social ideologies deeply rooted in the five thousand years of Chinese history, was taught by Confucious. It requires the young to respect, honor, and obey their elders, as well as to honor their ancestors. It is the basic foundation of the Chinese kinship system. The family system in Chinese society is the main source of social control and social protection. Each member of the family is expected to give to—and if necessary, make personal sacrifices for—the betterment of the entire family. In this kind of social system, a person defined his or her purpose in life not so much in terms of personal happiness but rather toward ensuring the survival and well-being of the family as a group.

When the Chinese spoke of their family, they were not referring to just the immediate family of father, mother, brothers, sisters, and grandparents. Instead, they were referring to the larger extended family or clan of kinship relations.[3]

The Stage of Liberation (1965–1985):

Since the Immigration and Nationality Act was amended on October 3, 1965, a total number of 20,000 immigrant visas from a single foreign state under the numerical restrictions and preference classes have been issued to

Asian countries. The Chinese immigrants felt liberated from the oppressive public policies. During this twenty year period, a large wave of more than 920,528 Chinese immigrants had arrived in the United States from Taiwan, Hong Kong, mainland China, and the Southeast Asian countries. Among them were many intellectuals, professionals, and political refugees who escaped from Communist rule in mainland China in the 1960s. They were large Mandarin speaking, and their philosophy and life styles were very different from the earlier Cantonese immigrants. Most of them engaged in scientific research, university teaching, professional practice, and government service. Their children are attending good colleges and professional schools in various technical fields, particularly computer science, engineering, biomedical research, medicine, and the health-care professions. Consequently, several thousand Chinese engineers in the high technology and space science industry in the United States today have laid a foundation for the development and growth of computer technology and engineering sciences in Chinese communities in both the United States and Taiwan.

Five major factors led to the rapid escape of these huge numbers of immigrants and refugees: (1) The national Chinese government lost its representation of China to the Communist Chinese government in the United Nations, a loss which raised the fear of the political and military occupation of Taiwan by the Chinese Liberation Army; (2) The visit of President Richard Nixon to Peking and his Shanghai Communique on the normalization of diplomatic relations with the People's Republic of China which brought a political-psychological shock to Chinese people in Taiwan and Hong Kong; (3) The withdrawal of diplomatic recognition from the Republic of China by the Carter Administration wiped out the trust and confidence of people who believed that American forces would protect Taiwan from an invasion by Communist China; (4) The Vietnam War pushed millions of refugees with Chinese ancestry out of Southeast Asian countries; (5) A large number of the immediate relatives of the first wave of Chinese Americans were qualified to enter America as new immigrants. Thousands have come with their young children and elderly parents.

Since 1980, the new immigration has brought rich business people, political escapees who held high offices, professionals, intellectuals, and many refugees without resources. These immigrants include Mandarin and Taiwanese speaking, and Fukienese-Amoy and Cantonese speaking groups. The life styles of these new immigrants are very diversified. They include multimillionaires who have invested their money in Hilton hotels, Holiday Inns, Ramada Inns, Asian-American banks, shopping centers, and real estate development projects in Los Angeles, Monterey Park, Long Beach, Anaheim, Irvine, San Francisco, San Jose, Chicago, New York, Houston, Phoenix, San Diego, Las Vegas, Miami, Boston, Seattle, and other major cities in the United States. The 1985 statistics of the Taiwanese Hotel and Motel Association of

Southern California indicated that there are over 650 motels and hotels of all sizes owned and managed by the first generation immigrants from Taiwan. There are thousands of Chinese restaurants, cafes, fast-food restaurants, coffee shops, and bakeries throughout the country. Daily business transactions among these new and old immigrants or with the American business community in general creates the real need for numerous bilingual lawyers, certified public accountants, real estate brokers, loan appraisers, property managers, gardeners, home designers, architects, landscape engineers, and medical care professionals. There are also thousands of young adults without professional education or vocational training looking for daily wages and willing to accept a low salary in Chinese communities in all big cities. Many of these young adults are attending English classes and regional occupational programs, improving their English proficiency and learning a job skill. The young children are attending public schools with bilingual programs. Many of them are also attending the Saturday Chinese schools to learn Chinese culture and languages. In San Francisco, one out of ten children attending school is a Chinese descendant. Also, hundreds of senior citizens who came with their relatives to this country have begun to face various psycho-social adjustment problems in Chinese American communities across the country.[7]

The social structures and social support networks in Chinese American communities changed drastically from the previous stage. The Tong associations and secret clubs were still functioning for the Overseas Chinese and Fresh Off the Boat from Hong Kong and Canton as their social support networks and mutual aid societies in Chinatown.

The new immigrants from Taiwan and mainland China, particularly the highly educated professionals and business people, started to organize their own support groups through Protestant churches such as Presbyterian, Methodist, Lutheran, Evangelical and many other independent local churches. These immigrants meet weekly in order to satisfy their psycho-social, economic, educational, informational, and political needs above their real spiritual needs since more than one third of the church attendees are non-Christian. There are over two hundred churches of different denominations organized and attended by Chinese immigrants in the Los Angeles and Orange County area alone. Also, hundreds of professional, business, social, academic, political, and self-help groups have sprouted during this period. Most of these loosely organized groups were only functioning within the Chinese American communities. Only a few of them had real contact and involvement in local or national politics with large social structures or American governments.

The "Tong Hsian Hoei," which is a club for people coming from the same village or same province, serves as an entity of geographic and political identity involved in the foreign politics of their nativeland. Since the racial-ethnic consciousness and civil rights movement began in the 1960s, there were a few Chinese American social work groups and community organization agencies started to address the socio-economic and socio-political issues of equal employment opportunity, community services, health care, and professional education for Chinese Americans in all major cities.

For example, the Chinese American Social Workers Association, Oriental Social-Health Society, and the Coordinating Council of Oriental Social Services organized and engaged in a dialogue with Los Angeles County and other City governments regarding their employment policy and cultural sensitivity toward community services for Chinese Americans. Some positive changes were made, but the effort of one ethnic group in combating the social injustice was not strong enough, therefore the joint effort of other ethnic groups emerged to form an Asian-American group and other community organization groups at the same time. Good examples were the Asian-American Social Workers Association and Asian-American Community Planning Council, which involved all Asian ethnic groups.

The Stage of Competition (1985–present):

The strong competition between the newly arrived immigrants and old Chinese Americans in the business world and professional practice as well as community leadership in the social and church groups are very evident at this stage. Not only do the Chinese Americans compete with each other for the political-economic and socio-religious leadership in the national and local Chinese American communities, but also, the socially conscious Chinese Americans have started to compete with the mainstream white political-economic power in government offices, industries, and businesses of all kinds. The academic and professional achievements in biomedical sciences, computer technologies, engineering, and Nobel Prizes are other examples of their successes.

Dr. S. B. Wu, who is a professor of physics, became the Lieutenant Governor of Delaware; Dr. March Fong Eu, who was an educational administrator, became the Secretary of the State of California; Ms. Lily Lee Chen, who is a social worker, served as the mayor of the City of Monterey Park; and the current mayor is Dr. Judy Chu, a Chinese psychologist. Both Dr. C. T. Lee, professor of physics at Columbia University, and Dr. Y. C. Lee, professor of chemistry at the University of California at Berkeley, have received Nobel Prizes. Dr. C. L. Tien was appointed as the Chancellor of the University of California at Berkeley. Dr. Wang-An's Computer Company is very popular in the computer field. These academic leaders are all first generation immigrants with bilingual and bicultural backgrounds.

The second generation of young Chinese Americans are competing with their white peers for the first-rate universities and colleges. This competition has always caused dissension in the public and private university administration. During this period, both Taiwan and mainland China are given a total of 40,000 immigrant visas each year plus the fact that there are many Chinese immigrants who were included in the special refugee groups from Vietnam or Cambodia or Thailand.

What are the Psycho-Socio-Cultural-Economic Characteristics of Chinese-Americans at this time? There are six characteristics that help to explain their present situation:

(1) The immigration of a large group who came to join the older immigrants was planned by their parents or relatives in advance. On the surface, over 60,000 young students are here to attend good high schools or colleges, but the underlying motive is to help their children obtain American citizenship in order to protect them when communist China seizes Taiwan or Hong Kong.

(2) The increase of extended family size and structure with three generations in a family (approximately 30 percent of the total population) has rapidly developed marital disputes, poor in-law relationships, and revealed generation gaps and cultural conflicts in many first generation families. There are also marital problems occurring between the new and old immigrants as well as between the ones from Taiwan and mainland China.

(3) The increase of absent fathers and female household heads (over 30,000 families) in families with young adults fostered child neglect and social isolation. Many fathers brought their wives and children here for the sake of a good education, and the security of property and investment in America, but they tended to return to their job or business activities in Taiwan and Hong Kong most of the time. The burden of supervising children and managing household activities eventually rested upon the shoulders of mothers. Some juvenile delinquency and gang activities have started to appear among the new Chinese American youth in junior and senior high schools around the urban communities.

(4) Competition for leadership of social and political activities between the new and old immigrants, the business people, and the intellectual groups became more visible. The older intellectual immigrants who have a good education, a high paying profession, and a good command of English tend to merge into the American community and assume political leadership and advocacy for the Chinese American community, but the business people and new immigrants who possess large sums of money and huge amounts of property may compete for community leadership and social recognition through the donation of money for political campaigns and church and community services. At times, they cooperate with each

other to achieve a higher goal for the whole ethnic community, such as the support and advocacy of positive immigration policy. Sometimes, they compete with each other for offices in city councils or boards of education. From time to time, the problems of leadership jealousy and individual heroism have become the stumbling block for effective community organization in Chinese American communities.

(5) The goals and activities of social-political groups and business-professional associations as well as Christian church groups have become diversified and broad-based. Some groups are oriented toward the social-political issues in Taiwan and mainland China; others are oriented toward local and national politics in this country. However, even among the latter, there is dissension. Some groups are geared to the interests of first generation immigrants, and others, to the problems of the second and third generation Chinese-Americans who were born here. Furthermore, some groups are interested only in marketing their business or professional services. They do not care too much about the community affairs or American politics.

(6) The psycho-social adaptation of the individuals and social-cultural adjustment of the groups to the American community appear to be so unique in the Chinese immigrant groups that there are nine types of self-images observable among them. The first type possesses a refugee image and mentality and is still running from political oppression and planning a mission of revenge and revolution in his dreams. The second type possesses a victim's image and mentality because she was deserted as a war bride or divorcee or suffered a broken family in this country. The third type, who keeps a face-saving image and consciousness has failed in business operations or marriage and family disputes in his or her nativeland and dreams of a second chance to rebuild the glory of the business or family in this country. The fourth type, who suffers from his or her own past experiences of family life, professional career, or business failure, tends to keep a sojourner image and consciousness in this new world. The fifth type, who holds a betrayed image and consciousness has felt cheated by his or her friends and business associates for encouraging him or her to invest money in the United States because so far he or she has earned nothing but lots of legal and emotional trouble. The sixth type, who keeps an opportunistic image and consciousness, maintains a detached attitude toward social and political changes on both sides of the Pacific Ocean. This person does not want to commit him or herself to the well-being of either the American or the Chinese community. He or she observes and criticizes when others are involved in the process of social and political changes. This type will sail when the political and economic wind is certain. The seventh type, who keeps preaching the five-thousand-year old Chinese culture and virtues or beats the drum of anticommunism, has built a psychological defense and a crusader image and

consciousness to justify his or her own existence in this strange land. The eighth type, who holds a strong pioneer image and a positive attitude, has dreamed of a beautiful tomorrow and a better life in the new world. This type respects the principles of godliness, honesty, liberty, thrift, democracy, industry, mutual aid, and self-government. He or she has courage to overcome frustrations and miseries in the hope of establishing him or herself and people in a new world and contributing their talents and resources to the well-being of their immediate neighborhood, their local community, and their relatives in the old world. The ninth type, who holds a participant image and consciousness, had adapted him or herself to the American way of life. He or she has learned "When in Rome, do as the Romans do" or "When in America, do as the Americans do." This group of people quickly become a part of the American social-economic and cultural community and will soon make themselves at home in this country. This type of person makes efforts to learn the American language and culture, to make friends with their schoolmates, business colleagues, and neighbors, and to participate in church, community, charity, and political activities. For a good and healthy psycho-social adaptation, the last two categories of self-image and consciousness are more constructive and realistic for the first generation immigrants to follow in this country.[7]

What are the implications of these characteristics for community organizers? The old Chinese classic *War Principles*, written by Sun Tsu, stated that in order to fight a victorious war, you must know yourself and your enemy. This war principle can be applied to community organization. Anyone who is interested in organizing in the Chinese American community must know him or herself and the Chinese-Americans as well. Without knowledge of the psycho-socio-cultural and economic characteristics of Chinese-Americans, organizers could not become sensitive to the very needs of Chinese-Americans. The organizing efforts will be in vain in either community organization or program planning. The next section will discuss community implications, program planning, and alternative strategies along with social adjustment problems the Chinese-Americans encountered in this country.

What are the Social Adjustment Problems of Chinese-Americans?

There are certain visible social adjustment problems and community concerns for new and old Chinese-American people. These problems are often discussed in various community meetings among the first and second generation Chinese-American. One is the social isolation of the aging group. Approximately 10 percent of the total Chinese-American population is aged retirees who came to join their adult children in this country. There are more than 30,000 retirees living in southern California alone. Even though the economic condition of their adult children is relatively comfortable, 33.3 percent of this aging group is receiving assistance—Supplemental Security Income from the U.S. Social Security Administration. The elderly expected kind treatment and due respect from their adult children and grandchildren when they arrived in this country, but instead, they have encountered cultural shock, status loss, and generation gaps as well as social isolation in their families and communities. The majority of them do not read, write, speak, or understand English. They watch English television programs without understanding the meaning. Most of them cannot drive; therefore, their daily activities have been confined to their immediate home environments. If their adult children or grandchildren do not have time to take them out for shopping or attending social activities in church or the community gatherings, they tend to become very lonely and isolated from social interaction and communication with other people. Sometimes these aging parents may develop emotional disturbance and depression which causes marital conflict for their adult children. The most serious problem, and one which has been observed as causing high anxiety in this group, is the issue surrounding medical care at acute hospitals and nursing homes. The language difficulty, social isolation, change in diet, strange environments, physical examinations, and blood tests by unknown persons all contribute to the fear of mistreatment and death in a foreign land. For example, a disabled aged patient in a wheelchair was cared for by his wife at home daily, but he was confined at home without care when his wife had to go to work. Another example is an elderly widow of a physician who recently arrived to join her daughter's family and immediately encountered a communication problem with her grandchildren and attendant social isolation.

How can one cope with problems faced by the elderly? The community and church leaders are planning to set up multipurpose retirement centers in southern California for those who are ambulatory and can function independently. The Formosan Presbyterian Church of Orange County and California Institute of Human Care in Garden Grove are organizing a biweekly senior ceramics program for a group of fifty elderly people who speak the same dialect of Taiwanese. In Echo Park, Los Angeles, there is a day-care center for Mandarin and Cantonese-speaking elderly, established by Ms. Alice Tsou of Chinese Community Services. The day-care center provides the first social-health program, lunch program, socio-recreational activities, and skilled nursing care for hundreds of Chinese elderly in downtown Los Angeles. For the senior housing project, there are only three projects available to the ethnic Chinese elderly in southern California: one for Cantonese-speaking groups in Los Angeles' Chinatown, one for Mandarin-speaking groups in Monterey Park, and one for Taiwanese-speaking groups in El Monte. These resources are far from meeting the many needs of the elderly group.

The Chinese-American, by definition, is neither a whole Chinese nor a whole American, socially or culturally. He or she is characterized by a "marginal" personality, in which he or she must live in a bicultural environment with certain incompatible social values, expectations, and role performances. Furthermore, the degree of socialization and acculturation for each individual in a family may not move at the same rate of speed. Therefore, value conflicts, ideological disputes, moral standards, behavior patterns, and sex-role perceptions in the new immigrant families become intense. Thus, family and marital conflicts eventually develop in the process of social adjustment and cultural adaptation of Chinese-American families. Fifteen to twenty percent of marriages which were united for situational needs, such as obtaining green cards (immigrant status) or for business purposes have recently failed miserably. The rate of divorce and intensity of marital conflicts are increasing among both the new and old Chinese-Americans. The American emphasis on individual freedom and the economic independence of the female has also affected marital stability among Chinese-American people who are struggling to break away from the traditional values of Chinese culture.

In southern California, the Chinese-American Social Workers Association and Chinese-American Mental Health Association are conducting seminars related to parent education, family counseling, and child abuse prevention, etc., to the general public. Many Protestant churches are organizing couple fellowships and women's associations to provide self-support and counseling services to the needy families. Their services are provided to cope with the crisis of their church members even though most of these services are fragmental in nature and also handled by the lay counselors. Some individual counseling services are provided by church pastors and elders who are not trained for family and marriage counseling in this country. At times, these pastors and elders gave wrong advice to their church members and made their family and marital problems more complicated and difficult to solve.

As a new immigrant group, Chinese-Americans place a great deal of emphasis upon the intellectual development and educational achievement of their youth, but 50 percent of their youth and young adults may greatly benefit from the basic occupational training after high school instead of higher education. However, there is a lack of occupational training opportunities for these young adults. Some of them, who are very frustrated by academic pressure and social adjustment, develop behavioral and emotional problems of delinquency, alienation, and identity crisis by being confused about which culture they belong in. Some of them become overly dependent upon their rich parents and suffer school maladjustment. Others complain and ask why their parents brought them to this country. Some of them start to form street gangs and commit crimes. The phenomena of questioning paren- tal authority, "ditching class," and running away from home, is increasing among the new immigrant groups. Most community and church leaders shy away from facing the delinquent youth because they want good reputations for having "nice youth" in their church and community. Proper school guidance services, recreational activities, youth camps, and occupational training programs will help these youth and young adults make more con- structive use of their time and energy. It may prevent some of the juvenile delinquency in Chinese-American communities.

In order to facilitate full-time employment for both parents, there is a need for adequate child care facilities in the Chinese-American community. Fifty percent of the preschool children are now staying home with their grandparents while their parents are at work. These children tend to develop language communication problems, inadequate socialization, and beha- vioral disorders. Conflicts of social learning and cultural values may also develop among three-generation families when grandparents insist on teaching the old Chinese traditions and the young parents want to teach the American way of life to their children. Sometimes the young children become very confused because of the incompatible social values and expec- tations of their parents and grandparents. Therefore, adequate child care facilities, staffed with qualified child care workers and supervisors will not only assist the full-time employment of parents, but will also reduce the men- tal conflicts and behavior disorders of these young children.

The need for bilingual human care professionals and social service agencies is greater than ever. There are very few social service agencies which exist to provide human care and social services geared to the various psycho-social needs and social-economic adjustment problems of new immigrants and the second generation Chinese-Americans in this country. Since most of the highly educated professional and intellectual Chinese- Americans are space scientists, engineers, and computer experts (over 60 percent of the professionals), there is a dearth of human care and social service practitioners who are specialized in helping people to make good social adjustment and to cope with mental health crises and life problems in American society. Less than 1 percent of the Chinese-American pro- fessionals are social workers or human care professionals. Of these, com- munity organizers are just about nonexistent.

The training of human care professionals for providing social services and mental health counseling or treating family and marital conflicts has become an urgent issue for the new and old Chinese-American. Both government and private sectors need to develop comprehensive plans for providing the necessary human care services to the "voiceless minority" and also for preventing the breakdown of supportive systems of the ethnic family structure and their cultural identity.[2]

There needs to be an aggressive leadership training in the democratic process and methods of community organization. There are several hundred formal organizations for social support groups; churches; mutual aid societies; political advocacy clubs; academic and professional associations; Chinese-American citizen Alliance; high school, university, and college alumni associations; hotel, motel, and innkeepers associations; Chinese culture and language schools associations; Chinese community services; Chinese medical and herbal associations; and Chinese-American Banks Associations, etc., listed in the Chinese Consumer Yellow Pages across the nation. In addition, there are thousands of small informal social support groups and grassroots organizations in this country.

There is a lack of leadership and coordination to bring these diversified formal organizations and informal groups together for the betterment of the Chinese-American community in this country. The majority of the first generation immigrants tend to limit their social participation to the primary social groups of family kinship, mutual aid, and religious groups typified by Christian churches or Buddhist temples. They may compete for the leadership roles in their own social groups or professional organizations, college alumni associations, or church groups, but seldom reach to the leadership post of the secondary social groups of labor unions, community organization, or American political advocacy groups, even if they have made an attempt to participate. This is because of the hard fact that they lack the leadership training in the democratic process and the knowledge of sociocultural dynamics of American society, human relations, and American language skills. Many Chinese-Americans tend to follow an authoritarian leadership style when they assume leadership roles in group activities or business associations that cause endless disputes and conflicts in the public affairs of Chinese-American communities in this country. Also, the concept of individual heroism inherited from the old culture has unconsciously influenced the Chinese-American to glorify his family name through his individual success or accomplishment. This is again a handicap in the process of group leadership. A few visible Chinese-American leaders either in the political arena, business world, professional associations, or community affairs are mostly the second and third generation Chinese-Americans who have opportunities to learn and to practice the democratic leadership in American society.

There is a Chinese parable that illustrates group leadership as "a dish of fish heads which contains only leaders and no followers." Its meaning is similar to the American saying that there are too many chiefs and not enough Indians. Even though the Chinese Benevolent Society, the Taiwanese Christian Church Council of North America, and the Taiwanese-American Citizen League have launched several summer youth leadership training programs to develop leadership skills among second generation Chinese-Americans, the result of their efforts has not been visible. Both first and second generation Chinese-American communities definitely need the leadership training and community organization knowledge to facilitate the transition of social adaptation and social cooperation within the mainstream leadership structures.[6]

Community Implications, Program Planning, and Organizing Strategies

The social, psychological, personal, political, and economic problems of Chinese-American communities underscores the urgent need for social intervention in the areas of community organization, professional training, and leadership development. It implies that Chinese-American communities needs self-empowerment, self-help, self-development, self-transformation, and self-liberation from the burdens of the old culture and historical traditions which are not compatible with the modern culture in America. It also implies that Chinese-American communities need a great number of community organizers, social workers, community mental health workers, socio-cultural experts, educators, and political-economic leaders in addition to many thousands of natural scientists, computer experts, engineers of all kinds, and restaurant and motel innkeepers. Above all, it implies that Chinese-American communities need leadership development for both first and second generation community leaders, professional staff, youth, and womens' groups regarding the democratic leadership process and skills, concepts of individual freedom, and group cooperation.

The concept of program planning suggests a socio-political and technical process. It also suggests an ability to guide an action system through the planning process in which a problem is identified, data are analyzed, alternative policies are evaluated, and feasible programs are formulated for social action and implementation. Following the community implications of Chinese-American communities, program planning can be conceptualized as follows: (1) Program Planning for Self-Empowerment and Self-Transformation. (A) In order to achieve self-empowerment, self-help, self-transformation, and to reach the level of self-liberation of Chinese-Americans, program planning should focus upon both the psycho-socio-cultural issues and social adjustment problems. For the psycho-socio-cultural issues, program contents should include community education programs, new immigrant seminars, English language skills, mental health seminars, parent education classes, and new American citizen programs, as well as psychological counseling and therapy services to change the self-images of the first generation immigrants and to help them select the positive values of American society. For the social adjustment problems, program planning must follow the immediate needs of senior citizens, youth, children, and family life. Program planning for the senior citizens may include health, medical, and nursing services, housing services, nutrition education, legal services of conservatorship, guardianship, tax and will, social support programs of day-care, religious and escort services, friendly visitors, home health aid, personal grooming, shopping and transportation, arts and crafts, and hot lunch and language skill services. For the family life and marital problems, program planning may include family and marriage counseling, parent education, legal system and sexual education, family planning, child rearing practice, home-economic management, child abuse, interracial marriage, and in-law relationships, etc.

These programs will definitely help all first and second generation families to make a better social adjustment to American life. For the youth and young adults, program planning should focus upon the social-intellectual development and career choice of the youth. A large majority of Chinese-American youths are adjusting well in the school setting, but there are still a few groups of youth who are not. For the youth who are going to colleges, program planning may include college guidance, career choice, social courtship with opposite sex, sex education, alcohol and drug abuse prevention programs, psycho-social counseling, economic independence program, premarital counseling, and group leadership training programs. These program interventions will help in better preparing a wholesome youth ready to face the intellectual and social challenges of the academic world. For the youth who are going to undertake a job in the community, program planning may include the presentation of career choices, occupational training, sex education and premarital counseling, alcohol and drug abuse prevention, human relationships, and group leadership training to equip the youth to face the real challenges of adult life. For the working mothers and child care needs, program planning should focus upon the resources of kinship ties and ethnic community resources to identify possible facilities and child care workers to provide the necessary services. The program design may include preschool education and day care as well as special classes for the handicapped and developmentally disabled. The program services may include day-care, weekend care, evening care, and holiday care for working mothers who assume different work shifts. The program contents may include bilingual and bicultural education, if feasible.

For the first generation group with hardships in American language and culture, the purpose of program planning is to develop professional staff to assist lay leaders in various community agencies or social organizations to carry out the organizing work and social service programs. The training content should include American culture; language skills; Chinese traditions and social values; community power analysis and organizing skills; conflict resolution; administrative and management leadership; and strategies and tactics of grassroots movements; in addition to the regular professional content. The program design should enable the current community leaders and volunteers to improve their knowledge and skills in community organization and social action programs. For the second generation group, the purpose of program planning is to develop community leaders and professional staff for the English-speaking Chinese-American groups to receive professional services and to merge into the mainstream American society. The program design should enable the second generation to affirm their self-identity positively as Chinese-Americans and to contribute their various talents to American society. The program content should include the history of Chinese-Americans, ethnic racial relationships, and the socio-cultural and political-economic trends of America. The professional leaders and community organizing specialists should be able to function as a bridge between the Chinese-American community and the mainstream American society. The schools of social work or other professional programs of laws, business, public administration, public health, and medicine should provide opportunity for admissions and scholarships to attract Chinese-American youth to enter professional education. The large majority of Chinese-American youth select their academic majors in Math and Computers (33.3 percent), Natural and Physical Sciences (22.9 percent), Health and Biomedical Sciences (19.0 percent) in colleges, and only a few of them try to enter the field of Social and Behavioral Sciences (4.8 percent). There are very few youth who would select social work as their major.[6]

The basic reasons for this peculiar phenomenon are the lack of understanding of social work as a profession and the difficulty of entering social work schools due to language and cultural gaps in understanding the application process and admissions policies. If the schools of social work make efforts in improving their applications, admissions, and recruitment policies with cultural sensitivity to ethnic groups, it can definitely encourage some of the talented youth to enter the social work and allied professions. The curriculum of graduate social work programs should include at least one required course on cross-cultural contents on all minority ethnic groups. In special cases, schools of social work may sign contracts with Chinese-American community agencies to accept their qualified staff as graduate students and specify that they must return to work one or two years for their original agencies in order to fulfill their accountability to their own ethnic community. One example is Dr. F. Wu, who was admitted to the D.S.W. program of U.S.C. with the intention to return to work for the welfare of senior citizens in a Chinese-American community, which she did after her graduation. It resulted in a process of community organization for the establishment of the Golden-Age Club and the Senior Housing Project in the City of Monterey Park.

Leadership development is defined as a process of influence between the leaders and the followers in the community. Leadership always involves goal setting, program planning, resource organizing, strategic functioning, and performance measuring. For the majority of people, leadership does not come naturally. There are many instances in which ill-prepared individuals suddenly become saddled with responsibilities and functions of leadership in community agencies or church organizations. For the Chinese-American community, there are too often many people who compete for leadership positions in the community eventually becoming enemies in handling community affairs. The purpose of program planning for leadership development in Chinese-American communities must be geared to harmonious leadership functions in coordinating various human talents and social resources for effecting positive changes. It will also initiate social action programs to improve the socio-economic conditions and psycho-social status of Chinese-Americans.

In order to achieve the goal of self-empowerment for the Chinese-American as a whole, the integration of leadership between first and second generations, between grassroots and professional groups, and between social and political groups must be made to form a solid foundation for ethnic identity and all necessary social action programs. The program contents of leadership development should include theories and skills of leadership in goal setting and clarification, program planning and problem solving, work facilitation and providing feedback systems, and making control adjustment and evaluating performance. Because the ultimate goal of leadership development is to effect the positive changes in Chinese-American communities, the professional and community leaders must educate their fellow citizens and followers to learn American ways of democratic leadership instead of the traditional model of authoritarian or autocratic leadership. The second generation leaders must learn the cultural traditions and must be sensitive to the decision-making process of their parental generation.

Who should be involved in the program planning for leadership development? All community groups, churches, social clubs, college alumni associations, chambers of commerce, and Chinese schools should start to launch the leadership development programs for their own staff and members. Without effective leadership development, it will be difficult to expect positive change in the Chinese-American community.

Strategy is defined as planning technique, approach, detailed operational program, foresight, and maneuver to carry out program plans in a community organization. For Chinese-American communities, the organizing strategy may start with the goal setting and program planning for self-empowerment, self-help, self-transformation, and self-liberation, then followed by organizing human resources, talents, and money powers in the community. It is important to bring together professional leaders and community volunteers who are willing and able to help.

Before implementing any community program, a comprehensive psycho-socio-cultural analysis of the first and second generation groups must be made to understand the needs of each group. Any program planning and operation must be sensitive to the self-images and consciousness of the first generation immigrants since many of them are still controlling the financial resources in the community. The organizing strategy for professional training programs should separate the first and second generation groups because there are many differences in social values and cultural practice. One of the professional training and leadership development programs may be encouraging the Protestant pastors and Buddhist priests or nuns to enter into schools of social work and to learn about modern social work knowledge and technology. They may develop insights and skills to transform their church or temple communities to meet the various expectations of contemporary society since all of them are engaging in a process of community organization and social service in this country. The schools of social work can make efforts to recruit the Chinese-American real estate agents to study social work and to make a difference upon the new immigrant communities because their contact and service with new immigrants are more frequent than the outreach social worker from community service agencies. For leadership development programs, the organizing strategy must involve both professional and lay community leaders from all social agencies, churches, and social groups. The reward systems must be designed to render the public recognition and service award to those who have made good contributions to the community. The evaluation and research of program effectiveness or organizing efforts should be made a part of the professional training and leadership development.

The transformation of Chinese-American community structures, leadership styles, self-liberation, and empowerment can be made with the cooperation of internal community organization and external professional assistance. For example, the Asian Family Service Center in Rosemead, California, has engaged in organizing the Chinese-American community to support social service and mental health programs for new immigrants from China, Hong Kong, Taiwan, and Vietnam. The Center has always invited the elected officials, professional staff, and volunteers from the main stream society to assist the community people to raise funds and to set up programs and services for Chinese-Americans.

Overall, the organizing efforts for self-help and self-development programs in Chinese-American communities for the past twenty years have been the establishment of hundreds of churches of all denominations in this country. They are organized according to the Christian faith and ethnic languages. The congregational development of the church as a strategy and tool of community organization has been considered as a successful event to achieve the concepts of self-help and self-development. It also preserves the ethnic identity of Chinese Americans in a multiethnic cultural society.

Even though the primary purpose of the church is to proclaim the gospel of Christ and to promote spiritual growth, its practical objective is to assist the church members to cope with various psycho-socio problems and social adaptation as well as to meet their socio-cultural needs in the ethnic community. Each local church can be considered as a community service center even though it may not be staffed with professional social workers or community organizers. The church needs people to attend its religious worship and needs money to support its community programs. The new immigrants come to church to make new friends and receive information about social adjustment and business opportunities. The young people come to church for seeking boy and girl friends. The rich and well-established people come to church for affirming their reputation and career success. Others come to church for mutual support and group belongingness. There are still many other reasons why people attend the church activities. But the basic reason for the existence of a church as a community agency is that the church programs are meeting the various needs of its members, otherwise, the church will disappear in the community. The most social gospel-oriented churches have developed community service programs for their neighboring communities. They usually provide services to the lonely elderly, frustrated women in family crisis, dependent children without parental care, and teenagers without proper supervision, such as the Good Shepherd Formosan Presbyterian Church in Monterey Park. It has provided child care and nursery school for children and youth programs for the teenagers. The Cameron House of Chinatown in San Francisco, which was set up for girls about a hundred years ago, has become the cradle for training the Protestant pastors, teachers, community organizers, social advocates, and youth leaders of Cantonese-speaking Chinese-Americans in this country. For the larger social network, the Chinese Benevolent Association represents the major family name associations and Tong associations from all Chinatowns in this country. Its organization has existed in this country for over a hundred years. Any community organizer or political leader who wants to make a major change in the life-style of Chinatown must seek approval and support from the Chinese Benevolent Association, which has been called "the City Hall" of Chinatown. Most property and business owners and people who live in the Chinatown area in the major cities in this country are mostly Cantonese-speaking Chinese either coming from the provence of Canton or Southeast Asian countries. The organizing strategy for Chinese-American communities must be diversified according to the different languages and dialects, different political orientation and social mentality, different generations, and geographical locality.

Conclusion and Recommendations

The agenda of community organization for Chinese-American communities for the next decade should include the two basic goals of liberating the first generation immigrants from the old cultural burdens and developing the second generation to merge into mainstream American society. In order to achieve the first goal, the organizing strategy must focus upon social adjustment and survival programs. To achieve the second goal, the organizing effort must focus upon ethnic self-identity, leadership development, and American culture. The leaders of Chinese-American communities and professional organizations, governmental officers of all levels, elected representatives, community organization experts, social work educators, and church leaders who are concerned about the welfare of Chinese-American communities must recognize that Chinese-Americans, like any other minority ethnic group, have a very painful history of oppression in this country. They have their own unique social adjustment and cultural adaptation problems as well as community service needs. Chinese-American communities need new and innovative, integrated systems and structures to provide comprehensive and coordinated human care services on all levels. They should include survival programs of individual care, family and marital relations, small groups, social development, community organization and planning, leadership training, welfare services, mental health, and health care institutions.

The primary social intervention should be focused upon the social adjustment and cultural adaptation of individuals and families through individual guidance, counseling services, adult education, citizenship training, group dynamics, psychotherapy, ethnic group psychoanalysis, sensitivity training business relations, social milieu treatment, marital therapy, group work with youth, development of self-help groups for women and the aged, new immigrant seminars. and employment services for both first and second generation Chinese-Americans. The Protestant churches, Catholic Social Services, and many Buddhist organizations can play a very important role in organizing community resources and providing social services to meet the psycho-social and socio-cultural needs of their followers and the neighboring communities. The hundreds of Chinese language schools operating on Saturdays can organize leadership training programs for the young people and parent education classes for the new immigrants. The regional professional and business associations can provide community education seminars, career guidance, and volunteer services to those who need vocational training, job placement, and selection of business careers. The associations of Chinese-American bankers and realtors should organize cross-cultural management training programs for the first and second generation youth to develop their management leadership. The Chinese-American faculty associations should provide volunteers to assist community and business groups to conduct various research projects related to community organization and social services. The most pressing needs that require immediate attention are the social-cultural and health care needs of senior citizens, family and marital counseling, mental health and group support for single adults, employment services and job training for young adults, child care services for working parents, legal and immigration services for the newly-arrived F.O.B., career guidance for small business owners, and emergency aid for the unemployed or single-parent families. In order to provide effective human care and community services to the needy people, it requires qualified professional providers, therefore, short-range and long-range programs of manpower training and professional education are urgently needed in the Chinese-American community. Bilingual and bicultural social workers, community organizers, mental health and vocational counselors, as well as bilingual teachers should be encouraged in both the Chinese-American community and graduate schools of social work and other related professional schools. Since the public agencies are not able to meet the various needs of the Chinese-American community, the process of self-help should be developed to organize the regional resources of several cities or counties and provide the bilingual social services. For example, the California Institute of Human Care in Garden Grove was established by a group of business leaders, professionals, and community volunteers to provide bilingual community services to new immigrants.

The Taiwanese Presbyterian Conference of Southern California is organizing a senior day care program for providing hot lunch and social religious services in Monterey Park. Furthermore, the contributions of volunteers can be a great support in all types of community services; therefore, spouses of well-paid professionals and business executives, as well as groups of retirees who are concerned with community services, can be organized to supplement the professional services. Various kinds of professional practitioners, such as physicians, dentists, social workers, nurses, lawyers, psychologists, dietitians, teachers, public accountants, computer experts, business consultants, and many other practitioners may also contribute a small part of their professional hours to the needy people as a volunteer service that eventually can become a very important human care program in the Chinese-American community.[10]

In order to merge and assimilate into the mainstream American society, the business communities should be encouraged to contribute their financial support to enhance the community organization, leadership development, and social services.[4] The well-established professionals should organize a "peace corp of volunteers" with technical knowledge and skills to serve the community at large and to develop harmonious working relationships with other ethnic groups. The community leaders should educate their followers to participate in the public affairs of the main stream society and political process. The Parents-Teachers Association in the local school may be the good place to start. The first generation Chinese-American must step out from their community to meet the challenges of socio-cultural tides of American society at large. The second generation Chinese-American must be oriented to future development with the vision and aspiration of a pioneer and participant in order to become a whole citizen in this country. The secondary social intervention should be focused upon changing group behavior and social ideologies of Chinese-Americans who are still the captives of traditional cultures and also changing the existing social systems and institutions and government rules and regulations through social planning, social action, and social reform to meet the special needs of Chinese-Americans. Therefore, the establishment of a community council in each region is strongly recommended. It will coordinate all segments of human care and social services as well as community organization services provided by various social groups and local churches in the Chinese-American community in each metropolitan area across the country. This community council can be organized through governmental and community sanctions with representatives elected by all groups providing financial support and human care services to Chinese-Americans.

The school of social work and other public service professionals can provide faculty and students to assist the new community council to formulate its goals and objectives for the provision of human care and various community services. With the technical assistance of social work professionals, the community council can engage in a community organization process to identify community problems, to assess social needs, to raise funds, to apply for grants, and to set up social service delivery systems for provision of direct and indirect services. The community council can become a part of the United Way Agency in the mainstream social system and become a bridge to other ethnic groups and public social service agencies. In concluding this chapter, it must be emphasized that the future destination of Chinese-Americans as a minority ethnic group in a majority white society depends upon the struggle for a firm self-identity and positive self-image and being a pioneer and participant in all phases of American community life, particularly the political-economic and socio-cultural affairs. The self-liberation and self-empowerment of Chinese-Americans can be achieved only through the process of raising the self-awareness and self-consciousness of community people and grassroots participation, to be emphasized by the professional and community leaders. Both internal community and external social-political forces of social change for improving Chinese-American communities must be based upon the principles of love, peace, humanity, and social justice. We must be able to sustain a humane community with a common purpose for all ethnic groups of people in this country.

Endnotes

1. Asian and Pacific American Federal Employees Council, "A Brief Chronology of Asians in America," (Washington, D.C.), with addition by the *Pacific Citizen,* May 1, 1981.

2. Monit Cheung, "Elderly Chinese Living in the United States: Assimilation or Adjustment?" *Social Work,* (September 1989):458, 459.

3. Daniel Chu and Samuel Chu, *Passage to the Golden Gate* (New York, Zenith Books, 1967), 27.

4. Milton M. Gordon, *Assimilation in American Life* (New York, Oxford University Press, 1964), 132–135.

5. Isaiah C. Lee, "Health Care Need of the Elderly Chinese in Los Angeles, With A Socio-Cultural Orientation," *Asian Profile,* 7 (April 1979):119, 120.

6. Isaiah C. Lee, "A Socio-Cultural Study of Youth Leadership in New Immigrant Communities With Parental Roots From Taiwan, Hong Kong, and Mainland China—1986," *Tunghai Journal,* 28 (June 1987):431–452.

7. Isaiah C. Lee, "The Psycho-Social Adaptation of Chinese Immigrants in Southern California," *Proceedings of The Seventh International Symposium on Asian Studies,* (1985), 501, 502, 505, 508, 509.

8. Rose H. Lee, *The Chinese in the United States* (London, Oxford University Press, 1960), 33–39.

9. Sterling, Seagrave, *The Song Dynasty* (New York, Harper and Row, 1985), 44.

10. There are thousands of talented Chinese professionals who can contribute a few hours of their professional services to their own ethnic communities.

CHAPTER EIGHT

Organizing in the Japanese-American Community

KENJI MURASE

Introduction

This chapter on the status and role of community organizations and community organizing among Japanese Americans will be divided into two historical periods: pre-World War II and post-World War II. World War II was the turning point in the history of the Japanese in the United States. The internment of Japanese Americans during World War II was a cataclysmic event that profoundly influenced the future course of their lives. Major emphasis in this paper will be placed on the significance of the internment experience and its consequences for Japanese-American community organizing in the post-World War II period.

Definition of Terms

In the discussion to follow, frequent references will be made to the terms used by Japanese Americans in identifying themselves: Issei, Nisei, Sansei, Yonsei. Montero points out that the Japanese are the only ethnic group to emphasize generational distinctions by a separate designation and belief in the unique character of each generational group.[19] Unlike the Chinese and Filipinos, neither custom nor law barred the earliest Japanese from bringing their wives to the United States. Within two decades of their arrival in the early 1900s, there were enough women to assure the birth of a second generation. The Issei (first generation), consisting of immigrants; the Nisei (second generation), their American-born children; the Sansei (third generation); and Yonsei (fourth generation) became reference groups for individual Japanese Americans, as each generation established its own rules of status and definition of behavioral boundaries. Accordingly, in this chapter, the terms Issei, Nisei, Sansei, and Yonsei will refer to each of the respective generations of Japanese Americans.

Socio-Demographic Profile

Unlike other Asian Americans, the population of Japanese Americans has remained relatively stable over the past several decades. Since 1980, when the Japanese, numbering 716,331, were roughly comparable in numbers to the Filipinos with 781,844 and the Chinese, with 812,178, they have not kept pace with other Asian groups in population growth. By 1990, it is expected that the Japanese population will be surpassed by the Korean and Vietnamese, and by the year 2000, they will be overtaken as will Asian Indians.[26] These differences in population growth reflect a marked decline in immigration from Japan at a time when there is increasing immigration from other Asian countries.

Analysis of the 1980 census data reveals that Japanese Americans are probably the most assimilated of all Asian populations in the United States. They have a greater proportion (96.4 percent) of persons aged 25 to 29 completing high school than any other ethnic group. Only 2 percent of Japanese Americans do not speak English, compared to 10 percent of Chinese Americans and 6 percent of Korean Americans. Among Japanese Americans 51 percent speak only English at home, in contrast to 17 percent of Chinese and 18 percent of Korean Americans. This data reflects the fact that foreign born members comprise 28 percent of Japanese Americans, compared to Chinese Americans with 63 percent foreign born and Korean Americans with 82 percent foreign born. The Japanese American median family income of $27,350 in 1980 was the highest of all Asian groups and substantially higher than the median family income of White families ($20,800). However, their economic status must be seen as a function of their longer history of residence in the United States and their having a smaller proportion of recent immigrants than other groups.

The Pre-World War II Period

The Early Immigrants

The initial period of migration for the Issei generation was from 1880 to 1924.[1] For the most part, the early Japanese immigrants were young, single males from rural areas who were lured by labor contractors, steamship companies, and representatives of agricultural, railroad, lumber, and mining industries who desired a supply of cheap labor. Despite their significant role in the development of rail transportation, mining, agriculture, lumbering, and other industries in the West, the Japanese, along with other Asians, were subjected to humiliating acts of racial discrimination and even mob violence. There were, for example, segregated schools for Japanese children in San Francisco, laws prohibiting racial intermarriage, antialien land laws preventing purchase of property and limiting leases to short-term, and a variety of local trade union restrictions on entry into skilled crafts and diversion into employment which was noncompetitive with white workers.[2]

Miyamoto's pioneering study of the Japanese-American community in Seattle provides an illuminating historical context.[18] He noted that the conspicuous characteristic of Japanese communities was their pervasive solidarity. Because Japanese Americans were a small group subjected to discrimination in housing and employment and because they followed nonmigratory occupations, the farmers, small businessmen, and service employees tended to settle in small urban ghettos and rural hamlets. These circumstances favored the development of a close-knit, highly cooperative, and tightly controlled ethnic community.

The Japanese-American community is comprised of a group of interacting family units rather than aggregates of discreet individuals. The Japanese concept of the extended household was transplanted to the United States and broadened to include the entire Japanese-American community. Families became interdependent with the ethnic community at large and this process provided the basis for a fundamental community solidarity to serve as a framework for social interaction and as security from outside hostility. Individuals were expected to behave in a way that reflects positively on all members of the community. One's sense of obligation flowed both ways; the individual felt a total commitment and loyalty to the group and the group in return was responsible for caring for each member. Within such a community context, opportunities for self-fulfillment were provided through Japanese language schools, churches and temples, cultural and recreational programs, and such institutions also served as a means for social control.

The Japanese, like the Chinese and later the Korean immigrants, became predominantly entrepreneurs and proprietors or "Middleman minorities."[5] Through the development of subeconomies in their communities, they could circumvent to some extent the economic discrimination and prejudice of white society. A common denominator to their status was the liquidity of their occupations; their jobs provided a portable or easily liquidated livelihood as personified by the trader, broker, gardener, truck farmer, service worker and small businesses such as laundries, barber shops, groceries, and restaurants. As a result of their occupational concentration and residential segregation, Japanese Americans were effectively excluded from the larger society. There were few horizontal alliances between the

Japanese community and their economic and social counterparts in the wider community. Within their own subeconomy and subsociety, Japanese employers and employees were vertically integrated and excluded from the external world. At the same time, the hostility of the larger society drove them deeper into their separate ethnic enclave.

With the coming of age of the Nisei generation, there were important changes in the social structure and processes within the Japanese community.[16] As the Nisei matured they found themselves subjected to two competing influences: the desire to preserve their own sense of ethnicity and the pull of socio-economic advancement made possible by their education. Benefitting from their education, the Nisei found opportunities for higher occupational status than had been possible for their Issei parents. They could find employment outside the ethnic economy which had been limited to small shopkeepers and farmers. However, the new employment opportunities meant that the Nisei would have to leave the ethnic enclaves of their parents. Gradually, the social and psychological values and comfort provided by the ethnic community began to diminish in importance in the face of the attraction of socio-economic advancement made possible by their higher education.

The process of Nisei integration into the dominant white society was further accelerated by the fact that the Issei generation preferred to remain in their ethnic enclave and were no longer present to ensure that their grandchildren, the Sansei, would receive a traditional Japanese upbringing. With their sansei children being reared and socialized in largely non-Japanese-American communities, and with the absence of other Japanese children to serve as agents of socialization, the integration process was hastened.

Community Organizations

Historically, the Japanese in America have a tradition of organizing formal associations for the purpose of taking collective action to protect or advance their interests.[3] Early immigrants in agriculture formed unions and engaged in work stoppages and boycotts as leverage to gain improved wages, working, and living conditions. As early as 1907, Japanese and Chinese immigrant coal miners were participating in collective action against coal mine operators in Wyoming.[13] Soon after their arrival in this country, Japanese immigrants formed associations for mutual aid and support, such as rotating credit unions and burial societies. Through their hard work, perseverance, and personal sacrifices, the Issei generation achieved a measure of financial security which enabled them to send their children, the Nisei generation, to colleges and other institutions of learning.

The early community organizations of the Issei generation were formed primarily to serve their economic and socio-cultural interests. They were not seen as vehicles to advance their political interests. Not until the

Nisei generation had grown to adulthood did community organizations serve political needs. As early as 1918 a group of Nisei in San Francisco met to consider their predicament and their future prospects.[12] They had grown up in a period of blatant racial persecution. Some had been banished to segregated schools for "Oriental" children. They had seen their fathers beaten for no reason other than race. Their family businesses had been picketed and boycotted, their homes vandalized while the police looked the other way. Their American citizenship conferred upon them no advantages over their Issei parents and they pondered about their future prospects. They concluded that Japanese Americans would have to claim their rights as American citizens and that the public must know that they too were Americans. The original name of their organization, the American Loyalty League, clearly signified their purpose.

The successor to the American Loyalty League was the Japanese American Citizens League (JACL) which was founded in 1930. One of its first acts was to petition Congress to amend the Cable Act to permit Nisei women, who had married alien Japanese, to regain their citizenship, and to permit Asian-born men who had served in the United States armed forces in World War I to be granted citizenship. Increasingly the JACL entered the political arena and began making representations on behalf of Japanese Americans before various federal agencies and commissions. In the period before the outbreak of World War II, the JACL was engaged in strenuous efforts to mitigate the rising anti-Japanese hostility that resulted from the rapidly deteriorating US-Japan relations. However, after the Japanese attack on Pearl Harbor, there was nothing that the JACL could do to stem the tide of hysteria and hatred which would lead to the eventual exclusion of Japanese Americans from the West Coast and their internment in concentration camps.

To summarize, community organizations and community organizing among Japanese Americans in the pre-World War II period was largely focused upon maintaining and sustaining survival and continuity. The Issei generation lacked the resources, the knowledge, and the energy to deal with abstract issues of social justice and to mount any effective to overturn discriminatory laws and judicial decisions. It was to become the fate of the Nisei and Sansei generations to confront the task of righting the wrongs inflicted upon them and their Issei parents.

The Post-World War II Period

Exclusion and Internment

At the time of the Japanese attack on Pearl Harbor, there were some 125,000 persons of Japanese ancestry living on the Pacific Coast. Approximately two-thirds of this population were American citizens. The presence of Japanese Americans in wartime became the focus of a virulent campaign for their removal, waged not only by racial bigots but also by agricultural interests that could profit by the elimination of competition and the expropriation of property.[4] Despite assurances from the military intelligence and the Federal Bureau of Investigation that there was no danger of subversion by Japanese Americans, President Franklin Roosevelt acceded to the demands of the military.[10] On February 19, 1942 he issued Executive Order 9066, ordering the removal of all Japanese Americans from the West Coast. Although the United States was also at war with Germany and Italy, the exclusion order did not affect German or Italian families.

The internment of Japanese Americans is perhaps the bitterest national shame of World War II. It represented the mass incarceration based on racial grounds alone, on false evidence of military necessity and in contempt of supposedly inalienable rights, of an entire class of American citizens, along with their parents who were not citizens in the country of their choice, only because that country had denied them the right to become naturalized citizens because of race. For Japanese Americans the internment is without question the one historical event which universally defines and symbolizes the Japanese-American experience. "Internment" is perhaps the one word which best evokes an understanding of what it is to be a Japanese American. Whether internment was personally experienced by the Issei and Nisei, or retold and learned by the Sansei and Yonsei generation, most Japanese Americans have been profoundly affected by what happened to America's Japanese during World War II.

The mutually shared experience of being uprooted and interned in concentration camps produced among Japanese Americans a deep sense of collective identity that persisted regardless of subsequent geographic dispersion to all parts of the nation. The kinship of experiencing a common misfortune for an inescapable physical trait, that of bearing the face of the enemy, and the humiliation and hardships endured during internment contributed to their sense of group identity which will survive throughout the remaining years of their lives.

The Concentration Camps

Approximately 110,000 Japanese Americans, two-thirds of whom were American citizens, were incarcerated in ten concentration camps located on deserts and inhabitable wastelands in Arizona, Arkansas, California, Colorado, Idaho, Utah, and Wyoming. Each camp held from 7,600 to 18,800 residents, housed in tar paper-covered barracks, that, according to military regulations, were suitable only for combat-trained troops and then only on a temporary basis. For Japanese Americans, these barracks served as long-term housing for a period up to three-and-a-half years. An average of eight people were assigned to twenty-by-twenty-five foot "apartments".

Communal kitchens, dining halls, and bathhouses provided little or no privacy. The camps were surrounded by armed guard towers and barbed wire fences. At one camp, several internees were shot and killed though not during attempted escapes; they died when guards fired into unarmed public demonstrations.

Each camp comprised an essentially self-sufficient community. Utilizing the labor and skills of internees, the camps produced most of their own food supply and provided essential community services. Community institutions were organized and run by the internees, including police and fire departments, health care, schools, churches and temples, social and recreational programs, cultural events, adult education classes, arbitration courts, and self-governance structures. Despite an economy based on a monthly income of $12 to $19, the internees operated successful cooperative stores and businesses, such as general merchandise stores, laundries and cleaning shops, beauty and barber shops, shoe repair, newsstands, and other enterprises.

For the older Issei residents, the internment marked a period of withdrawal from their previously active lives and an opportunity to pursue avocations, such as gardening, crafts, cultural activities, and hobbies. In contrast, the camps for the Nisei generation provided an unprecedented opportunity to assume new roles and responsibilities denied to them in the outside world. They became firemen, policemen, school teachers, managers, and administrators—occupations they may have aspired to but which were not attainable previously. Nisei personnel had a key role in the day to day planning and organizing of all institutional structures to sustain communal life. The camps thus provided a valuable training ground for Nisei leadership development that would come to fruition in the post-World War II period.

Psychologically, however, the internment was a devastating experience. To the Issei, the forced evacuation and detention symbolized a repudiation of their years of toil and sacrifice for their children. For the Nisei, internment meant rejection by the nation to which they had pledged allegiance. It precipitated an identity crisis because they had been taught by their parents to take pride in their ethnic heritage. Repression of the painful internment experience was a common reaction among the Nisei generation. It was not until their children, the Sansei, gave legitimacy to expressions of outrage and indignation about the injustice of the internment that the Nisei could confront their feelings and join in the movement with the Sansei to seek redress and reparations.

Rebuilding the Community

The end of World War II and the closing of the concentration camps in 1945 signalled the beginning of a new era in Japanese-American history. Upon their release from the camps, Japanese Americans had to recreate their former communities, which had been destroyed by their removal and internment. There followed a difficult process of recovery and rebuilding of their economic base, their social institutions, and their network of relationships for a viable community life. With an economic base established primarily in small businesses, the professions, and service occupations, Japanese-American community workers were soon able to address broader community concerns such as poverty, employment, housing, health care, crime, and delinquency. Over time there developed a network of indigenous community-based services and support systems that served to meet the economic, social, and psychological needs of the community.[20] This indigenous community care/support system was comprised of (1) institutions such as local churches, prefectural associations, credit unions, and social and fraternal organizations, and (2) individuals, such as ministers, priests, doctors, lawyers, teachers, shopkeepers, bartenders, and others who had gained a measure of respect in the community. Their role as community caretakers represented an extension of the traditional attitude and practice of collective responsibility derived from old-world values and customs.

Community Organizations and Community Organizing

In the post-World War II period, the Nisei and Sansei generations came into full maturity and took up the leadership in community affairs as the aging Issei generation withdrew. As Japanese-American community workers dealt with problems in their own community, they also became aware of the commonality of their problems with other Asian-American communities. This awareness led increasingly to collaboration with Chinese, Filipino, Korean, and other Asian communities in a common struggle to secure greater equity of resources from public and private funding sources. In several cities the United Way was a primary target for intensive organizing efforts in Asian communities to gain recognition and allocation of funding for social programs. Urban renewal also became a battleground for Japanese and other Asian community activists to preserve and extend low-income housing in the face of fierce resistance from redevelopment agencies and corporate interests.[25] This experience of Japanese Americans in collaborating with the leadership of other ethnic minority communities in various common causes resulted in the building of an interethnic network that was to provide the basis for future coalitions in the political arena.

In the vanguard of the Japanese community leadership were many Nisei and Sansei professionally trained social workers, whose knowledge and skills in organizational development, community outreach, constituency building, and research, were effectively utilized in organizing local and national campaigns. Some of the more significant organizing efforts will be discussed in the following.

Walter-McCarran Act of 1952   The first national political campaign undertaken by Japanese Americans, through the Japanese American Citizens League (JACL) was passage of the Walter-McCarran Act of 1952. This Act repealed the Oriental Exclusion Act of 1924, by extending to all Asian nations a token immigration quota and eliminating race as a barrier to naturalization. Henceforth, because the Issei were made eligible for naturalization, they could not be discriminated against as "persons ineligible for citizenship."

Repeal of Title II   At the height of the anti-Communist hysteria, the Internal Security Act of 1950 was passed. It contained the infamous Title II provision for imprisonment without trial of persons regarded as security risks in times of national emergency. Japanese Americans, as past victims of American concentration camps, were in a strategic position to lead a campaign to repeal Title II. It was also fitting that Japanese Americans, as passive beneficiaries of the civil rights movement, could take the leadership in removal of a law which threatened the abridgement of the civil rights of other Americans. Accordingly, Japanese-American activists initiated the formation in 1968 of a National Ad Hoc Committee for Repeal of the Emergency Detention Act. Because of the singular role of Japanese Americans as the first group in the United States to be interned in concentration camps, their appeal for support to prohibit further concentration camps was overwhelmingly successful. Two Japanese Americans, Senator Daniel Inouye and Representative Spark Matsunaga, introduced bills in their respective chambers and President Nixon signed the repeal in the Fall of 1971.

Recision of Executive Order 9066   Although the government's position was that of Executive Order 9066, issued by President Roosevelt in 1942 to remove Japanese Americans from the West Coast, it was a wartime measure that expired automatically at the end of the war. Japanese Americans demanded a forthright acknowledgement of its extinction. Their national campaign to secure recision of Executive Order 9066 resulted in a proclamation signed by President Gerald Ford on February 19, 1976. Among other things, it stated: "We now know what we should have known then, not only was that evacuation wrong, but Japanese Americans were and are loyal Americans . . . we have learned from the tragedy of that long ago experience forever to treasure liberty and justice for each individual American and resolve that this kind of action shall never again be repeated."

Redress and Reparations   Unquestionably the most significant community organizing effort among Japanese Americans was their national campaign to secure redress and reparations for their internment during World War II. This campaign involved all segments of the Japanese-American community and the unified support it commanded in terms of the scope and intensity of effort was without historical precedent. From the original formal approval in 1978 by the Japanese American Citizens League for a national campaign to take the Japanese American case to the American public, to the signing of the redress bill, H.R. 442 in 1988, required ten long years of persistent unflagging effort.

The concept of redress for the internment was introduced among Japanese Americans as early as the 1940s but at that time they were neither economically nor psychologically prepared to undertake such an objective.[9] Only after they had become secure financially could Japanese Americans revive the issue of the injustice of their internment and press for redress on moral grounds. It was not a matter of charity but a matter of regaining public recognition and restoration of their self-worth and pride. During the early 1970s, at their national convention, the JACL explored the idea of seeking an official apology from the government in the belief that even if the effort failed, the education of the American public would be of value. In 1978 the JACL established a National Committee for Redress and formally moved to seek redress and reparation from the United States government.

The initial organizing efforts of the redress campaign concentrated upon sensitizing awareness of the redress issue among Japanese Americans. In various cities, "Day of Remembrance" events were held to commemorate the internment. Pilgrimages were organized to former sites of concentration camps to recall and revive memories of the internment years. During this period the campaign organizers utilized effectively the available media and mass communication techniques to bring the redress issue before the larger American public. In the Congress were five Japanese Americans (Senators Daniel Inouye, Spark Matsunage, S. I. Hayakawa, and Congressmen Norman Mineta and Robert Matsui) who performed a pivotal role in the passage of a bill that was signed by President Carter in July 1980. It established a Commission on Wartime Relocation and Internment of Civilians to conduct hearings to determine whether any wrong was committed by the government when it interned Japanese Americans, and to make recommendations to the Congress as to possible remedies.

The Commission conducted public hearings from July through November 1981, in various cities throughout the country. Japanese-American groups in support of the redress movement mounted a massive campaign to publicize the hearings and to educate the general public. In February 1983, the Commission issued its report with the conclusion that the internment of Japanese Americans was not justified by military necessity as claimed by the government in 1942 (Commission on Wartime Relocation and Internment of Civilians 1982). It recommended to the Congress that the government provide a one-time per capita compensatory payment of $20,000 to each of the approximately 60,000 surviving former internees. The only dissenting member of the Commission was Representative Daniel Lundgren of California. His vote against reparations was not forgotten by Japanese Americans whose fierce lobbying efforts resulted in the California state senate's rejection of Lundgren's appointment to an important state post in 1988.

The campaign for legislation to implement the Commission's recommendation of redress and reparations took four additional years of sustained effort. After numerous bills were introduced and had failed, an all-out national campaign was mounted by the Japanese-American community leadership. Its target was the 1987 Congressional session in which both houses were controlled by Democrats. A massive letter writing and lobbying effort was launched in which hundreds of supporters visited their representatives in the Congress. Especially effective in the lobbying role were veterans of the celebrated 442nd Regimental Combat Team, made up of Japanese Americans, which was the most decorated unit of World War II. They enlisted the support of veterans of other military units that had fought alongside them. Endorsements of support for the redress bill was secured from hundreds of influential organizations, ranging from American Legion Posts in various cities, the national Veterans of Foreign Wars, the American Jewish Committee, Leadership Conference of Civil Rights, and city and county councils or boards of supervisors throughout California, Washington, and Oregon. However, the key players in the drama were the Japanese American members of the Congress—Senators Daniel Inouye and Spark Matsunaga and Representatives Norman Mineta and Robert Matsui. Even the most conservative members of the Congress were won over by their persistent lobbying efforts and H.R. 442 was finally enacted in April 1988. However, there was yet the hurdle of securing President Reagan's signature and every indication was that he would veto the bill.

The redress campaign then shifted to the White House and lobbying efforts focused upon contacts by Japanese Americans within the highest levels of government.[23] Although thousands of letters and telegrams had deluged the White House, the redress leadership was aware that the mail would not weigh heavily in the President's decision. The lobbying efforts would have to reach the very inner circle of the President's staff. Representative Matsui made personal contact with the White House Deputy Chief of Staff, Kenneth Duberstein. He also prevailed upon the Times-Mirror Company Washington representative, Patrick Butler, to talk with his former boss, the presidential chief of staff, Howard H. Baker, Jr. To offset the Justice Department's opposition, Grant Ujifusa, the JACL legislative strategist, persuaded the Education Secretary, William J. Bennett, and the presidential assistant, Gary L. Bauer, both of whose conservative credentials were impeccable, to support the President's signing of the redress bill.

Finally, it was time to make a direct approach to the President. According to one account, the foundation for the President's support of the redress legislation was laid by the Republican Governor of New Jersey, Thomas A. Kean.[23] It was known that the President would make a visit to New Jersey and that the Governor would be accompanying him. It also happened that the JACL legislative strategist, Grant Ujifusa, had edited a book written by Kean and knew of his personal conviction that the internment of Japanese Americans in World War II was one of the few events in American history to be ashamed of. Ujifusa persuaded Governor Kean to intervene with the President. At an opportune moment, the Governor urged the President to erase a black spot on America's past by providing restitution and an official apology to Japanese Americans who were interned during World War II. He then reminded the President that in 1945, when the city of Santa Ana, California would not allow a Japanese American soldier, heroically killed in action, to be buried in the local cemetery, a young actor named Ronald Reagan had the courage to participate in a ceremony awarding the Distinguished Service Cross to the dead soldier's family. In a follow up letter to the President, Governor Kean enclosed a note from the soldier's sister and snapshots of the award ceremony. He also pursued the matter further in a telephone conversation with the White House Deputy Chief of Staff Kenneth M. Duberstein.

With all this input from his own staff and the prospects of a veto-override battle looming immediately before the presidential election, in which the California vote would be critical, the President on August 10, 1988, signed the redress legislation. At the signing ceremony, the President recounted his 1945 participation at the postumous award ceremony for a Japanese-American soldier killed in battle and he commented that the blood soaked into the sands of a beach is all one color. Had not Governor Kean reminded the President of his earlier personal involvement with a dead Japanese-American soldier, it was an anecdote that he might easily have forgotten. It can be speculated that the reminder of his personal connection with the soldier was more influential in persuading the President to sign the redress bill than any rational argument. To Washington insiders, this episode was the crowning touch to a classic lobbying effort.

Involvement in Election Campaigns   A new development in the 1970s and 80s was Sansei participation in local and national election campaigns. Sansei were actively involved in mobilizing support for Japanese American and other Asian American candidates for local political offices and succeeded in electing a number of members of local county boards of supervisor, city councils, and school boards. In the Presidential election of 1988, Sansei, along with other Asian Americans, were prominently evident on the campaign staffs of all major candidates. However, their leadership role was most apparent in the Rainbow Coalition of the Jesse Jackson campaign where Asian Americans held such roles as National Field Director, California Campaign Director, and California Co-Chair. Over twenty-five Asian Americans were elected or appointed as Jackson delegates to the Democratic National Convention. Undoubtedly, as a direct result of the Asian-American leadership in the Rainbow Coalition, 46 percent of the Asian American vote in California went to Jesse Jackson.

Analysis and Assessment of the Japanese American Community Organizing Experience

Theoretical Perspectives

In reviewing the Japanese-American experience in community organizing, a clear pattern emerges of distinct styles of response to ethnic group issues and community problems, differentiated on the basis of generational affiliation. The Issei, preoccupied by survival issues, directed their efforts primarily to building indigenous community institutions and strengthening their family and community networks to provide a haven in their ethnic enclaves from the hostile world outside. They had neither the necessary resources nor the will to seek the overturn of discriminatory laws or judicial decisions and to confront the forces of racial bigotry and oppression. They saw their destiny as enduring hardships and making sacrifices for the sake of their children's education and economic future. They accepted the internment with characteristic stoicism and quiet dignity.

For the Nisei, World War II was the turning point of their destiny. They first had to rebuild their shattered communities which they had left behind to be interned. In time, their educational achievement brought economic rewards and the security to accept responsibility for dealing with community problems. There was also the beginnings of efforts to confront the injustices of discriminatory laws and to right the wrongs inflicted against Japanese Americans in World War II. However, it was not until the coming of age of the Sansei that there was a resurgence of community activism and direct confrontation of issues of concern not only to Japanese Americans but all other Asian Americans. Sansei youth began to challenge the legitimacy of their community leadership and the authority of American political institutions as well.

The changing styles of community activity among Japanese Americans historically and in the present may be understood in terms of several theoretical perspectives.

Accommodation   The style of both the Issei and Nisei generation may be characterized as essentially that of conservatism and accommodation. The accommodationist approach, as postulated by Maykovich, is used by members of minority groups who accept their segregated role while attempting to integrate wherever possible.[17] While they do not submit passively to an underprivileged situation, neither do they contend militantly against it. They are minority groups that adopt the values and expected behavior of the dominant group, yet are not accepted into personal and social relationships with members of the dominant group. The accommodationist style typifies the response of the Nisei leadership of the Japanese American Citizens League when they advocated cooperation with the exclusion and internment order of the government, in order to demonstrate their loyalty as American citizens.[10, 17]

The shift from the conservatism and accommodation of the Nisei to a style more protest-oriented and more politically left ideologically of the Sansei can be related to the issue of ethnic identity. In contrast to the Issei, who were secure in their identity, the Nisei faced an identity problem due to the conflict between their marginal status as American citizens and their heritage of traditional Japanese cultural values as transmitted by their Issei parents. For the Nisei there existed no reference group that could counteract their feelings of insecurity and marginality. Although the Issei functioned as a normative reference group, the Nisei also sought the approval of their white peers who rejected them on racial grounds. This identity dilemma then led to pressures on the Nisei to disavow their ethnic heritage and to embrace Americanism and to behave as super-patriots. Their faith was that acceptance of the norms and vlaues of the dominant white society, plus hard work and discipline to succeed in education, would be the way to surmount racial barriers.

The Sansei, on the other hand, did not experience conflict between their traditional cultural heritage and the need for white peer approval. The Nisei parents, unlike the Issei, were less bound by traditional Japanese values and exerted fewer controls on their Sansei children. More Americanized than their Nisei parents, the Sansei could more openly challenge adult authority and interact more freely with white society. At the same time, the Sansei, many of whom were born in the concentration camps, learned of the history of Japanese Americans. They realized that complete racial equality and integration was a myth and that Japanese Americans are basically only tolerated rather than fully accepted by white society. The awakening of the Sansei to their past then compelled them to question their values and to seek a redefinition of their identity.

The accommodationaist perspective was no longer viable for the Sansei. Their search for a redefinition of their ethnic identity led them to other Asian Americans who were similarly concerned by issues of ethnicity. Affiliation with a broader Asian-American community then became the basis for a new reference group. Whereas for the Nisei the major referent was their white peers, the key reference point among the Sansei became other community activists of Asian ancestry. This development was an outcome of the Sansei involvement in the racial and political turmoil of the 1960s and 70s, which took the form of participation in ethnic studies programs, broad-based community action, and a commitment to institutional change. Thus, the Sansei rejected the accommodationist mode of the Issei and Nisei generations and elected instead to challenge the established order in concert with other Asian Americans.

Exceptionalism   In contrast to many other ethnic groups in this country, Japanese Americans have been characterized as the "model minority" because of their low rates of poverty, crime, delinquency, and mental illness, and their high educational achievement.[22] Their transcending of racial barriers and their upward mobility have been attributed to the compatibility of their cultural values with those of the American middle class. The implication that follows is that other racial groups, who lack similar cultural compatibility, will continue to be confined to the lower levels of the social order. Therefore, in order for minorities to emulate Japanese Americans, they must somehow modify their "inferior" culture to make it more compatible with white middle-class values. For example, Light, in his comparative analysis of Asian and black ethnic enterprise, implies that lower-class urban blacks must develop a more "moral" community and a sense of "ethnic honor" if they are to be successful in business enterprises as are the Chinese and Japanese. This notion of exceptionalism, however, is flawed because it ignores the historical conditions responsible for the position of racial groups and overlooks the racial structure that restricted the development of "moral" communities for blacks and not for Asians.

Racial Subordination   An alternative view is to emphasize the impact of the political and economic context upon the changing behavior of the Japanese in American society.[26] According to Takahashi, the notion of racial subordination offers a historical point of departure to define the economic and political context in which Japanese Americans struggled to better their lives and achieve equality with other Americans. The status of the Issei, for example, as migratory cheap labor limited their organizing capabilities to alter their abject conditions of living. Their energies and resources had to be channeled into the development and maintenance of stable communities to secure their children's future. The racial structure thus restricted their economic development and their social mobility and undermined their ability to develop their power potential to combat their subjugation. Denied such assets as citizenship, land ownership, employment opportunities, political office, and access to the media, the Issei had no means to influence political behavior.

The Nisei, though citizens by birth, were still segregated from the social and economic life of the larger society. Despite their educational achievement, their college degrees failed to provide access to the more desirable white-collar jobs. They were still essentially dependent upon the Issei economy for their primary source of employment. Like the Issei, the Nisei also found few options for participation in organized forms of politics in the wider community and their focus was upon internal community affairs that had little or no impact upon the problems of their racial subordination. By the time of the coming of age of the Sansei and the birth of the Yonsei generation, societal changes had lessened the racial subordination of Japanese Americans. In turn they could capitalize on their education and achieve comparative economic success which expanded their life chances, including participation in the political arena.

Political Economy   Changes in the status of the Japanese in American life were also related to major changes in the American political economy. For example, the renewal and intensification of racial hostility that erupted in the 1930s may be traced to the Great Depression and the deterioration of the United States and Japan relations of that period. At that time, Japanese Americans were compelled to distinguish themselves from Japanese nationals for fear they would be lumped together as potential subversive agents of Japan. Any expression of ethnic identity would have made their loyalty suspect so identification with Japanese cultural traditions had to be suppressed. Again, as in their early history of discriminatory legislation, Japanese Americans lacked the power resources and the capacity to mobilize outside support to combat the prevailing public anti-Japanese hysteria. The passive acceptance of internment by Japanese Americans may be understood within the context of the dominant ideology of loyalty and patriotism that induced their obedience to the government's order for exclusion and internment. Rather than generate mass protest and public indignation, the internment process resulted in the stigmatizing of those few who actually protested the internment.[7, 21, 14]

As relations between the United States and Japan improved in the 1950s, the international context created a more favorable climate or race relations for Japanese Americans. The political conservatism of the Cold War period and the expansion of the economy during the Korean War were other factors in the political economy that enhanced their position. Finally, the cultural crisis and racial turmoil of the 1960s had a profound impact upon Japanese Americans, especially the Sansei youth. Their involvement in the student and Third World movement on college campuses resulted in a new political consciousness which was reflected in the patterning of their actions after the characteristic protest style of that period.

Summary

This review of the community organizing experience of Japanese Americans suggests that their actions were not always freely chosen but were responses shaped in relation to institutional or societal constraints. Within each period of history, they were faced with decisions on how best to promote their self-interest and achieve racial equality without incurring punitive reactions from the larger society. What was politically possible for Japanese Americans was largely a function of the structural limitations imposed by the legal and informal denial of citizenship to Issei and Nisei, the climate of the prevailing ideology of white America and the nature of the relationship between the United States and at the time. The result for the Nisei was the evolution of an essentially defensive and conservative posture characterized by such strategies as constructive cooperation with the internment, reliance on the courts, and faith in a gradualistic or incremental changes for the better in race relations.

With the Sansei there emerged yet a different political style in response to changing institutional and societal limitations. Amicable relations between the United States and Japan contributed to an international climate that enhanced the status of Japanese Americans. Changes in the economy produced a demand for a technically trained labor force which provided employment opportunities for the Sansei who were highly trained in such fields as engineering, electronics, and the health sciences. Also occurring during this period was the racial unrest of the 1960s which had a significant impact upon the Sansei in terms of their ethnic awareness and political consciousness that spurred involvement in social action and the political process. The concept of Asian American was a unifying force among Japanese, Chinese, Korean, and Filipino Americans. It provided the basis for an alliance with black, Hispanic, and Native American groups for collective action against the forces of oppression. These political and economic transformations profoundly influenced the life chances of Japanese Americans, especially the Sansei, in their social and political role in American life.

Problems and Prospects for the Future

Trends

Two countervailing trends are emerging that will shape the character of problems and issues in the Japanese-American community. On the one hand is a continuing and accelerating dispersal of Japanese Americans into the wider mainstream society, not only geographically but also economically and socially. At the same time there is an increasing recognition and awareness of the importance of maintaining their ethnic identity. This process is reflected in a renewed interest in language study and traditional cultural arts and a desire to learn about the history of the Japanese in America. The possible implications of these trends will be discussed in terms of community problems and issues, the response of community organizations, and the role of professional social work in the future.

Problems and Issues

There will continue to be problems related to family breakdown, drug and alcohol abuse, long-term health care, services for the elderly, equal opportunity in employment, and affordable housing. However, compounding the solution to those problems is the gradual decline of the informal support network that has traditionally taken care of many community problems. Increasingly, Japanese Americans will have to turn to the established systems of services as the alternative forms of community-based service organizations founded in the 1960s and 70s will have difficulty in surviving. In this transition, the challenge to social workers and social work education is to find ways to preserve the benefits and gains demonstrated by the experience with community-based social services. Those aspects of cultural sensitivity and ethnic-specific modes of practice that have been shown to improve accessibility and appropriateness of services to ethnic minority clients must now be incorporated into mainstream practice. Professional social workers with experience in Japanese American and other ethnic communities have a special role and responsibility to take the leadership in this process.

Earlier it was noted that, historically, the nature of United States and Japan relations has impacted upon perceptions of the Japanese-American community. If the present trade imbalance with Asian countries continues and grows, there is likely to be further exacerbation of anti-Asian hostility.[27] The massacre of Southeast Asian refugee children in Stockton, California by a mentally deranged Vietnam war veteran is seen as an expression of the pent-up hostility and frustration engendered by the trade imbalance.[15] Fueling the fires of hostility is the mass media's interpretation of the trade imbalance issue. Japanese and other Asian Americans need to take a much more active role in counteracting the media's influence in creating negative images about Asian countries and their role as trading partners.

A potentially divisive issue of concern to Japanese Americans in their relationships with other Asian-American groups is the widespread perception that Asian Americans are a model minority. This impression is based largely upon the academic and economic success of Japanese Americans and the model minority perception is then extended to apply to all Asian Americans, as if they constitute a single, monolithic group.[11] The fact is that among Asian Americans are many subgroups, such as Southeast Asian refugees, recent immigrants, the foreign born, the elderly, and single parents whose incomes are below the poverty level. Within the Japanese-American community are pockets of poverty among its elderly and single female-headed households. Because Japanese Americans are frequently singled out by the media as exemplars of the model minority, the leadership of Japanese-American organizations must exercise vigilance in challenging expressions of the model minority myth wherever it is manifested. They need to point out the model minority myth has overblown the "success" of Asian Americans and is based on erroneous conclusions. For example, the comparison of incomes between Asian Americans and whites fails to note that Asian Americans are concentrated in California, Hawaii, and New York—states with higher incomes but also higher costs of living than the national averages. Also overlooked is the fact that Asian-American families have more persons working per family than white families and that Asian American family incomes reflect the presence of more workers in each family rather than higher incomes. Also not recognized is that Asian-American employees, although highly trained and qualified, are generally excluded from the upper levels of management and decision-making and confined to lower levels of technical or professional positions.[27, 6]

A long-term problem is forecast by new population projections by the United States Census Bureau which estimates that the Asian American population grew nearly 50 percent during the period 1980 to 1985, from 3.7 to 5.5 million. In 1970, Asian Americans were 3.2 percent of California's population; by the year 2000 they are expected to comprise close to 12 percent of the state's population. Although the growth in the Japanese-American population is not expected to keep pace with more recent Asian immigrant groups, their future will undoubtedly be affected by problems associated with such a dramatic rise in the Asian population.

Role of Community Organizations

To counteract the trend towards the physical dispersal of their community and the diminution of ties to their ethnic heritage, Japanese-American community organizations and community workers must seek new ways to perpetuate and strengthen ethnic identity. Opportunities have to be created for collective activities for the renewal of old ties and the beginning of new relationships that will endure. One avenue for this process would be the offering of programs celebrating important ethnic holidays and festivals, commemorative events to refresh memories, and tributes to pioneers of the past. Cultural programs of exhibitions, performances, and films on lectures could focus on traditional Japanese cultural arts. In several cities community centers have been built to serve as a focal point for bringing together the Japanese-American community. The local school system provides another means of access to educational materials and instruction about Japanese-American history. There needs to be continuing support of bicultural education programs in the public schools and ethnic studies at the college level to sustain interest in ethnic history and literature. A special role for ethnic studies would be to record and transmit the history of the Japanese-American community for future generations. A structure such as the new Japanese American Museum in Los Angeles would provide a setting for the accumulation and display of artifacts and memorabilia pertaining to the Japanese in America.

Parallel to these activities, which are essentially internal community affairs, Japanese Americans must increasingly go beyond their own community to respond to the problems and issues common to all Asian-American communities. Japanese Americans, now well-established and financially secure, must perform a special leadership role in efforts to improve the quality of life of other Asian Americans. One model of such a role is offered by the Nisei Student Relocation Commemorative Fund, which each year since 1983 has awarded scholarships to Southeast-Asian refugee high school students. The Fund's rationale is that since the Nisei were helped by church and civic groups during World War II to leave the concentration camps to go on to college and have prospered because of their college education, they now have an obligation to help others who are less fortunate.

Such organizations as the Japanese American Citizens League, with its history of successful national campaigns, can well serve as a model for other Asian-American organizations. With the largest national membership of any Asian-American organization and a proven record of legislative and legal accomplishment, the JACL has the resources and the experience to impact the national political and legal process on behalf of other Asian-American groups. The JACL is now undergoing a critical time of transition from Nisei to Sansei leadership. The time may be propitious for the JACL to expand its base to go beyond the Japanese-American community and to merge with other Asian-American organizations to make the Asian-American presence felt on the national scene. Such a development would be symbolic of the political maturity of an ethnic group that was once singled out by the government to be potentially subversive and required to be confined in concentration camps. Japanese Americans are now presented with a new opportunity to justify the trust and faith and the sacrifices made by their Issei and Nisei forebearers.

Endnotes

1. For a comprehensive account of the early history of Japanese immigrants, see: Y. Ichioka, *The Issei: The World of the First Generation Japanese Immigrants, 1885–*

1924 (New York: Free Press, 1988); also H. Conroy and T. S. Miyakawa, eds. *East Across the Pacific: Historical and Sociological Studies of Japanese Immigration and Assimilation* (Santa Barbara: Clio Press, 1972).
2. For a detailed history of discriminatory acts against Japanese Americans, see F. F. Chuman, *The Bamboo People: The Law and Japanese Americans* (Del Mar, CA: Publishers, Inc., 1976); also R. Daniels, *The Politics of Prejudice: The Anti-Japanese Movement in California and the Struggle for Japanese Exclusion* (Berkeley: University of California Press, 1962); and C. Williams, *Prejudice: Japanese Americans—Symbol of Racial Intolerance* (Boston: Little, Brown & Co., 1944).
3. The history of Japanese-American participation in unions and other collective action is chronicled in Y. Ichioka, *The Issei: The World of the First Generation Japanese Immigrants, 1885-1924* (New York: Free Press, 1988). For a highly personalized account, see K. Yoneda, *Ganbatte* (Los Angeles: Asian American Studies Center, University of California at Los Angeles, 1983).
4. An extensive literature is available on the exclusion accounts are: A. R. Bosworth, *America's Concentration Camps (New York: Norton, 1967)*; R. Daniels, S. C. Taylor, and H. H. L. Kitano, eds. *Japanese Americans: From Relocation to Redress* (Salt Lake City: University of Utah Press, 1986); M. Grodzins, *Americans Betrayed: Politics and the Japanese Evacuation* (Chicago: University of Chicago Press, 1949); and J. tenBroek, E. N. Barnhart and F. W. Matson, *Prejudice, War, and the Constitution* (Berkeley: University of California Press, 1954).
5. E. Bonacich, "A Theory of Middleman Minorities, *American Sociological Review* 36 (Month 1973):583-594.
6. A. Y. Cabezas, "Disadvantaged Employment Status of Asian and Pacific Americans," In U.S. Commission on Civil Rights, *Civil Rights Issues of Asian and Pacific Americans: Myths and Realities* (Washington, D.C.: Government Printing Office, 1980), 434-444.
7. F. F. Chuman, *The Bamboo People: The Law and Japanese Americans* (Del Mar, CA: Publishers, Inc, 1976).
8. R. Daniels, *Concentration Camps U.S.A.: Japanese Americans and World War II* (Hinsdale, IL: Dryden Press, 1971).
9. R. Daniels, S. C. Taylor, and H. H. L. Kitano, eds. *Japanese Americans: From Relocation to Redress* (Salt Lake City: University of Utah Press, 1986).
10. R. Daniels, *The Politics of Prejudice: The anti-Japanese Movement in California and the Struggle for Japanese Exclusion* (Berkeley: University of California Press, 1963), 54.
11. K. Gould, "Asian and Pacific Islanders: Myth and Reality," *Social Work* 33 (February 1988):142-146.
12. B. Hosokawa, *Nisei: The Quiet Americans* (New York: William Morrow, 1969).
13. Y. Ichioka, *The Nisei: The World of the First Generation Japanese Immigrants, 1885-1924* (New York: Free Press, 1988).
14. N. R. Jackman, "Collective Protest in Relocation Centers," *American Journal of Sociology* 63 (March 1957):264-272.
15. L. Jue, "Asian Violence: Confronting an Old Demon," *East Week News* (May 18, 1989):1.
16. C. W. Kiefer, *Changing Cultures, Changing Lives: An Ethnographic Study of Three Generations of Japanese Americans* (San Francisco: Jossey-Bass, 1974).
17. M. K. Maykovich, *Japanese American Identity Dilemma* (Tokyo: Waseda University Press, 1972).
18. S. F. Miyamoto, "Social Solidarity Among the Japanese in Seattle," *University of Washington Publications in the Social Sciences* 11 (February 1939):57-130.

19. D. Montero, *Japanese Americans: Changing Patterns of Ethnic Affiliation Over Three Generations* (Boulder: Westview Press, 1980).

20. K. Murase, "Alternative Mental Health Service Models in Asian Pacific Communities," In T. C. Owan ed. *Southeast Asian Mental Health: Treatment, Prevention, Service, Training, and Research* (Washington, D.C.: Government Printing Office, DDHS Publication ADM, 1986), 85–1399.

21. G. Y. Okihiro, Japanese Resistance in America's Concentration Camps: A Re-evaluation, *Amerasia Journal* 2 (January 1973):20–34.

22. W. Petersen, *Japanese Americans: Oppression and Success* (New York: Random House, 1971), 131.

23. B. Stokes, "Behind the Scenes: Dynamics of Redress," *National Journal* 20 (October 1988):2649–2654.

24. R. Takaki, *Strangers From a Different Shore: A History of Asian Americans* (Boston: Little, Brown, 1989), 000.

25. S. Tatsuno, "The Political and Economic Effects of Urban Renewal on Ethnic Communities: A Case Study of San Francisco's Japantown," *Amerasia Journal* 1 (January 1971):33–51.

26. U.S. Bureau of the Census, *U.S. Summary, Characteristics of the Population: 1980*, 1 (Washington, D.C.: Government Printing Office, 1983), 1–20.

27. U.S. Commission on Civil Rights, *Recent Activities Against Citizens and Residents of Asian Descent* (Washington, D.C.: Government Printing Office, Clearing House Publication 388, 1986).

References

Anderson, "U.S. Asian Population, Up 560% 1980–1985," *Asian Week* (June 1989):1.

Commission on Wartime Relocation and Internment of Civilians, *Personal Justice Denied* (Washington, D.C.: Government Printing Office, 1982).

R. W. Gardner, B. Robbey, and P. C. Smith, "Asian Americans: Growth, Change and Diversity, *Population Bulletin* 40 (October 1985).

H. Kitano, *The Japanese Americans* (New York: Chelsea House, 1988).

L. H. Light, *Ethnic Enterprise in America: Business and Welfare Among Chinese, Japanese and Blacks* (Berkeley: University of California, 1972).

A. I. Mass, "Psychological Effects of the Camp on Japanese Americans," In R. Daniels, S. C. Taylor, and H. H. L. Kitano, eds. *Japanese Americans: From Relocation to Redress* (Salt Lake City: University of Utah Press, 1986).

J. H. Takahashi, "Changing Responses to Racial Subordination: An Exploratory Study of Japanese-American Political Styles," Unpublished Doctoral Dissertation (University of California, Berkeley, 1980).

R. A. Wilson and B. Hosokawa, *East to America: A History of the Japanese in the United States* (New York: William Morrow, 1980).

CHAPTER NINE

Organizing in Central American Immigrant Communities in the United States

CARLOS B. CORDOVA

Central American Migrations to the United States

Since the early 1900s, Central Americans have migrated to the United States, motivated by political and economic reasons. During the 1930s, the economic crisis and political instability affecting the Latin-American countries created the foundations for the first large scale Central-American migrations to the United States.

In the early 1930s, the military hierarchy ascended to the top of the government structure to share the political power with the oligarchic families that had ruled most Central-American countries since the 1860s. In Nicaragua, for example, the military, under the leadership of Anastasio Somoza Garcia, created a repressive dictatorship in Central America, resulting in large numbers of people leaving the country. Nicaraguans trying to escape political persecution by the military dictatorship arrived in the United States during the 1930 to 1940s and resettled in San Francisco, Los Angeles, Houston, and New Orleans.

During the 1960s, Central American legal immigration to the United States rapidly increased as a result of liberal immigration policies reflected in the Immigration Act of 1965. The new immigration policies granted quotas to countries that historically had not been included in the U.S. immigration policies. The 1965 law encouraged professionals and skilled laborers to migrate to the U.S. and permitted the resettlement of large numbers of young working-class and middle-class families from Latin America.

It was during this time that Central Americans created the economic foundations necessary for the development of ethnic enclaves in San Francisco, Los Angeles, Houston, New York, and Washington. Many cities had established Latin-American immigrant neighborhoods that acted as a magnet attracting Central Americans to their municipalities. Newcomers resettled in the Latin-American neighborhoods because of the familiar cultural traditions and support systems maintained there.

Since the 1970s, immigration from Latin-American countries has accounted for approximately 40 percent of the immigrants arriving into the United States. The influx of Central-American immigrants has sharply risen during the past two decades. Presently, the Central-American countries rank as the second Latin American region contributing significant migrations to the United States. Prior to the late 1970s, most Central-American immigrants arrived with legal immigration status as permanent residents. In the 1980s, changes in the migration patterns became evident as large numbers of El Salvadoreans, Guatemalans, and Nicaraguans entered without legal immigration status or as political asylum applicants. The pre-1979 migrations were mostly economic in nature, while the post-1979 migrations have been generated by political motives.[1, 4, 5]

Demographic Characteristics of 1970–1990 Central-American Immigrants to the United States

The demographic figures of Central-American immigrants in the United States have dramatically increased since the 1970s as a direct result of socioeconomic and political instability in that region. The Central-American countries suffer from widespread poverty created by an economic system that is internally controlled by interrelated oligarchic families and the military hierarchy. The Central-American economies are unstable as a result of their dependency on the monocultivation of agricultural cash crops, the international trade markets, and foreign economic aid.

The Latin-American population in the United States has increased to more than 20 million people in 1989, demonstrating an increase of 5.5 million people since the 1980 census. The Census Bureau reported in October 1989 that there are 12,567,000 people of Mexican origin in the U.S. The fastest growing population is Central and South Americans, which add up to 2,545,000 people. It is important to note that these demographic statistics appear to be low since they do not include the numbers of undocumented people now residing in this country. The House of Representatives decided to take into account the undocumented population figures during the 1990 census and their numbers will be used for purposes of reapportioning districts.

The actual numbers of legal and undocumented Central-American immigrants in the United States are not available at the present time. The demographic statistics calculated by the Immigration and Naturalization Service (INS) estimate the numbers of Central Americans in the U.S. at approximately two million people. These figures are not accurate because the majority of Central Americans arrived in the United States during the post-1979 migration as undocumented workers or as political asylum applicants, and they have not been included in any of the demographic surveys conducted by the government.[1]

The Central-American sociopolitical and economic crises have been important determinants for the present migrations patterns to the United States. Such are the cases of Guatemala, El Salvador, and Nicaragua, which have been affected by armed insurgency against the established sociopolitical systems. Since 1980, more than 70,000 people have been assassinated by right wing paramilitary death squads in El Salvador. Labor leaders, intellectuals, community organizers, catholic priests, agricultural workers, and anyone that attempted to change the social system has been a target for assassination. These political factors must be taken into account with the 1951 United Nations Convention definition of a refugee, which states that a person who, having demonstrated a well-founded fear of persecution because of race, religion, nationality, or membership in a particular social or political organization, is outside the country of his or her nationality, and is unable or unwilling to receive the protection of that country. The majority of Central Americans in the United States would qualify as refugees, but the criteria for accepting individuals as refugees are designated by the President in consultation with Congress and must be of special humanitarian concern to the United States.

Factors considered are the plight of refugees, human rights violations in the country of origin, and family, historical, cultural, and religious ties of these populations to the U.S. The likelihood of finding sanctuary elsewhere, as well as previous contacts with the U.S. government are also taken into consideration. Presently, the Central-American countries are not in the priority category of humanitarian concerns of the United States, therefore, refugee status has not been granted to Central Americans. In addition, the U.S. criteria states that if individuals are outside their native country, then they are no longer in fear of persecution.

Many Central Americans in the United States have applied for political asylum, and the criteria that the U.S. government and the I.N.S. follows state that political asylum may be granted to individuals that are residing in the U.S. territory only if refugee status and humanitarian considerations have been granted to their countries of origin. Furthermore, political asylum may be granted to individuals who are deemed refugees and who are in the United States or are applyiing for admission at a land border or port of entry. Asylum is a discretionary act exercised by the Attorney General that allows the refugee to remain in the U.S. as opposed to being deported. It is not the equivalent to refugee status, as refugees may have their status changed to permanent resident after a specified period of residence in this country. A person granted political asylum may not change their status as easily, even though the law stipulates that they can become permanent residents after living one year in the United States.

It has usually been the case that countries from which refugees seem to have difficulty obtaining asylum often have close political relations with the U.S.. Because the U.S. government perceives Central Americans as economic immigrants, it denies their claims of persecution. In order to be granted political asylum the refugee must prove that he or she is a legitimate refugee.

It is important to consider these social and political factors when analyzing the present demographic makeup of Central-American communities in the United States. It is a difficult task to attempt to generalize the demographic, political, or socioeconomic characteristics of this population because of the complex nature of the Central-American population and their migration determinants. The Central-American communities have divergent political ideologies, from conservative right wing views to orthodox Marxist orientation. A community in a single geographical area may represent a wide diversity of political views as in the cases of San Francisco or Los Angeles, or they may hold a unified political perspective, such as in Miami.

The socioeconomic backgrounds of Central-American immigrants are also diverse. In the U.S. urban centers one might find upper-class individuals, such as in Florida and California. There are strong cultural similarities between the upper classes in the Central American countries. The upper classes in the different countries have often intermarried or have very close social, business, and cultural relations among themselves.

The majority of Central Americans in the U.S. are middle- or working-class individuals, with their original occupations in Central America and include teachers, high school and university students, secretaries, accountants, homemakers, domestic workers, office workers, and skilled factory workers.

Guatemalans in the United States

In Guatemala, entire Indian communities have been destroyed, relocated in strategic villages, or people have been forced to migrate to Mexico and the United States as a result of intensive military repression.[6] In areas of conflict, civilian populations were forcibly removed and relocated in refugee camps throughout Central America and Mexico. The refugees have been subjected to government military actions resulting in the massacres of the elderly, women, and children, who make up the vast majority of the refugee population.[1, 2, 3, 6]

In the rural areas in the U.S. Southest, the Central-American population is made up mostly of rural people who made a living from agricultural activities in Central America. Agrarian people are tied up to the rhythm of the agricultural seasons and prefer rural over urban lifestyles. The majority of Guatemalan Indian immigrants are unskilled young males with low educational backgrounds, and are employed as seasonal migrant workers in the agricultural farms throughout the sunbelt states. There are numerous Guatemalan Mayan Indian people working in the agricultural fields of Florida, Texas, Arizona, and California.

The situation of Indian peoples is more difficult than that of most Central Americans in this country because they hold nonwestern cultural values, and are often monolingual in their traditional Mayan languages. These indigenous groups represent the large majority of Guatemalan immigrants to the U.S. during the past decade. The majority of Guatemalan Indians working in Florida come from the town of San Miguel Acatlan in the northern province of Huehuetenango and are Kanjobal-speaking people.

In the U.S. urban centers the majority of Guatemalans are of urban backgrounds and the majority originate from working-class backgrounds in Guatemala. This population is Spanish speaking and some individuals may also speak any of the various Guatemalan Mayan languages.

El Salvadoreans in the United States

El Salvadorean immigrants in the U.S. come from different socio-economic and cultural backgrounds. During the late 1970s and the early 1980s members of the ruling classes left El Salvador and resettled in Florida and California. These upper-class individuals had economic, cultural, and political ties in the United States. For years the El Salvadorean upper-class had taken their fortunes out of Central America and deposited them in U.S. banks. Because of their economic and educational status, and their bilingual skills, they had legal residency or citizenship in the U.S. This phenomenon is characteristic of Latin-American revolutions as it was observable in the case of Cuba and Nicaragua.

On the other hand, the most recent El Salvadorean immigrants arriving in the U.S. are undocumented and come from middle- and lower-class backgrounds. They lack the economic and social support available to upper-class El Salvadoreans because of their socioeconomic and class backgrounds. Many do not have the educational and language skills needed to succeed in this country. The working-class populations in the different Central Americas have strong similarities in their social and cultural experiences and have little in common with the upper-class social and cultural experiences.

An important observation in the cultures of El Salvador, Honduras, and Nicaragua is the large body of cultural traits that are similar among the national groups. This common background may be attributed to the long history of migrations from Mexico to the Central American pacific coastal regions. Since Pre-Hispanic times, large migrations of Mexican people have resettled in the area diffusing their language, culture, and religion to the Central-American populations. Presently, El Salvadoreans, Hondurans, and Nicaraguans on the Pacific Coast speak a form of Spanish mixed with the Nahuat language brought by Mexican immigrants around the year 700 A.D. In Guatemala, the dominant culture is Mayan, manifesting important linguistic and cultural differences from the rest of Central America.

Nicaraguans in the United States
The Nicaraguan cultural and social experience in the U.S. is similar to that of El Salvadoreans. The main difference is the political orientation of their migrations. The first Nicaraguans to arrive in the U.S. during the 1980s were upper-class individuals that were fleeing the country because of their former ties with the Somoza dictatorship and their disagreements with the Sandinista government policies. The majority of these Nicaraguans resettled in Florida and brought with them their wealth and their right wing political ideology. More recently, Nicaraguans are young working-class people who have left the country to escape the war and the military draft.

Hondurans and Costa Ricans in the United States
The numbers of Honduran and Costa Rican immigrants in the U.S. are not very extensive. The majority of Hondurans reside on the East Coast from Florida to New York. Their social and cultural experience has not been studied in depth.

The Structure of Central-American Communities in the United States

Central Americans arrive in the United States metropolitan centers following already established ethnic and family networks. The pioneering immigrants bring their spouses and close relatives to the U.S. after they have established themselves economically in the host of society. Friends or relatives may give a temporary place to live to recent arrivals with no close family ties in the area. The new arrivals often use ethnic or family contacts to secure employment, housing, or to meet any immediate needs they encounter in the host society. Once the person is settled and able to save money other relatives begin to arrive.

After a few years of living in the Latin-American neighborhoods, many Central-American immigrants are able to socially adapt to the new environment and acquire the necessary employment skills and education to fully participate in the mainstream economic life. Many relocate in other ethnically mixed neighborhoods or suburban cities. Other individuals take advantage of the economic opportunities and develop extensive ethnic business enterprises in the Latin-American neighborhoods and utilize the immigrant labor force to maximize their profits.

The ethnic enclave is the place where the new immigrant becomes familiarized with their new social environment and provides the proper mechanisms and institutions to gradually introduce the new arrivals to U.S. society. The Latin American enclaves maintain the culture, language, religion, foods, and traditions present in the Latin-American region.

There are concrete features that demonstrate the clear distinctions between an ethnic enclave and ethnic immigrant communities. As a rule, immigrants initially relocate in ethnic communities while developing a few small business enterprises to meet local consumption demands. However, ethnic neighborhoods lack the sophisticated economic structure and the extensive division of labor of the enclave.[8] The Central-American enclaves in San Francisco, Los Angeles, Washington, and Houston, among others, demonstrate a well-diversified economic base and division of labor.

The economic structure of the enclave provides for a wide range of bilingual professional services to be available to the community, from legal, educational, immigration, medical, dental, accounting, income tax consulting, counseling, employment training and referrals, food services, etc. These professionals are not only immigrants, but first and second generation Central Americans and Latin Americans that provide the professional services in the enclave. Other bilingual ethnic and Anglo professionals and merchants also provide services in Spanish within the enclave.

The enclave provides the familiar settings by allowing the development of regional associations that support the immigrant with cultural, social, and recreational activities. Regional associations and the enclave provide new immigrants with support structures and resources that develop cultural identification, security, and a sense of belonging in the host society.

Regional associations allow the preservation of cultural traditions and the retention of a strong cultural and national identification as a Central American on the individual and the family. Many regional associations are named after towns, cities, states, or regions where the immigrant populations originate in Central America. Some organizations may be affiliated with religious societies, sports clubs, artistic or cultural organizations, or social service organizations as they exist in Central America. The most popular regional associations are identified with soccer or baseball clubs with membership in the Latin-American sports leagues or the mainstream leagues. These associations have a well-structured organization, a large membership, their members pay dues, and they rent a small place as a recreation center.

The study of Central-American enclaves and the immigrant's social interaction in the community may be analyzed under the Neo-Gemeinschaft Model developed by Rivera and Erlich.[9] This model is based on Toennies concepts of Gemeinschaft or community as the primary relationships involving intimacy and privacy, and Gesellschaft or society, the individual's public life or the pursuance of secondary relationships for utilitarian and survival reasons.[10] Rivera and Erlich expanded Toennie's model to explain the formation of ethnic groups in this country. Enclaves develop as subgroups within society as a result of an antagonistic social environment where the members of the immigrant or minority group are victims of discrimination and economic exploitation.

According to this framework, the immigrants will only develop secondary relationships at the societal level (Gesellschaft) where the individual experiences discrimination as a result of racial, cultural, and linguistic differences. Primary relationships (Gemeinschaft) are restricted to members of the same national or ethnic group.

The Emergence of Political Power and Influence in Central-American Communities

Because of the socioeconomic and political diversity observed in the Central-American communities, they have limited political power and influence within the United States political structure. The Central-American communities are divided on issues related to national identity and origin, political affiliations in Central America, ethnicity, and socioeconomic status. These divisions do not allow the necessary social cohesion needed to become a strong political body that will be able to seek viable political solutions to the problems and realities faced by the community. There is a need to develop responsible and accountable political and social activists within the Central-American community in order to critically affront the wide range of problems that they face in this country.

Another drawback to empowerment in Central-American communities is the common belief on the part of the immigrants that their stay of residence in the United States will be of a temporary nature. Therefore, the immigrant becomes isolated and neglects to participate in political affairs at the community, municipal, state, or national levels. Unless the individual has some degree of political sophistication or experience, the common attitude among the majority of immigrants is of political apathy.

There have been attempts made to work among Latin-American immigrants to try to convince individuals to become U.S. citizens and to register to vote. These activities in the community have been fruitless because large numbers of Latin Americans believe that becoming a U.S. citizen is a betrayal to their national identity and citizenship. There are organizations in the Central-American communities throughout the United States that strive to achieve political power. Some organizations are closely associated to political parties or associations in Central America. Casa El Salvador, Casa Nicaragua, and some Guatemalan organizations have close ties with Central-American popular revolutionary movements. Another example is the Frente Democratico Nacionalista who represented the Nicaraguan Contras.

In California, the popular revolutionary groups have been successful in their actions against U.S. policies in Central America. Their success is based on the fact that they have not limited their activities within the Latin-American communities. They have reached out to the mainstream and have created multiethnic coalitions by working closely with international solidarity coalitions and networks such as CISPES, Amnesty International, or the Emergency Response Network. Their main objectives deal with issues that affect directly the Central American region, but do not place their main emphasis on empowerment efforts within the local community.

The Paulo Freire Model of Community Empowerment   The Freire method of community empowerment is based on the development of educational strategies that bring about critical consciousness on the individual and the community at large. Freire's methodology has been widely used in Latin America by the Catholic base communities in the empowerment of rural and urban political activists, campesinos, and students. The methodology has been designed to teach basic literacy skills to adults while providing the students with basic notions of political awareness to develop praxis and community social action.

Freire pedagogy has been used by base community organizations and educational centers to effectively teach English language skills to Spanish monolinguals. Their pedagogical objectives are to teach basic concepts of social and political awareness in their language lessons as the means of empowering new immigrants in our society. In San Francisco, the Mission Reading Clinic, Project Literacy, and the High School Step to College Program at San Francisco State University have accomplished great success in their educational efforts while utilizing the critical education method.

Other successful organizations include the refugee self-help committees in various U.S. cities, such as San Francisco, Los Angeles, Washington, D.C., and Houston, among others. Three refugee organizations are important to mention because of their successful and effective activities in the internal affairs of the Central-American community, as well as with the mainstream society and local political structures. They are (1) the Comite de Refugiados Centro Americanos (CRECE), (2) the Central American Refugee Center (CARECEN), the legal immigration services and advocacy agency of the refugee organizations in San Francisco and Los Angeles, and (3) is El Rescate in Los Angeles.

One important aspect of the two organizations is that refugees themselves provide empowerment to refugees since they have been created and are operated by refugees. These organizations are designed after the organizational models of Freire's Critical Consciousness and the Central American Catholic base communities. Because of their organizational structure, philosophy, and empowerment efforts these two community organizations are widely recognized as providing the leadership in the Central American refugee community. They address a wide range of issues affecting the lifestyle and adaptation processes of Guatemalan and El Salvadorean immigrants and refugees.

CRECE provides the refugee community with basic survival services such as food and clothes distribution, emergency housing, medical services, job referrals, and skills development workshops. They also provide educational information to the mainstream communities by making presentations at schools, universities, churches, and home meetings, where they give testimonies of their experiences in Central America. CRECE has also been an active advocate of refugee rights in Central America, and has been actively involved in the repopulation of refugees in El Salvador.

CARECEN is involved in the legal representation of refugees in immigration court in political asylum hearings. CARECEN also gives health referral services, trains health promoters, and produces literature for the Central-American refugee community. CARECEN has played an important role in the formation of the Central American National Network (CARNET), that includes thirty-eight refugee agencies and grassroots organizations in the U.S.

CARECEN and CRECE have demonstrated a strong commitment to empowering the Central-American community so that they can actively participate in their own legal defense and advocacy of their rights as refugees. The development of local leadership is an important priority in their selection and training of low-income refugees who work as Refugee Rights Promoters and Refugee Advocates. The promoters provide services to the refugee community; speak in public forums; and monitor and try to impact legislation affecting the Central American refugee community at the municipal, state, and national levels. One of their achievements in the San Francisco Bay Area has been to influence a number of cities to declare themselves cities of refuge in which the local governments and law enforcement agencies will not cooperate in Immigration and Naturalization Service (INS) raids against undocumented workers. These organizations work closely with religious organizations such as Catholic Charities, the network of churches associated with the Sanctuary movement, the Baptist Ministries, and others. They receive funds and direct services from religious organizations and private foundations.

What Needs to be Done in the Near Future

The Need for More Research Studies

Further theoretical and practical research studies are necessary to fully comprehend and resolve the acculturation issues faced by Central-American immigrants in the United States. The specific areas in need for a greater scope of examination are legal, medical, psychological, educational, professional and occupational skills retraining, nutrition, and counseling. These studies are needed in the major metropolitan and rural centers where the Central-American populations are resettling. It is imperative for mainstream professionals and researchers to develop the critical awareness necessary to effectively address the needs of Central Americans in the United States.

Institutions of higher education must implement broad curricular offerings across the varoius disciplines that address the cultural, socio-economic, and historical backgrounds, and the basic needs of this rapidly growing population. In cities with high numbers of Central Americans, universities must include specific curricular offerings and training programs for students enrolled in their undergraduate and graduate studies. Course offerings must develop in the students a critical understanding of the ethnic, cultural, economic, and sociopolitical backgrounds of Central Americans residing in their geographical areas.

A priority for universities should be the recruitment, enrollment, and retention of Central American students in order for them to enroll and succeed in their academic programs. It is an obligation of universities to be accountable to the communities that they serve in their geographical areas. The success of recruitment efforts also serves as empowerment activities for the Central-American communities. Furthermore, the research activities conducted by Central-American professionals will provide the academic and professional community with a native perspective in the study, research, and analysis of the problems and processes experienced by this population in the United States.

Further academic research is needed in the study of the incidence of Psychosocial Trauma and Post Traumatic Stress Disorders (PTSD) in Central Americans in this country. Only a small number of social workers, psychologists, and psychiatrists have researched the problem. More scientific and psychological studies need to be conducted to fully understand and successfully treat individuals affected by the various forms of PTSD manifested in the Central-American population. Schools of Social Work, Medicine, Psychology, and Sociology must take a leading role in the study and research of various manifestations of Psychosocial Trauma and PTSD observable in Central Americans living in this country.

The Need For Immigration Changes

The undocumented immigration status is the most serious problem faced by the majority of Central Americans in this country. There is a great urgency to modify the governmental policies and practices at the macro level in order to have position impact in the economic, social, and cultural experience of this population. The American Civil Liberties Union and the United Nations High Commission on Refugees have declared the position that El Salvadoreans and Guatemalans in the U.S. are prima facia refugees and should not be deported or forced to return to their countries of origin. Temporary refuge and extended voluntary departure status must be granted to this population as an effective solution to a complex problem.

Furthermore, it must be noted that Extended Voluntary Departure has been granted in the past to other refugee populations. Extended voluntary departure should be granted on a temporary basis until the U.S. Congress determines that hostilities have ended and personal safety has been restored in Central America.

Central-American activists and refugees strongly believe that when individuals escaping the terror and political violence of the civil war arrive in this country, the U.S. government has a legal and moral obligation to treat them in a humane manner consistent with U.S. and international laws. If Central Americans were granted refugee status, their most difficult acculturation problem would be resolved, thus resulting in their gradual adaptation and incorporation into the U.S. society.

The immigration status of these individuals prevents their adaptation and incorporation into U.S. society and culture. Undocumented Central Americans have a difficult time finding employment because of their immigration status. This creates an underclass of workers that can only find subminimum wage employment in the ethnic enclave, the domestic, and secondary labor sectors.

The Need for Counseling Services

It is important to reframe the immigrants' perceptions regarding counseling and social services. In Latin America, the extended family provides the economic, emotional, and social support to individuals. Family cohesion and support is strong, providing security and stability to the individual and the community. Social services are seen as charity in the traditional Central-American culture and receiving charity is not considered a positive communal action. People must work to make a living and only the lazy or disabled are expected to receive charity. A problem developed a few years back when the Commission for Social Justice of the Catholic Church changed its name to Catholic Charities, the Central American community perceived the name change as a negative political move and many did not want to seek services provided by the agency.

This attitude may create further complications. For instance, individuals may not seek medical help until the illness or problem becomes a serious emergency. It is a common belief that if one cannot afford to pay for a medical service then one seeks home remedies or assistance from family or friends but not from the government.

It is essential to inform undocumented Central Americans of available social services. They must know their legal rights as well as the legal implications of their undocumented status. Although there are community agencies providing information and referral services, organizations need budget increases to provide more efficient services. Financial support is needed to expand available facilities and services, and effectively train their professional staff.

Presently, there is a need to develop culturally sensitive counseling and social services at low cost or free of charge, which provide support to Central Americans in their relocation and acculturation. At the micro level, community organizers must offer population classes or workshops that provide the necessary cultural, social, and political awareness and survival skills. Workshops must include an introduction and orientation to the U.S. cultural patterns and the legal and social systems to assure understanding and familiarity with the cultural and social dynamics of the U.S.

Basic cultural differences must be explained to newcomers to generate clear understanding of the host society. It is important for the newcomer to become oriented to cultural attitudes, values, and laws of the United States. Concepts of time and punctuality are themes to discuss with newly arrived immigrants. In Central America, the pace of life is slower and punctuality is not considered as important as it is in this country. Individuals need to be acquainted with proper procedures and expected behavior such as scheduling appointments, cancelling appointments, and punctuality when they cannot attend interviews or meetings.

Other important subjects for community organizers and school professionals to discuss with recently arrived immigrants are the values, attitudes, and laws dealing with child rearing practices and child abuse. It is common practice in Central-American culture to discipline children using corporal punishments such as spanking or belting a child even in public situations. What is accepted behavior in Central America, however, might be considered child abuse in this country. In the Central American culture, it is expected of a parent to discipline a child with corporal punishment; the punishments may range from spanking, belting, or forcing a child to kneel on the floor for prolonged periods of time. If a parent does not punish a child during an expected situation, people might feel that the parents are too permissive and are allowing the children to run their lives. In U.S. culture, corporal punishment is not widely accepted. Spanking a child on the buttocks may be accepted, but only in extreme situations, and even then the child may not be hit with a hard blow.

A high incidence of child abuse by undocumented Central Americans is reported by community agencies, clinics, hospitals, and schools. Parents must be aware of the different values, attitudes, and laws dealing with child rearing to prevent any legal problems for the family. It is imperative to develop cultural awareness and sensitivity on the part of school administrators and teachers, community organizers, doctors, and other professionals that frequently interact and treat Central Americans. A problem was brought to my attention by a high school counselor in the San Francisco Bay Area when a Salvadorean father had belted a young teen student in the legs. The child showed several bruises from the punishment, and the school administrators called the father to a meeting to discuss the problem. The father was greatly upset at the school administrators for threatening to report him to the authorities for child abuse. In anger the father told the principal that if he was expected not to discipline the child in the traditional ways, then the child would be the responsibility of the school officials and that they had to assume the cost of the expenses of bringing up the son.

There are also instances in which the children begin to threaten to report the parents to the authorities for child abuse. This situation creates discord within the family because the parents see their traditional roles being challenged by what they consider disrespectful children.

The majority of family problems encountered by this population arise from the values and cultural systems held in the U.S. society and the contrasting nature of the Central American values and traditions. Children and adolescents, especially girls, are given more rights and privileges in this country. This practice is considerably different than the traditional family values held in the Central-American society. Problems are created for the family resulting in intergenerational conflict between the parents and their children.

Family conflict is observed when children and adolescents find part-time employment to meet the family's financial responsibilities. Emotional problems are created for the father since it disrupts the traditional image of the father as the provider. This situation is aggravated if the father is unemployed at the time.

Other family problems may arise because the young usually acculturate faster than the older adults. They learn English at a more rapid pace than the adult family members. Children are used as interpreters assuming more responsibilities for the family. When the parents interact with the mainstream society the children are called upon to serve as interpreters for the family business affairs. This may include interactions with the utility companies, school officials, landlords, etc. These interpreting responsibilities empower the children in the family and places them in a bargaining situation with the parents. Children begin to negotiate with parents for privileges as well as for access to more material things that they desire for their social activities.

Educational Needs

Language acquisition is an important aspect of the acculturation processes faced by Central-American immigrants in the United States. Mastering the English language is necessary to improve the socioeconomic and cultural experience of recently arrived immigrants. Besides giving cultural awareness of the host society in the basic English language curriculum, educational programs must include counseling to newcomers. Also, it is important to implement empowerment pedagogies such as those of Freire's Critical Education to develop social and political awareness on the part of newcomers.

Professionals, university professors, and teachers encounter serious obstacles because they cannot find employment in their areas of expertise. Many professionals experience downward social mobility and are often employed in menial occupations that generate frustration and emotional, and psychological problems on the individuals. It is difficult for attorneys, architects, or professors to earn a living as dishwashers, janitors, or babysitters. Their high expectations of the opportunities available in the United States, and the disappointment of not fulfilling their expectations, creates a high degree of stress.

Occupational retraining programs are needed for individuals employed outside their areas of expertise. Professionals need to find employment in fields related to their areas of expertise and should receive academic counseling and training to prepare them for accreditation by the appropriate professional qualifying boards. The development of English language courses designed for professionals are needed so that they acquire the language proficiency to pass the accreditation examinations to practice their professions in this country.

Medical and Mental Health Care Needs

Culturally sensitive health care services are needed by the Central American population in the United States. There are special needs in health and nutrition. Recent immigrants suffer from tropical diseases such as parasites, gastroenteritis, malnutrition, tuberculosis, and high mortality rates. Medical and health problems are of concern due to the fact that many immigrants do not seek medical help because of their fears and apprehension of deportation or different medical belief systems. There is mistrust of officials in institutions such as hospitals, clinics, police stations, and schools.

Most Central Americans are not very familiar with Western mental health concepts and psychological treatment. It is commonly believed in Central America that healthy and sane individuals do not seek the services of psychologists, only the mentally ill do. The incidence of mental health problems such as Post Traumatic Stress Disorders, alcoholism, and abuse of pharmaceutical drugs is reportedly high among Central-American immigrants.

Central Americans suffer psychological and physiological stresses created by the civil war and their relocation experiences. These stresses are categorized as various forms of psychosocial trauma by Latin American psychologists.[7]

Psychological stresses common in political refugees are also manifested in Central Americans. Individuals may suffer from Post Traumatic Stress Disorders (PTSD) associated with the environment of violence and the effects of the civil war in the region. They are reported to suffer anxiety and acute depression that may result in hospitalization and intensive psychiatric treatment. Individuals who were victims of political violence in Central America often manifest various forms of psychological problems upon their arrival and settlement in the United States. Torture victims suffer from PTSD, exhibited as severe depression, guilt, nightmares, hyperalertness, insomnia, suicidal tendencies, and withdrawal. Psychiatric evaluations of Central Americans conducted by refugee centers in the San Francisco Bay Area have concluded that a significantly large number of their clients suffer from psychosocial trauma and PTSD.

Reports documenting the impact of psychological disorders on the immigrants and their families suggest that marital and family relationships are negatively affected by the above-mentioned mental health problems. Conflicts, depression, alcohol and drug abuse, frustration, physical abuse, separation, and divorce are the recurring consequences.

At the macro level, the medical profession has the moral and social obligation to develop critical awareness of the cultural perspectives of health and disease as believed by the Central-American population. Psychologists, psychiatrists, doctors, nurses, and hospital staff need to understand the traditional healing concepts and methodologies used by Central Americans to effectively treat the medical and mental health problems of this population. Workshops or coursework need to be developed by universities, hospitals, and clinics to offer professionals a critical awareness of the socioeconomic, political, and cultural backgrounds of undocumented Central Americans. Culture bound diseases in Central American patients have been reported by doctors in hospitals and clinics. Many illnesses are perceived as supernatural or magical. Patients usually do not respond to western medical methodologies unless they undergo the necessary rituals or take remedies as determined by the traditional cultural beliefs in Central America. There are community health agencies such as the Instituto Familiar de La Raza in San Francisco, that have incorporated western and traditional healing methodologies in their medical and mental health practice while treating Central-American immigrants.

In California, efforts are being made to develop effective methodologies and programs to treat Central-American patients in hospitals and community agencies. Because of the high incidence of torture cases reported on recent Central-American immigrants and refugees, a National Coalition of Medical and Mental Health Professionals and Organizations was created to treat survivors of torture. These efforts need to be supported and expanded to provide adequate treatment to individuals who have suffered psychological and physical torture.

Employment Needs

Employment is a major issue concerning the social adaptation and economic stability of Central-American immigrants in the U.S. Employment opportunities are closely dependent on the immigration status of the participants, a situation that forces the majority of undocumented individuals to find employment in the ethnic enclave, in the secondary labor sector, or in domestic labor.

Working conditions in the enclave appear to be more acceptable to newcomers and undocumented workers because cash wages are often paid. Cash payments minimize the fears of disclosing a person's immigration status to strangers and do not require necessary documentation to work as required by the Immigration Reform and Control Act of 1986 (IRCA), such as a social security number or an alien registration card.

Conclusion

The spectrum of problems faced by Central Americans may dishearten many community organizers in the United States. Their challenges and responsibilities are many and range from the development of a body of knowledge and understanding around immigration issues, educational concern, housing, and the broad dynamics of acculturation. Added to these responsibilities are the cultural sensitivity and critical awareness required for successful community social work.

Since there is a scarcity of literature on organizing with Central Americans, community organizers will be required to make modifications and adaptations in existing methods of practice while they mix and phase strategies and practice. Social action models, though dramatic, are the least favored, because of the attention drawn to the people involved in the process. They might bring a negative outcome as the police or immigration officials become aware of the individuals and their possible undocumented immigration status in this country. Furthermore, because many Central Americans live marginally in our society, they may have a strong reluctance to engage in this level of social change and advocacy. Traditionally, the poor and disenfranchised tend to be conservative in nature and are reluctant to engage in direct confrontation tactics. Community and economic development models are more acceptable and effective in working with Central Americans in this country. They are more status quo in their orientations and offer more real material gains like employment, housing and the development of an economic exchange market that may exist parallel to the traditional mainstream market systems. The utilization of Paulo Freire's methods for developing critical awareness and empowerment are especially relevant in organizing with Central Americans because they do not possess false expectations, emphasizing very real material and educational rewards. Furthermore, many Central-American immigrants are already familiar with Freire's methods, as they were implemented in the Central-American Catholic base communities.

Because of the psychologically sensitive nature of many Central-American communities and individuals suffering from a wide range of manifestations of Post Traumatic Stress Disorders, organizers must be knowledgeable about the dynamics of community psychology and the ebbs and flows of communities' mental health. This in turn would dictate when to suggest particular organizing strategies and when to implement alternative strategies that may be more ameliorative in nature. These challenges are obvious; the strategies have to be determined on a day-by-day basis as we work with and learn to develop a critical understanding of the communities.

Endnotes

1. American Civil Liberties Union, *Salvadorans in the United States: The Case for Extended Voluntary Departure*, National Immigration and Alien Rights Project, Report No. 1 (Washington, D.C., April 1984).

2. Amnesty International, Annual Report (Washington, D.C., 1983).

3. R. Camarda, *Forced to Move: Salvadorean Refugees in Honduras* (San Francisco, CA: Solidarity Publications, 1985).

4. C. B. Cordova, *Migration and Acculturation Dynamics of Undocumented El Salvadoreans in the San Francisco Bay Area*, Unpublished Doctoral Dissertation (University of San Francisco, San Francisco, CA, 1986).

5. C. B. Cordova, "Undocumented El Salvadoreans in the San Francisco Bay Area: Migration and Adaptaton Dynamics," *Journal of La Raza Studies* 1 (1987):9–37.

6. B. Manz, *Refugees of a Hidden War: The Aftermath of Counterinsurgency in Guatemala* (Albany, NY: State University of New York Press, 1988).

7. I. Martin-Baro, "Political Violence and War as Causes of Psychosocial Trauma in El Salvador," *Journal of La Raza Studies* 2 (Summer/Fall 1989):5–15.

8. A. Portes and R. L. Bach, *Latin Journey: Cuban and Mexican Immigrants in the United States* (Berkeley: University of California Press, 1985).

9. F. G. Rivera and J. Erlich, Neo-Gemeinschaft Minority Communities in the United States: Implications for Community Organizing, *Community Development Journal* 16 (October 1981):189–200.

10. F. Toennies, "Gemeinschaft and Gesellschaft," In Talcott Persons, et al., eds. *Theories of Society* (New York: Free Pess, 1961), 1–191.

References

K. Andersen, "The New Ellis Island: Immigrants from All Over Change the Beat, Bop and Character of Los Angeles, *Time* (June 1983):18–25.

E. Burgos, *I . . . Rigoberta Menchu* (London: NLB [New York: Schocken Books], 1984).

C. B. Cordova, "The Mission District: The Ethnic Diversity of the Latin American Enclave in San Francisco, California," *Journal of La Raza Studies* 2 (Summer/Fall 1989):21–32.

J. Fallows, "The New Immigrants: How New Citizens and Illegal Aliens are Affecting the United States," *The Atlantic* (November 1983):45–106.

M. E. Gettleman, P. Lacefield, L. Menashe, D. Mermelstein, and R. Radosh, eds., *El Salvador: Central America in the New Cold War* (New York: Grove Press, 1981).

G. Gugliotta, "The Central American Exodus: Grist for the Migrant Mill," *Caribbean Review* 11 (January 1983):26–29.

T. Muller and T. Espenshade, D. Manson, M. de la Puente, M Goldberg, and J. Sanchez, *The Fourth Wave: California's Newest Immigrants* (Washington, D.C.: The Urban Institute Press, 1985).

R. C. Nann, *Uprooting and Surviving: Adaptation and Resettlement of Migrant Families and Children* (Boston: D. Reidel Publishing Col., 1982).

National Lawyers Guild, *Immigration Law and Defense* (New York: Clark Boardman Company, 1981).

A. M. Padilla, "The Role of Cultural Awareness and Ethnic Loyalty in Acculturation, In A. M. Padilla, ed. *Acculturation: Theory, Models and Some New Findings* (Boulder: Westview Press, 1980).

A. Portes, R. Nash Parker, and J. A. Cobas, "Assimilation or Consciousness: Perceptions of United States Society by Recent Latin American Immigrants to the U.S.," *Social Forces* 59 (September 1980):200–224.

T. Scudder and E. Colson, "From Welfare to Development: A Conceptual Framework for the Analysis of Dislocated People, In A. Hansen and A. Oliver-Smith, eds.

Involuntary Migration and Resettlement: The Problems and Responses of Dislocated People (Boulder: Westview Press, 1982).

United Nations Human Rights Commission, *Report on the Situation of Human Rights in El Salvador* (Washington, D.C., 1983).

CHAPTER TEN

Southeast Asians in the United States: A Strategy for Accelerated and Balanced Integration

VU-DUC VUONG   JOHN DUONG HUYNH

Introduction

April, 1975, marked the end of American military involvement in Cambodia, Laos, and Vietnam, and at the same time opened a new chapter in the ongoing saga of immigration to the United States: the Southeast Asian wave.[1]

By the end of 1989, over a million Southeast Asians have migrated to the United States, both as refugees and immigrants. The Southeast Asian diaspora in the United States is thus the largest in the world and, thanks to the resources and circumstances in this country, potentially the most influential one as well.

This chapter will briefly profile this community, raise some of the critical issues for the 1990s, and advance a strategy that can enable it to achieve its full potential in the twenty-first century.

Southeast Asians in the United States: A Profile

When the Phnom Penh and Saigon regimes fell to the communist in April, 1975, there were no more than a few thousand Southeast Asians living in the United States. Most were students in American universities and the rest were diplomats, bureaucrats serving in the United States, or military personnel in training. Virtually overnight the United States admitted over 130,000 refugees, mostly from Vietnam, to these shores. This earliest group was dispersed throughout the country, from Duluth to New Orleans, and from Maine to Hawaii, in a deliberate policy of minimizing the impact on local communities and of accelerating, one hoped, the integration process.

During the next three years, 1976 to 1978, refugee outflow from the three countries dwindled down to a trickle, to about 37,000. More than half came from Laos alone. In Cambodia, it was the reign of the Khmer Rouge, that massacred at least one million of their fellow countrymen, including the majority of the professional and educated class. In Vietnam, the incarceration of tens of thousands of former public servants and officers of the overthrown regime and the initial, somewhat hopeful "wait-and-see" attitude among many who did not escape in 1975, that accounted for the reduced outflow of refugees.

By the end of 1978, and during 1979, two major events in Southeast Asia unleashed another exodus from that region. In the South, Vietnam invaded Cambodia, overthrew the Khmer Rouge, and set up a new Cambodian government under its protection while to the North, tensions between China and Vietnam, close allies during the war, led to harassment of the Chinese population in Vietnam and open warfare along the border. Anti-Chinese policies in Vietnam caused a massive, unprecedented exodus of "boat people" from Vietnam that included both Chinese ethnics and Vietnamese who had given up on hope for a better Vietnam. And, by the time Vietnamese tanks rolled into Phnom Penh, they also awakened and unchained a population incapacitated by the Khmer Rouge's atrocities. Hundreds of thousands of Laotians, predominantly of the Hmong hill tribes, also crossed over into Thailand; hundreds of thousands of new refugees braved high seas in their miniscule boats to reach Thailand, Malaysia, Indonesia, the Philippines, and Hong Kong. During the four year period from 1979 to 1982, the United States alone admitted well over 400,000 refugees from Southeast Asia. This group was often referred to as the "second wave" of Southeast-Asian refugees. Since 1983, the level of Southeast Asians admitted to the United States as refugees has leveled off and hovers between 35,000 to 50,000 annually.

In terms of status, most Southeast Asians were admitted as refugees, but in the last few years, a small number were admitted as immigrants, often sponsored by their close relatives already in the United States. Both refugees and immigrants were allowed to seek work immediately but only refugees were eligible for government assistance, from English and vocational classes to welfare benefits and medicare. After residing in the United States for one year, a refugee became eligible for permanent residence status, and four years later, he or she was allowed to petition for citizenship. It was estimated that by the end of 1989, at least half of all Southeast Asians in the United States have become citizens.

In terms of procedures, most Southeast-Asian refugees and immigrants arrived in the United States in one of two ways: a few directly from the home country such as under the auspices of the Orderly Departure Program (ODP), and the majority through a selection process in refugee camps throughout Asia.

ODP essentially was an escape valve for people who had reason to leave Vietnam, (persecution of some sort, for instance), and who had been accepted for resettlement by another country, to leave Vietnam legally and safely. The procedure required two authorizations; from the Vietnamese side, authorization to leave and from the recipient country, authorization to immigrate. It was therefore very susceptible to political caprices on either side, and indeed ODP had often delayed, scaled down, or was simply held hostage by one side or the other during the first ten years of operation following the 1979 agreement. Nevertheless, ODP had provided safe passage for well over 100,000 Vietnamese during that period. Today, ODP remains a much more humane and sensible alternative to clandestine escapes on land or by boat.

For the vast majority of Southeast Asian refugees, however, clandestine escape was the only available means. In general, Laotians and Cambodians crossed the Thai border while the Vietnamese left by boats to a country of asylum. By the end of the Federal Fiscal Year, 1989, over 1.8 million Southeast Asian refugees had reached a country of first asylum. The number of people who perished during these flights will never be known with certainty; they disappeared in the jungles or at sea.

First asylum countries provided shelter and basic needs with funds from the United Nations and contributions from other developed nations. Under the best of circumstances, which almost never happened, refugee camps in these countries epitomized the welfare state that can cause debilitating dependence if continued too long. More frequently, however, most governments resorted to mistreatment of refugees as a way to discourage more from coming. Thus, in 1981, for example, Thailand "pushed back" Cambodian refugees across the border into a mine field; in 1983 Hong Kong established the "closed camp" system, a jail-like facility with little service beyond subsistence and no opportunity for resettlement elsewhere; in 1988, Thailand, Malasia, and Indonesia pushed boats back out to sea often at great imminent risk; and most recently, Hong Kong simply used force to repatriate a number of Vietnamese people.

Of the 1.8 million who made it to a country of first asylum, most were able to petition a third country to accept them as refugees. The potential recipient country set up interviews and from that point on, procedures varied from country to country as to eligibility criteria and preparation for resettlement. The United States, for example, sent admissible refugees to one of the three refugee processing centers for some cultural orientation and some rudimentary English instruction before sending them to this country for resettlement.

Overall, the developed world has admitted some 1.6 million refugees worldwide with Australia, Canada, China, France, and Germany as major resettlement countries after the United States.

Similarities and Differences

Numbers and circumstances aside, Southeast Asian refugees in the United States make up a most varied community in virtually every aspect. Beyond the mere fact that they come from three different countries, thus at least three separate languages, Laos and Vietnam also contain linguistic minorities. The Hmong and Iu Mien, two primary hill tribes resettled in the United States, speak two different languages, from each other and from the mainstream "low-land" Lao language. In Vietnam, a number of Chinese ethnics still cannot read or write Vietnamese. More on this group later in the chapter. In each country, there are sufficient numbers of illiterates in their own language, making English instruction a Herculean task.

Their respective pasts also vary greatly. Cambodians have suffered the most—physically, emotionally, psychologically—under the genocidal Khmer Rouge. It is safe to say that no Cambodian family—from the royal down to the poorest—was left untouched by tragedy during that brief but atavistic reign. Before the war, however, Cambodian life was easy, with ample food and a leisurely lifestyle. Many believe that the Khmer (another name for Cambodia) Empire peaked in the 12th century as illustrated by their sophisticated waterworks and celebrated temples of Angkhor Wat. The Khmer Empire encompassed today's South Vietnam and the Eastern part of Thailand.

Vietnam had been at war almost constantly since the 1930s, first against the French, then against the Japanese, then the Americans, and most recently against the Chinese and Khmer Rouge, and almost always against each other. Instead of genocide, Vietnam suffered a half century of steady hemorrhaging of its best and brightest youths.

Even Laos, though not completely embroiled in the recent wars, was not spared from the fighting. During the American phase of the Vietnam war, Laos provided cover for the Ho Chi Minh Trail, a major supply route, and the Hmong tribesman were recruited, paid and trained by the CIA to assist the American war effort.

Vietnam was the most urbanized of the three countries, although agriculture remained the backbone of all three economies. Constant warfare in Vietnam had driven many people from the countryside to cities in search of some measure of security. In 1954, when the country was divided, nearly one million Northerners moved South and often were resettled on the outskirts of major towns. In Laos and Cambodia, by contrast, a more agricultural way of life prevailed until very near the end of the war, thus people were still able to live on their lands and the hill tribes were still able to practice slash-and-burn farming.

Education levels also vary. At the risk of gross generalization, it can be said that the majority of Vietnamese and Chinese Vietnamese were literate in some language, having received some form of formal education. The proportion goes down in Cambodia—particularly Laos, where some hill tribes did not have a written language until a few decades ago. Urbanization would most likely have played a role as well, at least to the extent that one would have to rely more on literacy to function.

The predominant—and in a sense unifying—religion in all three countries was Buddhism. Only in Vietnam was there a significant minority of Catholics and Protestants. Since Buddhism was not a highly structured religion, such as Christianity, Islam, or Judaism, most people believed in their hearts and seldom displayed their faith with outward practices or observances.

Due to the protracted war and the presence of several million Americans supporting the war effort, many Vietnamese had ties to the defeated regime, either as government officials, armed forces personnel, or support personnel for the Americans. Likewise, the Hmong in Laos who fought alongside the Americans during the war found themselves in the same situation. In Cambodia, unfortunately, most of the former government officials, most of the educated class, and most of the trained professionals had been decimated by the Pol Pot's Khmer Rouge.

After 1975, instead of a blood bath that many had feared, the communist regimes in Laos and Vietnam incarcerated the people from the "old regime" in re-education camps where they were usually put to hard labor during the day, indoctrinated at night, kept isolated from their families except for an annual or occasional visits, fed at subsistence levels, and generally mentally tortured. These people—estimated at about 100,000—would qualify as political refugees under both the United Nations and the United States standards. But it took until September, 1989 for the United States and Vietnam to agree on their fate. By this time, most had been released from re-education camps but were not allowed back into normal life; they were denied job opportunities and food rations. The United States agreed to accelerate these refugees' and their families' resettlement in the United States while Vietnam agreed to let them go.

Another vestige of the war with an even more direct link to the United States was the Amerasians, literally the common children of Vietnam and the United States. Estimated at between 7,000 and 15,000, these are the children that American servicemen fathered while serving in Vietnam, and in most cases abandoned after returning home. The children, although most are now adults, and their mothers and often their siblings survived as best they could in a society that, for the most part, refused to accept them. After 1975, they also became the living reminders of the defeated enemy.

Congress passed a bill in 1982 giving preference to the admission of these children and their families, but it took until 1989 for them to begin to arrive in any significant numbers. They too are an integral part of the Southeast Asian community in the United States, and perhaps particularly in the United States where they function as natural bridges.

The Chinese-Vietnamese Refugee

In contrast to the numerous waves of late nineteenth and early twentieth century European immigrants, the Chinese Vietnamese are a population of individuals whose migration has often been forced. For some, there was very little time to prepare financially and/or emotionally. The journey itself was both dangerous and frightening for those who drifted for days at sea and those waiting in temporary refugee camps. Such circumstances of the refugee experience would tend to favor the young and more physically able. This fact is clearly evident in the overall sex and age distribution of the Chinese-Vietnamese population in the United States, which tends to be both more male and considerably younger than either the general population or other refugee groups migrating to this country under more favorable circumstances.

Political migrations tend to favor the wealthiest and most influential members of the Southeast Asian society. It is usually these individuals who have the motivation and financial means for leaving their country in times of political instability. This tendency has been magnified somewhat in the case of the Chinese Vietnamese by the strong political ties between the United States and South Vietnamese governments. This well-established relationship made it both necessary and easy for persons associated with the American occupation to leave South Vietnam as its government began to cave-in under pressure from the North. In most instances these individuals were social elites, often fluent in English and highly Americanized in their outlook and way of life. At the same time, a good number of these initial migrants entered the country with significant personal capital.

These political circumstances have had an important impact on the social composition of the Southeast Asians in this country. The earliest arrivals were disproportionately elite groups when measured in terms of their educational and occupational positions. The social background of the latest waves of refugees is considerably different from that of the earlier waves. This difference has been characterized by a decrease in the number of predominantly elite, urbanized refugees, as increasing numbers of the rural-based, less educated, and less Americanized continue to be admitted. The latter arrivals need more assistance and support from the community and the local refugee programs.

Among the general population of refugees being admitted by the United States, large numbers are ethnic Chinese from Vietnam. This ethnic subpopulation is playing an important role in creating a more social and economic community. Their actual influence in the business environment needs to be examined in light of other forces of change characterizing the community. One recent study of the California Vietnamese refugees suggests that the addition of the ethnic Chinese in recent months have some impact on the overall socioeconomic status of the community.[2]

The Chinese-Vietnamese community, like any other community, has problems now, has had them in the past, and will have them in the future. Most refugees are not well prepared for the American way of life. They have high hopes that all will be well as soon as they arrive in the United States, but they quickly learn that American streets are not paved in the proverbial gold. The initial reaction is one of shock. Their dreams are based on popular misconceptions that soon vanish.

Few refugees have adequate financial resources. They hope to find employment soon after their arrival; but there are few jobs that do not require English as a means of communication. Even such professionals as accountants, doctors, and college professors, who are successful in their native language, must accept low-paid jobs that are below their dignity and self-respect. Many react to stressful conditions by becoming depressed.

Housing is scarce and rents are high; most refugees have no choice but to live in high-density housing. They also face external pressure and racial discrimination. Consequently, building a community to help these refugees is an urgent and immediate necessity. Churches and nonprofit agencies such as Catholic Social Services, and Lutheran Social Services, play an important role in supporting the community and providing needed resources.

The community itself has to become active, developing appropriate strategies for action. The success and survival of the community depends on the voluntary participation of its members. The community is aware that the only true guarantee for refugee assistance programs to be sensitive to their needs is first to achieve effective social, economic, and political power. Unity within the Chinese-Vietnamese refugee community is needed to work towards common goals. Through efforts to unify and help themselves by addressing problems such as social adjustment, refugees try to demonstrate that they do not want to be dependent on the Government. The future status of refugees will depend on community development, planning, and the administration of programs for them, as well as community empowerment and self-determination.

Southeast Asians in the United States: Critical Issues

Issues that are of critical importance to Southeast Asians in America in the 1990s and beyond can be roughly separated into two categories: Issues that are particular to Southeast Asians, or maintenance issues. They are neither mutually exclusive nor are they exhaustive.

Issues specific to Southeast Asians range from the obvious ones like language, acculturation, and employment to the more subtle ones like overcoming the traumas, regaining a sense of stability, of security, and of order, to name a few.

The English language is a barrier for virtually all Southeast Asians who did not go to grade school in the United States. To the extent that one overcomes that barrier, by learning and practicing, the issue recedes. However, for many adult Southeast Asians, effective mastery of English remains an elusive goal. The chance of becoming fluent in English becomes even more unattainable for the small segment of the population who did not have any formal education, thus lacking even the fundamental building blocks of learning. Moreover, there are levels of fluency appropriate for different lines of work or positions in society; the level that enables a shopkeeper or a keypunch operator to function often is not adequate for a loan officer or a software engineer. It becomes therefore an almost unending process of self-improvement if one wants to progress and move up.

But far more intractable than the language issue is acculturation, in the sense that one not only understands what surrounds him or her, but also that one can take part and function well in that environment. In this context, the newcomers essentially must be able to build their own support networks and to be at ease enough in whatever circumstances, from lunch counter to the boardroom, from the ball park to the church pews, to be able to function effectively.

If language is the prerequisite for basic communication, then social skills are the prerequisites of acculturation. Sometimes, these are just basic, elementary skills such as the ability to strike up new friendships, to express displeasures, to make oneself heard, to cite a few examples. But at times these skills can also be quite sophisticated and complex, such as playing the corporate culture and dynamics to one's own advantage, or competing openly, successfully, in the electoral process.

By this standard, Southeast Asians still have a long way to go before achieving acculturation. Witness a few situations. In schools, it is true that many Southeast Asian students excel academically, but often glossed over is the fact that many of the same students are quite isolated from the rest of the student body, unable to cross over the invisible walls that separate them. Many simply hang out with fellow Southeast Asians only. When does a support network become a crutch? How does a student balance his or her need for a secured identity and the need to participate fully in school activities, to build up new friendships that will carry on into their future?

At the workplace, few Southeast Asians have developed lasting, trusting friendships with their coworkers. While many have managed to move up to skilled professional levels, it is still rare for Southeast Asian professionals to function as effectively in social settings as in their respective assigned duties, or to perform public duties as easily as their secluded tasks. At first glance, it may seem irrelevant. The type of "as long as I can do my job well, it will be recognized" mentality is still prevailing. Unfortunately, recognition seldom comes automatically, and in the workplace, racial stereotypes and outright prejudice are still a fact of life. Thus, the deadly combination of corporate discrimination against minorities in general on the one hand and our own inability to build allies on the other can and does lead to untold numbers of blocked career paths in the Asian and Southeast Asian communities. It is not a coincidence that in the electronic industry, where Asians provide a disproportionate range of engineering skills, yet get very few leadership, decision-making positions, the frustration has led to very high incidence of job switches and the growth of small, privately-owned firms. Many realized that they could not win the corporate battle and opted for independence and more risk but where they could exercise both skills and leadership.

In the political arena, Asians contribute a disproportionately high amount of money to candidates, yet very few get political appointments and fewer still get their issues seriously considered. As for elected positions, they are still few. For Southeast Asians, by and large, the situation is even bleaker; they are still well outside of the arena.

It is therefore a long and difficult road ahead before Southeast Asians— and to a lesser extent other minorities—can truly achieve full acculturation, full integration. As with most problems, the sooner they can recognize them and find ways to remedy them, the easier it will be for us to cope.

In addition to language and acculturation, Southeast Asians in America also face many other collective and individual road blocks. On the collective side, the lack of a democratic tradition in all three counties becomes an impediment to efforts at organizing the community in the United States. From the lack of basic practices such as a tradition of open debate, open disagreement without becoming enemies, to more fundamental dynamics such as a peaceful, honorable way to retire the old leadership to make room for a new one, Southeast Asians often are unable to tolerate different points of view that can move the community forward.

Compounding the lack of a democratic traditon is the half century of warfare, of clandestine operation, of deceit and betrayal, and corruption and incompetence that make many of us unable to function in the broad daylight of public scrutiny. And without public scrutiny and debate, allegiance and loyalty must be based on factors other than the intellectual or moral correctness of the cause. To this day, Southeast Asians, and Vietnamese in particular, tend to take things or people as serious only if they had a few layers of secrecy about them.

The protracted way left another piece of luggage: distrust of one another and the facility with which one labels one's enemy. Factionalism and the "us versus them" mentality might have been necessary and useful to protect war secrets; in the open, democratic society they greatly hinder our efforts to integrate and build bridges with other people, including our former enemies. During colonial times, many people lost their lives after having been fingered as "collaborators" with the French. Never mind if the proof was unconvincing, or that many others also lost their lives on the mere suspicion of being a resistance fighter. In our times, being labeled as "communist" carries the same stigma and danger. Unfortunately, the tradition is alive and well in the United States and at times still practiced with gusto, at least within the Vietnamese community.

On the individual side, let us first consider the issues that were caused by circumstances. The most obvious one is the assault on one's status, sense of dignity, sense of security and the ability—however limited—to control one's own life and destiny. Becoming a refugee is, by definition, to lose everything: job, status, wealth, friends, even family members. Some may be replaceable, some are not, and as refugees, they know they will carry these physical and emotional scars for the rest of their lives. But they lost more than wealth and loved ones, they lost something deep inside themselves: the security and the ability to control one's own life to some extent. During the escape, they were at the mercy of traffickers, of pirates, of bandits, of troops from several governments, these people acted swiftly and often mercilessly. In camps, they were at the mercy of the soldiers who ran the camps, at the mercy of the United Nations that fed, clothed, and took care of them. When applying to a resettlement country, they were completely at the mercy of immigration officers. At any point in the steps along the way, there were no reconsiderations, no appeal. It is this sense of helplessness that they must overcome, and the only way to do it is to regain some sense that they are back in control of their own lives, and if nothing else, that they finally found a place where they belong.

Depending on the specifics of the escape and conditions in camps, some of them may have to recover from survivor's guilt; from atrocities inflicted upon them, upon their families, or merely witnessed; from rape, robbery, and beatings and from starvation. And the list goes on. It will be a long time, if ever, that some of us will not jump at the sound of a car backfiring, before some of them will forget the rapes and beatings suffered, or for that matter, that some of them will accept that earthquakes are only natural phenomenons and not the expression of some supernatural discontent.

The same traumas of escape, and the ability to escape itself, often cause other types of dysfunctions within the family as well. Many families are divided and separated, many children are separated from their parents and must fend for themselves. While separation is usually a burden, sometimes even being reunited causes other tensions no less serious; one of the spouses, for instance, has moved on with life beyond the moment they were separated and the mutual expectations are no longer valid. How to restore harmony, mutual respect, and love? How to avoid dwelling on the past traumas, to avoid becoming bitter or paranoid?

Even under the best of circumstances—a rare painless escape and resettlement, for example—external changes in the new society can cause serious disruptions in the family life of most refugees. Spousal roles often have to be readjusted where life requires two or more bread winners instead of one. Difficulties in understanding, helping, and controlling one's own children can lead to abuse, bitterness, or breakup. Disparity between children's potential and parents' expectations can easily lead to alienation.

Southeast Asians also have their share of other generic problems, literally from the cradle to the grave. As is the case with many poor people, prenatal and neonatal care is not yet widely practiced. Many preventable diseases, particularly those associated with diet and lifestyle, still continue unabated and some such as heart disease and cancer are increasing.

As children grow older, many parents still lack adequate understanding of how the school system works in order to supervise and help their children. By the teenage years, many parents—and young people—have difficulty coping with the bewildering youth culture in this society and sometimes their reactions range from excessive to virtual neglect.

On the other end of the age spectrum, the romanticized myth of the Asian "extended family" begins to break down as well. Older Southeast Asians, even when they live with their children, are increasingly being isolated: few can learn a new language, few can afford to drive, very few can find employment even if they are very motivated to work. During the daytime, when the adult children go to work and the grandchildren are at school, many elderly are virtual prisoners in their own home, unable even to answer the phone or the door. Where there are preschool age grandchildren, often grandparents become built-in babysitters without pay. In the worst scenario, they may even be abused, mentally if not physically, often neglected by their own children.

It follows that among the Southeast Asian elderly population, depression is rampant, due in part to such external conditions and in part to their own sense of loss, of uselessness, of isolation, and frustration. Sadly, they are often given perfunctory respect and filial duty. But, throughout the whole country, there are fewer than half a dozen programs specifically designed to assist the Southeast Asian elderly.

Community Building

In addition to seeking to re-establish the traditional family structure, Southeast Asians also seek to locate and build their communities. Soon after arrival in the United States, most refugees make desperate efforts to get in touch with as many family members as possible. They get together in small groups to exchange information, share their feelings over their present circumstances, and mourn their losses. This search for a support system and traditional community network gradually gives rise to a pattern of secondary migration. Growing Southeast Asian communities in California, for example, are evidence of this migration.

Local refugee programs are responsible for providing orientations to newcomers. Successful orientations can prevent serious problems from developing. The purpose of such programs is to attempt to get the new arrivals familiarized with their new environment. The newcomers will attend a series of workshops and training sessions for the next several months.

The first task is to provide practical information to newcomers, such as medical facilities, public schools, housing, social services, location of grocery stores, and other such survival information. These basic resources will give extra encouragement to newcomers on how to use personal initiative in the resettlement process. This is the initial connection to the network of people within the community, an early phase in developing a sense of community.

The second task is to acquaint the newcomers with others who are also new to the community. This will enable them to establish an identity in relation to the new and old members of the new community. As Erickson wrote, "Identity is the establishment of the person as an identifiable being within the social reality of the community."[3] A person works towards a future in the new location by breaking ties to old networks and struggling to remake a fresh network of connections in the new environment.

During this process, personal identity will be tested as it was during adolescence. The testing takes place as members of the community recognize the newcomer as someone who may be accepted for what he or she is, and who, being the way he or she is, is assimilated into a place in the community. Being a member of the community will give the individual a sense of unity with the group and mutual assistance within the group.

During these sessions the members will have the opportunity to discuss stressful aspects of relocation, to share among themselves their own experiences, and express their feelings of loss and generalized anxiety. They will also learn to adapt to the new community systems. As Meyer wrote, "In order for the individual to adapt to a new community, the complex of service systems and individual systems which make up a community must be individualized for each newcomer."[4] This task is accomplished in ways that are particular to each individual and to each system. The results of this individualization may be considered as the individual neighborhood organizations, such as churches, sponsor the meetings. It is essential that all members have access to the meetings. At these meetings, members learn to support each other and express a common position. For example, meetings may be called to announce plans for a fund raiser, support a local refugee program, or create a neighborhood watch against criminal activities.

In San Diego, California for example, a recent "Refugee Coalition" was formed to promote not only the interests of refugees, but those of individuals and organizations involved in resettlement activity. This organization lists no less than twenty-two members, engaging several hundred people as part of its roster. Two units are Chinese-Vietnamese "friendship associations" staffed by volunteers from the refugee community, the remainder are federally funded language, mental health, and employment-training programs. Also included are several county social services units employing full-time personnel and a variety of voluntary relief organizations (VOLGAS), whose primary function is the initial placement of refugees in the community. The work performed by many public and private agencies has helped to ease the refugee community's serious problems of finding adequate housing and obtaining needed social services. These organizations have also helped newcomers to obtain support and friendship from community members.

The community organizer who works with the Southeast Asian community as a whole should not ignore ethnic differences in the community. It is the point at which the individual creates a personal system, using the resources of the community and giving back to the community what is unique about his or her personality.

At this time, the boundaries between newcomers and community have not been fixed. People are still struggling with beginning tasks of locating resources and defining their new roles and the needs for community knowledge and interpersonal skills.

The overall goal of the community is to assist individuals and families to open existing community boundaries and negotiate a place for themselves in the new situation. It is the task of the community to assume the role of mediator, giving out vital information and helping newcomers improve their communication and coping skills. Individuals and families are helped through a major life transition. This will increase each participant's sense of identity, establish cooperative working relationships among groups in the community, and stimulate interest and participation in community affairs. The newcomers will be able to learn more about the community and its resources, to identify specific needs, set priorities, and plan to satisfy these needs from resources available in the community. The community, seeking

to reinforce social power, involves members and service providers committed to the social ethnic group. The attachment of refugees to these new community groupings serves to maintain their old identity until a newer identity
and clearer status within the United States can be worked out.

In its turn, the community pulls together all available resources to form
an identifiable ethnic support system. Religious groups, friendships,
extended families, and groups of professionals begin to coalesce. Traditional
activities involving the various national and ethnic groups' holidays—
religious ceremonies, preparing ethnic foods, and banquets—are opportunities for them to meet and discuss problems in the community. These
traditional rituals transform the individually experienced crisis into a
socially recognized event with lasting associations.

Khinduka, in describing the process of community development,
writes that

> ". . . locality development is a process of consciousness-raising whereby
> local citizens are empowered to deal with local concerns in a more
> competent fashion. Consciousness-raising includes the ability to make
> critical judgments on local situations, to understand the causes of prob-
> lems, and to take an active role in reform and transformation. . . Any
> social movement must start with an appreciation of the felt needs of the
> residents of a community.[5]

The new Southeast Asian community slowly begins to serve as a focus
for a collective mourning of losses and a "family" for new ideas, support, and
self-help. It becomes a buffer between the old, familiar life style and the new,
modern one. People in the community are involved in future development
projects. They define short- and long-term goals. They develop workships
and social, cultural, educational, and recreational activities. Particular tasks
such as obtaining resources and funds, printing a local newspaper, and promoting the community to local government are long-range plans and must
be carried out by elected community leaders. The essence of the community
depends on the voluntary cooperation of its members and a strong foundation of the community viewed as an entity. People must be encouraged and
sustained in working at a defined task. They must feel that what they are
doing what will benefit themselves and others in their community. They
should have a sense that they are involved and that their ideas are important.
Communication within the community is also another means to keep people
involved in the community. People must understand what has been done,
what is being done, and what is going to be done. Face-to-face communication must take place between individuals or in groups.

The groups strengths and weaknesses can sometimes be utilized for
action. For example, Asian people have the tendency to hide their problems
because of their strong sense of shame and pride. This conservative behavior

in the community can be utilized constructively to mobilize them to do something for the community before the outside public finds out about these problems. Changes should be taken gradually with respect to traditional customs. The following are steps that may be taken as part of a long-term effort to aid the Southeast Asian community:

- Dissolve myths and stereotypes by informing and educating both the general public and the refugee community. It is necessary to make the rights and privileges of being an American citizen known to the refugees and to inform the general public of the problems confronting the community.
- Develop community resources to cope with the existing problems by initiating social services to serve the refugee community and stimulate the existing social welfare agencies to provide new and meaningful programs to meet the growing needs of the refugees. Facilities are needed for employment, physical and mental health, housing, education, and recreation. Programs such as vocational and on-the-job training must be developed for the refugees.
- Promote social action. Develop leadership in the community so that people will cease to be passive recipients and become active participants in solving their problems.
- Educate and train bilingual and trilingual social workers. It is essential to encourage schools of social work to include courses in the training of multilingual Asian students and social welfare agencies to provide services and training for them.
- Educate the public. Community people should be informed about the planned activities in their communities and its problems. A good understanding of their own problems would facilitate organizers in obtaining their support. This can be done by regularly scheduling meetings; using community newspapers, locally sponsored ethnic television, radio, direct mail, and personal outreach; and existing informal communications networks.
- Conduct research and surveys to study the social change and social behavior within the community to help determine what is feasible in developing long-range strategies and tactics as well as to reach a greater understanding of the community's needs.

A Strategy for Accelerated and Balanced Integration

After some fifteen years of working with refugees from Southeast Asia, we have concluded that it is possible for newcomers in the last part of the twentieth century to join the American mainstream much faster and much more effectively while still keeping a balanced identity.

As one can readily see, this is a marked departure from the traditional "Americanization"—or what used to be erroneously called the "melting pot"—of immigrants and refugees, where normally the first generation stays out of the mainstream, labors hard, and invests in the second generation, who join the professional ranks, and by the third generation, one becomes a monolingual, monocultural, homogenized "American."

It is now possible—and indeed indispensible—to, on the one hand, collapse the two-to-three generation process into one while on the other hand developing a new model of a truly pluralistic "American," fit for the new age of economic and human cooperation. It is possible to expedite the integration process because circumstances have changed drastically in the last half of this century.

First and foremost among these changes are the achievements of the civil rights and related movements. Equal protection of the law and equal opportunity for all people regardless of race and sex open up whole new vistas that used to be off limits to newly arrived immigrants. Better housing, better employment, and better educational opportunities, in turn, promote a sense of belonging and dignity among the newcomers.

The second major change is the revised immigration law itself. The 1965 changes in the Immigration and Naturalization Act are still unrecognized as an important milestone in the development of American society. It abolished the racist Asian exclusion and the inherently self-perpetuating formula of admitting immigrants according to the existing percentage of each ethnic group in the country. It replaced those policies with the comparatively more equal admission quotas: a maximum of 20,000 people per country per year under a ceiling of 180,000 per year for the western hemisphere and another 180,000 per year for the rest of the world.[6] Beginning in 1968, when this law took effect, the United States as a society underwent a radical change in its demographic complexion. Only very preliminary data is beginning to trickle in and, among these, a faster integration of newcomers.

The third major change lies in the domestic and global economies. The United States lost its predominance abroad while at home the economy shifted noticeably from production to service industries and while also developing new technologies at breakneck speed. Newcomers, thus, are no longer confined to a few labor-intensive sectors; but, because of the changes and their own education, find themselves excelling in technological fields. It does not take much skill to deduce that a first generation immigrant today who happens to be an engineer in Silicon Valley or a medical researcher would look at the United States—and at the same time be perceived by the rest of society—very differently from his or her counterpart of a couple of generations ago who toiled in fish houses, steel mills, or laundries. We are not assuming that these changes have been easy and consistent; rather, the changes have taken place in spite of racism, exploitation, and sexual harrassment of the refugees. But, because of these major changes, Southeast Asians have more avenues within which to develop their potential.

It is also necessary for the United States to evolve into a truly pluralistic society, and in this context, recently arrived refugees and immigrants—who happen to be more brown-skinned than any other pigment, reflecting the world we live in—serve both as the catalyst and the vehicle toward this goal in the twenty-first century.

We cannot repress a sense of wonder about the profound human instinct for improvement as well as about the momentous events of 1989 to 1990. Through this roller coasting year we witnessed the Soviet withdrawal from Afghanistan; the Vietnamese withdrawal from Cambodia; the United States cutting off the Nicaraguan Contras, then invading Panama to impose its order; the euphoria of the Peking spring followed by the June massacre and the aftermath of repression; recognition of Tibet's struggle for independence; the Prague civilized revolution; the taking down of the Berlin wall in Germany, the bloody and swift retribution in Rumania; the secessionist movement within the Soviet Union; the almost universal acceptance of democracy; and so much more. The human race seems determined to redeem itself from the brink of self-annihilation and to make the world into a better place.

The basic needs for human happiness and dignity can be reduced to two simple components: food and freedom. The common threads running through virtually all people's movements in the last half century, from independent struggles to civil rights marches, from Tienanmen Square to Tibet, from Rhodesia to Rumania, from Pretoria to Prague, from Nicaragua to Sri Lanka, from the Baltic to Burma, from boat people to migrant workers, from Seoul to San Salvador, are either basic physical well-being or a sense of freedom, thus dignity, and often both. Food means not just a full stomach but also a sense of security toward tomorrow, opportunities to improve one's economic situation, and a reasonable belief that one's children will live in an even better world. Freedom, likewise, prescribes not only individual liberty but also a democratic society, respect for human rights, and a process where citizens effect changes. In a real sense, people no longer live by bread alone, they also want to determine their lives, and collectively with others, their futures.

In this context of global evolution and interdependence, no country can afford to be an island or can mandate deference from the rest of the world. Rather, we depend on each other for materials, for markets, for the environment, for peace, and for travel, among other things. Conversely, successes or disasters in any part of the world can be instantly felt on a global scale. Witness, for example, Chernobyl, the Brazilian rain forest, Tienanmen Square, or the Berlin Wall.

The United States, consequently, has to learn to deal with the rest of the world not as a commander but as a partner, more powerful to be sure, but inherently equal. The popularity of English, rock music, and blue jeans notwithstanding, we as a country can no longer dictate the political regimes or the terms of trade as we used to do until very recently. Rather, we have to market our products, negotiate our terms like everyone else, and respect other people's self-determination. In other words, we have to persuade rather than prescribe, convince rather than conquer, and therefore, to be successful we must be able to communicate with our partners. This is precisely where the "melting pot" model of assimilation must be discarded and replaced by a balanced integration approach. This delicate balance functions at least at two levels: between the old and the American cultures and among the three key aspects of modern life: social, economic, and political.

Certain portions of the Southeast Asian community, most notably in the San Francisco Bay Area, have deliberately adopted this model of accelerated and balanced integration. Field-tested for only under ten years, it is evidently still too early to render a verdict on its validity and usefulness. However, based on the early results, one may draw some preliminary conclusions. At the very least, this chapter can serve both as an interim report from the field by a community development practitioner as well as a restatement of the strategy. By necessity and in fairness to other practitioners who pursue alternative models, we must narrow the scope of this strategy to our working and ongoing experience at the Center for Southeast Asian Refugee Resettlement (the Center or CSEARR).

Started in 1975 and incorporated in San Francisco, California as a social service agency assisting newly-arrived refugees, CSEARR has evolved over the years and expanded its services to meet the needs of a growing and diversified constituency. By 1985, CSEARR operated throughout the San Francisco Bay Area with offices in four adjacent counties, providing a nearly comprehensive spectrum of services, from greetings at airports when refugees first land, to making business loans to help him or her start his own business enterprise. In between, the Center teaches English, finds jobs, upgrades skills, translates, counsels, helps people become citizens, and generally trouble shoots on any issues involving refugees or Southeast Asians. It was established as a community-based organization (cbo), a nonprofit corporation, and it continues to be led, managed, and staffed predominantly by former Southeast Asian refugees. Each year, the Center serves from 10,000 to 12,000 clients with a staff of sixty. Three quarters of the staff come to this country as refugees; in this sense we spring forth from the community, we empathize with the people we serve, and we understand and anticipate the community needs.

As a community-based agency, CSEARR's mission, philosophy, and ultimate goal is to integrate and empower the Southeast Asian community in the United States. The single guiding principle running through all of CSEARR's services and activities is the empowerment of the people it serves.

The Center teaches English so that newcomers can function in this society. It offers vocational training and employment services so that fellow refugees can get back on their own feet financially. It provides a wide range of social services—from orientation to earthquake preparedness, from the reduction of smoking to AIDS prevention—so that its served communities, young and old, male and female, can keep their bearings in this bewildering environment. It facilitates citizenship naturalization and voter registration so that its fellow citizens can begin to regain some control of their own lives. It provides business technical assistance and small business loans so that the pioneer entrepreneurs can lay a solid economic foundation for the community. At the same time, the Center also facilitates the maintenance of former languages and cultures so that these new Americans and their children retain their roots, their identity, and their dignity as complete human beings.

We want both integration and identity for several reasons. First and more practical, being an ethnic minority with distinct skin tone and facial features, there is simply no way for Southeast Asians to become white Anglo Saxons as the "melting pot" would like. We could accommodate and acculturate, but we can never assimilate. Second, the United States has changed and is well on its way to becoming a truly pluralistic society. Thus, the ability to retain one's culture and language is fast becoming a source of pride rather than a cause for embarrassment. Third, it is an advantage for the United States—economically, politically, and diplomatically, to mention just a few areas—to have citizens who are multilingual and multicultural. Having statespersons, professionals, scientists, business people, and artists who are fluent not only in English but also in another language is a definite asset for this country in dealing with the rest of the world. And lastly, it is the right thing to do.

To reach this balance of integration and identity, we at CSEARR pursue a three-pronged strategy: social services, economic and community development, and political participation. Essentially a social service agency, we also know that the Center is only as stable and effective as the community is influential, thus this strategy.

While social services are the fundamental requirement that every community has to provide to its members, those same services are effective and lasting only if buttressed by a certain amount of political and economic weight. On the other hand, pure economic or political power, without ties to community services, runs the risk of losing its proper perspective and often ends up chasing power for its own sake. And naturally, political power does not exist in a vacuum without economic power, either as cause or effect, or both.

Firmly rooted in this strategy, the Center has provided consistent quality and innovative social services to fellow Southeast Asians since 1975 and will continue to do so in the future. It has facilitated the establishment and development of hundreds of small businesses owned and operated by Southeast Asians. It has formed a revolving loan fund to help businesses that have no access to standard capital. It has encouraged community people to become citizens, to register to vote, to actually vote, and increasingly to run for offices as well. Concurrently, it has hosted candidates' forums without endorsements and used communications media to educate the community on issues of importance. These economic and nonpartisan political activities will continue in the foreseeable future.

The social, economic, and political integration is thus only one side of the equation: to enable Southeast Asians in the United States to function effectively in this society. The other side of the equation—maintaining the former language, culture, and identity—enables the same people to live happily and with dignity; they preserve the past to help maintain them for the future.

As we enter the last decade of the millennium, no one among us is immune from the effects of the revolutionary changes taking place all around this planet, and few of us can remain unmoved by these events. It is hardly an overstatement any more to claim that all of us are taking some part in these momentous events and that we are, in effect, shaping a new human dynamic for the next century. These are heady days; a little scary, but full of hope.

It is in this context of global revolution that the very small Southeast Asian community in the United States intends to make its modest contribution to human development by replacing the "melting pot" assimilation model with a new strategy of accelerated and balanced integration. It is applicable not only to ethnic minorities in the United States, but to all ethnic groups everywhere. Before 1990, such a strategy was deemed excessively optimistic, if not altogether unrealistic. In light of the ongoing fundamental changes in the way we think and behave, anyone who can live in only one culture and function in only one environment will be a disadvantaged person. An accelerated and balanced integration—not just by the minority community but also by the majority population of society—has become the best vehicle to brave the new world. This is what community organizing is all about.

Endnotes

1. For the purpose of this chapter, "Southeast Asian" refers to refugees from three countries only: Cambodia, Laos, and Vietnam. It is accurate when used in the context of the refugee status because the United States currently recognizes no refugees from any other Southeast Asian country. The authors concede that the term

is less accurate in a more general sense, though more preferable than the "Indochinese," a vestigae from the French colonial days. The use of Southeast Asian is also a vehicle to unite and organize the three nationalities by emphasizing the common bonds and circumstances of people in similar situations but who had much to disagree about in their respective pasts.

2. R. Bass, *The Impact of Indochinese Migrants on California* A paper presented to the California Policy seminar. [1989] (University of California, Department of Community Medicine, San Diego, 1989).

3. E. Erickson, *"Identity and the Life Cycle,"* Psychological Issues, 2 (July 1959).

4. C. Meyer, *Social Work Practice: The Changing Landscape* 2nd ed. (New York: Free Press, 1976).

5. S. K. Khinduka, "Community Development: Potentials and Limitations," In *Strategies of Community Organization* (Itasca, Ill.: F. E. Peacock Publishers, Inc., 1987), 358.

6. *Refugee Reports*, U.S. Committee for Refugees. A project of the American Council for Nationalities Service. (Nashville, Tennessee: December 29th, 1989).

CHAPTER ELEVEN

Community Development and Restoration: A Perspective

ANTONIA PANTOJA   WILHELMINA PERRY

Introduction

Community work in the United States has been arbitrarily divided into two broad major areas: economic development and community development. These two areas of theory and practice are separated by the professions and disciplines. Policy makers, government agencies, and funding sources support the separation. In this artificial separation, economic development is viewed as a highly technical area dominated by the professions of business, economics, and planning. Experts in these areas, predominantly males, labor to create a community economic infrastructure of housing, physical facilities, and local economic ventures as well as the introduction of large outside industries that will create employment for residents of the targeted communities. This work is generally devoid of considerations of human development, community control, community education, and community ownership of the enterprises that create employment and create local wealth.

The separation is further sustained in communities because the human service and the social work professions work in services unrelated to the economic development activities. They create the social services, the human development, and community education programs, and the broad array of social welfare programs.

In the real world of community practice and in the world of academia, these two groups function with little or no contact with each other. The lack of an approach that is holistic, integrated, and culturally relevant has sustained the dependency of our communities and impeded the authentic processes of empowerment, community participation, community control, and the emergence of a local economic system that would provide local employment and develop local wealth.

This is not to naively argue that a holistic and integrated approach, in and of itself, will magically dismantle the institutionalization of neocolonialism but, without such an approach, we surely deny our communities the opportunities for meaningful engagement with the problems that they face.

If development work continues to be imposed and orchestrated from the outside or by the technical experts, there will be no sustained physical or human development. Economic analysis and understanding will escape the community residents and human development efforts will continue to avoid the crucial need for the groups to attain their own economic empowerment.

In our work, as faculty practitioners and members of oppressed communities (African-American, Puerto Rican, and women) we have been searching for ways to integrate theory and practice for community economic development. In our minds, the artificial separation must end. Economic development is central to the work of community development.

The values and the method that we use in our work have a philosophy that is developmental and nurturing. The knowledge base is holistic and does not fragment the human experience into separate distinct pieces. The method of work is nonaggressive. The acquisition of power is not a central objective, although power is recognized as an essential resource. Evaluation and corrective mechanisms are constants in our teaching and work processes.

This chapter is written for people who want to find a way to liberate their communities. We have used our teaching and practice to find a way to organize and test conceptual and practice models for restoring our communities to more holistic and productive functioning—communities that fulfill the needs of its members. Mythology aside, we do not live in an integrated society. We live in pluralistic communities within the larger white society. These communities are created both by chance, preference, and exclusion. They must be given the necessary resources and help to survive.

What is Community? Definitions

Community as Geographic Locale: Vignette #1

In early January 1985, we arrived at our farm in Cubuy. Living in the hills and on a farm was entirely foreign to both of us. We quickly learned that two women living alone would need some help with the heavy work. John Luis, a young man in the area, was a member of a crew of handymen that helped us out. As custom requires, he became like a family member rather than simply a "stateside" handyman. He was unemployed and his prospects for a job were dismal. We began to informally involve him in sessions on entrepreneurship skills. Eventually, he asked whether his friends and family members could join him in these sessions. Before we could proceed to accept his suggestion, John Luis explained that we had to talk with his family and the parents of other youths who would be coming. We visited homes to introduce ourselves and explain the purpose of the youth sessions. Before long, the sessions expanded to formal Saturday morning meetings with eight of his relatives and friends.

Word spread around the small village that two "American" teachers from California had come to live in the area and that they were teaching the children. Within a week, John Luis brought a verbal invitation for us to present ourselves at a meeting of the local association. Not knowing what to expect, we arrived at the meeting fully equipped, carrying documentation as to who we were. We were seated in a small room opposite eight older gentlemen and one woman who never spoke throughout the meeting. The men were dressed in the true "jibaro" style. They wore sparkling clean and ironed "guayaberas." We introduced ourselves and they asked why we had come to their village. We spoke for several hours. At the end, fully satisfied, the association asked us to work with the entire community in solving its serious unemployment problem. We told the association that we needed a planning and action committee. They named a committee, immediately including some of those present and others whom they could notify. Our work began that night. Every Thursday evening we met to plan and create a model for action. As a result of our work, Producir, Inc., an economic and community development corporation, was legally incorporated in June, 1986.

The two barrios are connected by custom, history, language, church affiliation, and family relationships. In spite of hardships, people wish to remain in the area. Our distance from the municipality (thirty minutes by car) binds us together as residents to handle and solve problems that we must face together, such as electricity blackouts, the shutoff of water, lack of public transportation, difficult and ill-kept roads, flooding caused by continuous rain, and lack of all the basic services that one takes for granted in an urban area.

Community of Interest: Vignette #2

I can remember as a child attending a Black Holiness church with my dad. My dad was a deacon and the treasurer of the church. We were "Deacon Ward's daughters" and members of an extensive network of relationships. Just as we had our identity and the accompanying expectations for conduct and behavior, the sisters, deacons, mothers, and ushers had their respective identities, and we all lived out a full set of behavior during the week and on Sundays. We performed a standard unchanging set of behavior at funerals, and we celebrated in song and worship the new members that joined the flock. I can remember longing to be "saved" and to have the opportunity to participate in these joyous activities. Those who violated the customs and rules were called "back sliders," and they were dealt with severely. However, punishment was always delivered with compassion and forgiveness. We knew of each other's problems and we cared for each other.

In my memories, the doctrines of the particular religious teachings have long disappeared. What I remember is the sense of belonging, identity, and community that was created in a small building on 141st Street in Harlem.

A second type of community can be a group of people who have no physical location that they own or inhabit, but that are bound together by historical and/or contemporary circumstances; racial, religious, or national origins; and who share a common set of values, mutual expectations, and aspirations. In this typology of community there are many groups that we consider reflective of the cultural pluralism movement. Among these groups are communities of ethnic groupings, homosexuals, women, seniors, physically impaired, environmentalists, religious groups, etc.

Most of our work has been done in locality-based communities and we will proceed from this information base. However, we maintain that our model of community development also has usefulness for emerging communities of special interests.

Community Origins and Functions: Vignette #3

A tragic and violent incident occurred in our community last year. Two young men from two large families were drinking in a newly opened discotheque and they became involved in a bad argument. Rumor had it that they were drunk or under the influence of drugs. Harsh words were exchanged and one of the men hit the other. A more serious fight was avoided by removing the contenders from the premises. The next weekend, members of both families were at the discotheque when it opened for business. The man who had struck the first blow the week before was about to apologize when his victim shot him. He also shot his brother who had come to his aid. Everyone ran out of the bar, including the two wounded men. One of them fell to the ground. the gunman jumped into his truck, ran over his two victims, killing them, and fled into the woods.

The next day, the news of the terrible incident was being discussed all over the close-knit community. All agreed that the discotheque was not a desirable addition to the community. Everyone agreed that the shooting was a terrible thing, but to have run over the wounded men was brutal and insane. A delegation of three neighbors, members of the Board of Producir, went to see the police officer on duty at the local station. The police officer's response was that the community was blowing the incident out of proportion and that the incident was the result of a feud between the two families. Police action would take place in due time. The officer told the delegation to stay out of the situation and leave matters to the police. By the following day, the community was boiling with discussion groups. Some urged speaking to the family of the victims. Members of the family wished to go after the killers and still others wanted to hold a community meeting to discuss the situation and to take some action before things got out of control. Everyone agreed that the discotheque must be removed.

Community leaders asked the president of the community development corporation to call a community meeting that Thursday. The meeting was announced at churches; notice was sent to parents with school children and announced by loudspeaker throughout the area. Preparations for the meeting started Monday. The announcements were made Tuesday. The family of the victims was invited. On Wednesday, a delegation asked the regional police to attend the meeting. The meeting packed the community center. Residents gave their condolences to the relatives of the victims. The regional police were represented by the area commander, the chief of the drug and vice squad, the captain of the township, and local officers. The mayor also came. The meeting covered an agenda designed by the residents, the "Asociación Cívico Social," and the Community Development Corporation.

The first order of business, after introducing the purpose of the community meeting, was to hand over to the grieving mother of the victim an amount of money collected in the community to help with the funeral and other needs of the family. Residents insisted that the police give assurances that the suspect would be apprehended and brought to trial. The brothers of the victim said that they would abide by the police handling of the matter. The assembly then discussed the matter of the discotheque. Both the police and the mayor said that the business was proper because it had its licenses and permits. The community was adamant. Outsiders from downtown established the discotheque, and were suspect. These outsiders could introduce illegal activities in the barrio which the community would find difficult to prevent. The business, located next to a church, violated the law by selling liquor, the residents said. They added that the business was bringing in women from the outside to work as waitresses and entertainers, that the law against serving minors was not observed, and that they were not convinced that drugs were not being sold in the establishment. The meeting concluded with everyone requesting that the law and other persuasive methods be used to close the discotheque. The discotheque never reopened. The murder suspect was apprehended, tried in court, and found guilty.

Many traditional sociologists, writers, and social observers will say that communities no longer exist. They characterize communities as inventions of primitive and prehistoric people. We are even taught that a desire to belong to a community is an outdated need not entertained by sophisticated people who are socially or physically mobile. They arrived at this conclusion by noting the following conditions:

- Neighborhoods (geographic entities) are no longer intact because modern people come and go, meeting their needs in different institutions of the total society.
- The community functions of mutual support, social control, socialization, and defense, that were once met in local neighborhoods, are now met for all people by the state through commonly shared and supported government agencies.
- Work, as the basic economic function that once held people together, is now performed wherever it is best for the production process and the market, and companies no longer feel it is necessary to be located where the workers live.

These statements serve three purposes: (1) they postulate the idea that the human person is an island unto him or herself and that this condition of "aloneness" is the natural and preferred state, (2) they deny and negate the tenacity of the human community and the inventiveness of people to sustain themselves within social groupings that meet their needs, and (3) they promote the destructiveness of human communities by devaluating all forms that do not meet some traditional norm.

Why is it necessary to destroy the realities of communities and even to deny the concept of community? We think that by doing so a process is set in motion that separates the individual from his or her group and standards of behavior, expectations, and support systems. Each person is rendered vulnerable and weak, and each person becomes a potential employee left to negotiate his or her own "contracts" in the marketplace. Each person who is not a member of the dominant group of the society becomes a potential absorber of the products and behavior of an "idealized" dominant culture. The processes that are the prerequisites and reasons for destroying the community are also the foundations for securing our society's inequitable functioning.

In a political environment, where individuals are constantly being disconnected from their communities, the dominant group in our society retains control. No equally strong community group or coalition of smaller communities ever effectively challenges its power base.[1]

Community: Model for Analysis

Over time, we have developed a model for analyzing community to provide an organized way of approaching community development work. We found it necessary to proceed in this way because we found in our work with learners that they held unexpressed ideas that communities were created by metaphysical processes, or they had never intellectually examined the origin of community. Their knowledge base of anthropology and sociology had been so completely fragmented or discarded that learners who were members of oppressed communities were not able to understand and accept that their people had originally made communities and had the power, capacities, and right to continuously search and recreate more perfect forms for their well-being and meeting their basic needs (See Figure 11-1).

Once learners acquired an understanding and acceptance of the right and need for change, it became necessary to have a guide (road map) by which analysis and action could occur within some rational, orderly, and sequential series of steps by which community restoration/development could occur.

Using a multidisciplinary knowledge base for our work, we have organized a coherent explanation as to how and why the human group invented community. Based on a perspective of the human person that is multidimensional, the model helps the community worker to understand how people, who are the creators of communities, can reconstruct them again and again when changes are required and/or desired for the continuing survival of the group. Our working model relates each human need to a system of institutions that were invented by people to fulfill their needs in a collective human system, that is, the community.

In our model of community development/restoration (of which parts are presented in this chapter) the most crucial and essential function of com-

Dimensions:

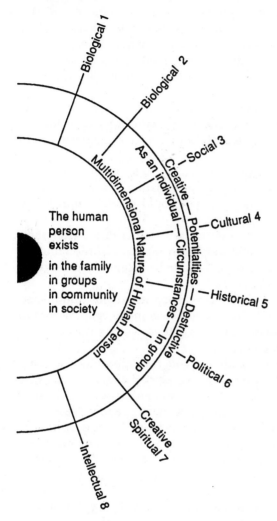

Basic Needs To and For:

1. Food, water, shelter, clothing, medicine, exercise, rest, recreation, work tools, machines, sexual expression
2. Love, belonging, identity
3. To exist in groups and patterns of relationships, to locate oneself in relation to others, to form groups and associations, help from others in time of emergency
4. Express ideas in symbols (language, art); to celebrate life in ceremonies, rituals and festivals; to establish norms, values and customs
5. To tell and record the deeds of the group and of individuals, to study the past to evaluate the present events
6. To use power to control, to attack, to defend, to protect, to create order through rules, laws, organizing systems
7. To depict the past, the present and the future through pictorial forms, color, sound, words, acting, movement, to explain that which is not known
8. To find explanations, interconnecting the nature of things: environment, the elements, nature and natural phenomena; to develop knowledge to control the elements of nature; to investigate and experiment

FIGURE 11-1 • *Nature of the Human Person: Her/His Dimensions and the Needs These Create*

munity is the function of production, distribution, and consumption.[2] This function is performed by a series of institutions related to human work that form the economic system of a community. Without this function and the systems that perform it, the human group cannot adequately survive.

Other functions of community were invented by humans to satisfy other needs and to support the economic function. These functions include:

- *The socialization function*, to teach the members of the community the accumulated knowledge (the science and technology, the history of the group, the language to communicate, the norms, rules and customs).
- *The social control function*, to create rules, laws, accepted behavior, and the punishments or rewards for violating or accepting these standards and the institutions that would create, enforce, and reward.
- *The social placement function*, to institute associations, groupings, and ceremonies that would help each member of the group to accept it and find a position in it, and to be accepted and be given recognition by the group.
- *The function of mutual support*, to develop an array of institutions and relationships that would insure that each member of the group would be assisted and provided for in times and circumstances of emergency or extreme need.
- *The function of defense*, to create a manner through which the group and its members would be protected against attack and dangers from within the group and from outside the group.
- *The function of communication*, including mobility and expression, to create a common language and symbols (verbal, written, pictorial, and expression through sound), to create methods of moving in space, and methods of expression of ideas and expressions of the senses.

These functions and the institutions that perform them vary from one human community to another according to geographical, historical, cultural, and other circumstances that surround the particular group (See Table 11.2).

Communities Becoming Dysfunctional: Forces at Work

We do not believe that minority communities want to live in slums with dilapidated housing and drug-infested schools. People suffer these con-

TABLE 11.2 • *List of Human Needs and the Systems and Institutions that Function to Satisfy Them*

Dimension	Need	Systems of Institutions	Functions
Biological	• Food • Shelter • Water • Tools/Machines • Clothing • Medicine • Rest & Recreation	• Economic Systems	Production Distribution Consumption (Work-convert resources into goods & services)
Social Psychological Cultural	• Medicine • Sexual expression for pleasure and recreation • Patterns of relationships Language verbal & non-verbal	• Family System • Education System • Religious System • Linguistic System	Socialization Communication
Political	• Using controlling/destructive potentialities of power • Need for protection from inside and outside forces that would destroy, capture assets, resources, people	• The State/Nation • Government System • Family System • Religious System • Judicial/Penal System • Legislative System • Nation/State • Police • Military System • Family System	Social Control Defense

(continued)

TABLE 11.2 • *(Continued)*

Dimension	Need	Systems of Institutions	Functions
Historical Cultural Psychological	• Tell and retell events and acts of heroic figures • Provides a way of locating oneself in a social context • Need for identity and belonging	• Civic Participation System • Historical Societies • Museum Associations • Clubs, Civic Organizations • Social Organizations	Social Integration
Creative Imaginative	• Record in symbolic and actual language life of group • Need to explain that which is not immediately known • Need to depict the world as it was, as it is, as it would be using common symbols and the senses	• Folk object festivals • Art disciplines • Religious institutions • Philosophical schools of thinking	
Intellectual	• Desire to find explanations, relationships, connections, answers about nature of things, events, environment and its elements • Use of knowledge to control the elements of nature	• Education System • Scientific & Technological System • Philosophical System	Socialization
Social Psychological Cultural	• Help to individual or group when established functions go wrong	• Social Welfare System • Religious System • Family System • Friends • Neighbors	Mutual Support

ditions because they become powerless and unable to correct the situations that destroy their well-being. We believe that our communities have been abandoned by the institutions to whom we have relinquished control for community services. Our children are not educated by the public schools. Our housing is inadequate or nonexistent. The police do not protect our neighborhoods. The churches in our neighborhoods preach and talk to each other. The public welfare services operate as instruments to define and promote morality and behavior. With all these circumstances, the tenacity and perseverance of the human community is clearly demonstrated in the retaining of their language, their families, their culture, the secure and enduring social affiliations, and mutual support systems.

We maintain that people who live in rural and urban communities function with kinship bonds, communication networks, and communal relationships. These are the functions that the larger society allows to exist or does not destroy in processes of institutional controls or cultural domination (internal neocolonialism). Dysfunctional internal processes are precipitated by the destruction of the "economizing function" that is primary and central to a community's stability. Once this function is destroyed, all other supportive functions become severely impaired or deteriorated. Without the right to work, to be productive, there can be no legitimate roles. Community members are rendered economically impotent and dependent with some subsequently internalizing this dependency and abandoning their rights and privileges to be in charge of their own communities.

Throughout history, all communities have developed the functions of community that we have discussed above. However, some communities have emphasized one function over another. We do not know why some communities expand, become aggressive, and use their power and technology to conquer and absorb others. It is as if the function of defense had been viciously twisted and turned into attack. Various explanations can be found in literature and in the writings of other disciplines. To our knowledge, there is no empirical data to explain these activities. Therefore, we use world history and analysis as the basic sources for our understanding.

Historically, some human communities have attacked other communities to use their economic productivity, their territory and natural resources, their scientific and technological knowledge, or the labor-power of their people. Over time, through aggressive activities of conquest and annexation, these communities become nations with great accumulated wealth, large landed territory, slaves, armies and low-paid workers. These nations acquire colonies to provide raw natural resources and to provide potential customers to purchase finished manufactured and processed goods and products. Members of the conquered and colonized communities have been brought into the metropolises of the great aggressive nation-empires to become part of the large numbers of unknowing and low-paid workers. These imported groups become the impoverished internal colonies that suffer great social problems.

Today and within the context of our national sphere, these destructive forces are institutionalized and sanctioned, not only through public policies, but through traditions, customs, and values taught in school to the general population. Minority group communities are denied their rights, access to information, and knowledge. They are denied access to protection of the law by denying them participation in the political processes that govern the country.

The dynamics and mechanisms of destruction are now less direct and obvious. Because they are covert, they are more difficult to identify. Their impact is so insidious that the victims are blamed for their own situation and, ultimately, they learn to blame themselves. We are at a time in the history of our minority communities when conditions of racial oppression, political and economic disenfranchisement, withdrawal of basic social supports and services, and internal crime threaten to completely destroy any solidifying ties that hold people together in the ghettos and barrios of the United States. The threat also applies to any solidarity that existed among different groups of disenfranchised and oppressed peoples. We know, however, that no matter how destroyed a community may appear to be, there are members willing to rebuild their lives and the life of their community to obtain a better situation for themselves and their families.

It is around these desires and expectations that community development and community restoration take root. In the U.S. during the 1960s and 70s, as people grew in consciousness of the forces of destruction described above, they began to analyze how their communities become destroyed. It is within this analysis and learning that members acquired "conscientization" and that community building and development must take place.

The work of community development must begin with the worker and the community identifying:

- What functions of the community have been destroyed?
- Which are still functional and which are dysfunctional?
- What are the forces at work that destroy the community?
- What are the destructive forces emanating from the colonizing process?
- What are the destructive forces that are set in motion in the total society to keep colonized members of the community in a state of oppression?
- What are the forces that keep community members subjugated and colonized and in a state of subjugation and oppression?

Once these realities are understood, the rebuilding process can begin on solid group.

What Makes an Effective Community Development Worker? Vignette #4

It is not my purpose to tell a story, but rather give you a slice of my life and the types of experiences that have shaped me as a community worker. I grew up in a barrio of Santurce called Barrio Obrero (the village of workers). This was a section of the new city of San Juan that had been built as a housing project for World War I veterans. Our family was well-known throughout the community because my grandfather, my uncle, my mother, and one aunt worked at the cigar factory at the entrance of Old San Juan. Grandfather knew all the other cigar makers who lived in Barrio Obrero and worked at the American Tobacco Company. When the idea to organize a union to secure better wages for the workers in the factory began to take root, my grandfather was a key person to hold meetings in that area. The contacts were made in the evening on Avenue A where there was a gathering place around a "friquitín" (a corner business where a woman fried codfish wrapped in dough, "bacalaítos," and plantain dough with stewed meat in the middle, "alcapurrias"). Men came to buy the fried products and take a shot of rum. They discussed politics standing around a homemade stove, a large can where wood would burn and a large iron cauldron with boiling oil fried the frituras. This was an excellent place to meet everyone if a meeting was called and to present and debate ideas. Meetings where more formal agendas were decided were called in a worker's house.

I was six years old, a very curious, introspective, and quiet child. My grandfather, Conrado, was a very dear person to me. I thought him to be handsome, distinguished, and very wise. Periodically the group of men organizing the union would meet in our humble house till late hours of the night. My grandmother would prepare a salad called "serenata," made of boiled potatoes cut in slices, raw onions, scales of dried codfish, slices of pepper, olives, oil, and vinegar. The men discussed mixing loud cursing phrases interspersed into their arguments for this or that point.

I had been put to bed to get me out of the way of adult business, but I would get up and sneak near the bedroom door so that I could peek at the group. The discussion would reach me in pieces, I would hear cursing, which would scare me, but I remained glued to the scene of the men around the table, with long spirals of gray smoke going up from their heads from the cigars they smoked. At that age, I did not know why they held the meetings, why they were angry, but one evening a group of men carried my grandfather in arms and everyone commented that the union breakers at the friquitín, where cigar workers gathered, had thrown boiling oil on his hands. Grandmother was very upset and I began to cry but then I stopped whenI heard the men say that the nurse at the dispensary had said the hands were not badly burned. Since this incident, I concluded that organizing is done by and with working people; that organizing is a dangerous activity since people who do not want you to organize could attack you and hurt you. Although I never understood then the full meaning of the meetings in our house, later I learned that they met to ask for changes in their wages and in the conditions of their work place. The owners retaliated employing people to hit the main organizers. The workers went on strike and were out many, many months. I heard adults in our house talk about the strike being a success. Since that strike, our family suffered from the deterioration and the extreme poverty that comes from unemployment of all the wage earners in a household. The workers won the strike, but the owners packed the machines and tools in crates and left Puerto Rico. The factory was closed.

This experience, early in my childhood, gave me an opportunity to suffer close to me injustice and to incorporate in my self what all adults, whom I respected, were saying about this event. My grandfather and his friends said: "Rather than share the wealth they were making from the skill of our hands, those bastards removed our source of honest work. They left us to starve with our successful strike. The sons of bitches. All we asked was a miserable increase to help us feed our families." I learned that life for those people, "like us," was hard and that we had to learn how to fight against "the sons of bitches" (words I was not supposed to use but which I repeated in my head in quiet murmurs). I also learned that to struggle against whatever evils will come, one had to join together with others who suffered also. I began my education early.   A.P.

Vignette #5

I am the daughter of a union organizer. My father became the founding president of the first integrated union for employees of the Pennsylvania Railroad System. Talks of discrimination and the system's inequities were a constant part of our getting together at the dinner table. We were taught that strategies of picketing, demonstrations, and legal petitions were rightful actions to correct social injustices. Social change has always been something that I considered necessary to correct injustices that Black people experienced. Change was a goal to make the larger society better, but changing ourselves was also a requirement to make ourselves more prepared for opportunities. My father, with his strong union background, taught us not to be afraid to fight for our rights and to never deny our racial heritage or our people.

Fiery and angry words at the dinner table were moderated in the outside world by a strong religious affiliation typical of most black families, with roots in the South. Religion contributed a mixture of forgiveness, peacefulness, and perseverance.   W.P.

In our model of community development, there is no particular profession or discipline that has a monopoly on the capacity to prepare people for the work. A community development worker can be a priest, an artist, a human service professional, a social worker, a planner, or an environmentalist, among others, but all these persons must share a philosophy, a political perspective, knowledge, and methodology for working with people. We do not think that one can be fully prepared in a formal educational institution because we do not believe that the dominant society's institutions prepare people to value cultural differences—the ultimate desirability of a truly pluralistic society—nor are students taught to examine, analyze, and challenge the society's practices of inequality. We believe that education in a formal institution partializes and fragments knowledge so that it is impossible to acquire the necessary conceptual lenses to approach the holistic work that community development requires.

The worker, as a member of the community, must bring enormous energy and personal resources that can only be sustained if she or he has a deep and unswerving commitment to eliminating circumstances of economic oppression and social injustice. The decision to work in community brings one face to face with the inconsistencies of our country's professed values and democratic principles and the actual practices of institutionalized inequality and injustice. It is frequently impossible to institutionalize the desired changes or the gains accomplished. The business of oppression and racism does not go away, and social change efforts can often be characterized as "one step forward, two steps back, and so forth."

Ultimately, in community development work, it is the members of that community who will decide who is with them and who is not. They choose who they will work with and who they want to work with them. Community residents make these choices based on their gut reactions, their ideological views of people, and the demonstrated and informed results of their work together.

"Conscientization" is an important process in our model of work. It means that the community development workers must bring a political perspective, knowledge, and skill that community members may not initially possess. This being the case, the community development worker must face the task with willingness and conviction to allow her or his knowledge, access, influence, and resources to be used by and in behalf of the community. This permits that the work will proceed on relationships based on equal rights. The partnership will result in services, resources, knowledge, skills, and increased rights becoming available to community members. What characteristics make for an effective community development worker and how does effectiveness come about? Obviously there is no litmus test that can be applied. Table 11.3 illustrates the knowledge base, skills, characteristics, and values that we consider necessary for an effective community development worker.

What Is Community Development and Restoration?[3]

New communities are constantly being created and existing communities are being adapted to survive in a changing, frequently hostile, environment. In the U.S., people will move in and out of several communities to meet multiple needs. Investments and affiliations will vary, based on the needs being met, but most people still consider that they have a "home-base community." In fact, human beings have lived in communities throughout history because the human person cannot survive alone. We invented community because we need community.

Starting with every newborn infant and ending with the aged person and going through every age and stage of the group, people need each other to sustain activities that support life and insure full development of the group and each of its members. Accumulated knowledge, from biology, sociology, psychology, history, the sciences of government and political relations and economics, to knowledge of art and religion attest to and explain the fact that the human species survives, even though more powerful and physically better-equipped forms of life have disappeared. This survival into full development can be traced to the human being's capacity to think (remember, analyze, synthesize, and integrate). Human groupings have used these capacities to provide for the basic needs of the group and its members using

Basic Formal and Preparatory Experiences	Basic Prerequisites, Philosophical and Political World Views	Basic Characteristics and Skill Base	Knowledge Base
• No particular prior profession and/or educational experience is required. • Positive experiences in which the person experiences her/himself as a member of a community. • Direct experiences with discriminatory circumstances and/or practices of being excluded because of one's membership in a particular group. • A member (by birth and/or acceptance) of the community in which work is to be undertaken. • Sufficient skills in working with people who have gained knowledge confidence in her/his interactional skills and her/his abilities to understand and influence others.	Believe that: • The human person should be viewed as a multi-dimensional person with multiple needs emanating from this nature. • People do not choose to live or survive alone. • The human community is an invention of people to meet current and changing human needs. • Culture groups differ in their environmental context and adaptation to environment, and it is around these adaptations and choices that cultures are made. • Intolerance for justice and commitment to equal opportunities and access. • Human persons cannot realize maximum produc-	• Planning and management skills. • Communication skills. • Problem-solving skills. • Analytical and conceptual skills. • Flexibility. • Investigative and evaluative skills. • Creativity and inventiveness. • Curiosity and an exploratory approach to problem-solving. • Self-confidence and integration as a person. • Ability to recognize, mobilize, and integrate resources within a work effort. • Ability to work, within time constraints, to realize product and process goals. • Ability to learn, acquire	• A working conceptual base that allows for an acceptance and willingness to use knowledge holistically from these areas: • Definitions, functions and origins of community (Anthropology). • Social systems functioning (organizational theory). • Basics of economic anthropology. • Political science (theories of community power, use of power in political arenas, origins, functions, processes of social policy, analyzing social and group interaction policy arenas). • Social change theories, strategies, community organizing models (social work). • Leadership development

- Sufficient skills in working with people to have understanding and appreciation of others, their personal differences, cultural context, and behaviors as members of groups and communities.
- Physical strength and endurance to work hard and long hours.

tivity and fulfillment living alone and/or isolated from relationships with others.
- Human groups that identify themselves as communities have the right to define their needs and create/control the systems necessary to meet these needs.
- The human community is made dysfunctional when their needs are controlled from the outside.
- A community that may appear to be in the process of dysfunction has the desire and internal capabilities for restoration/redevelopment processes.

new knowledge, integrate, change and adapt to new ideas and information.
- Specific skills as may be required by particular program activities such as fund-raising, entre-preneurial, business development.
- Patience and respect for a truly democratic way of working with others.
- One must become a continuous learner with an appreciation of the fact that learning can come from many sources.

theories.
- Perspectives on racism, feminism and agism.
- Traditional and radical analysis of the development of U.S., particularly U.S. history as it relates to its colonies, internal and external.
- Definitions, manifestations and uses of culture.
- Definitions and perspectives on cultural pluralism.
- Origins of language and relationship of language to culture.
- Comparative philosophies and definitions of the human person.
- Basic concepts and principles of logic and community.
- Sociology of knowledge.
- Perspectives on "creative education" and analytical thinking.
- Theories of role performance, social and group interaction.

the human resources and resources of the environment in different ways according to the natural circumstances in which they find themselves. These differences are called culture.

In our community development restoration activities, we are intervening in an environment that has become destructive to people, and we are acting to influence, direct, and reshape energies, values, and work efforts towards a more desired functioning. We use community development/restoration with a specific meaning. It has philosophy; a definition of goals and products. It also has a methodology consistent with the philosophy and an evaluatory process from the beginning to the end.

We emphasize development to reinforce the participatory and educational goals involved in community work. Community development, as we define it, rests heavily on a series of developmental processes, but the tangible, concrete end-product goals are equally significant, and development/restoration cannot take place unless process and product goals are equally valued and operationalized. Community development requires timely realized products that have both short- and long-term accomplishments and impact. We are talking about products and outcomes that include worker/owner business ventures, cooperatives owned by the community members, cultural activities, and celebrations reinforcing and securing the group's history and values, and social service delivery systems cooperatively or collectively owned by community members.

In our definition, community development/restoration is the work with people through which members of an economically dependent and politically disenfranchised community accept to work together with the following purposes:

1. To understand the forces and processes that have made them and keep them in their state of poverty and dependency.
2. To mobilize and organize their internal strength, as represented in political awareness, a plan of action based on information, knowledge, skills, and financial resources.
3. To eradicate from individuals and from group culture the mythology that makes them participants in their own dependency and powerlessness.
4. To act in restoring or developing new functions that a community performs for the well-being of its members—starting with the economizing function.

Development involves people working in a process of understanding, acquiring skills and knowledge, and learning how to use new information that can change the circumstances of their lives. By development, we mean:

• A process of education that allows people to analyze and understand forces that create and sustain the integrity and conditions of exclusion for persons such as themselves.

- A process of education by which people come to know they possess strength, knowledge, and skills; they can access, value, and utilize their individual and collective resources as they can be integrated into community development goals.
- A process of education in which people are learning how their activities, values, fears, and behaviors allow them to be victimized.
- A process by which community members learn to defend themselves against forces, inside and outside their community, that would deny them their rights, resources, and privileges.

What Is Community Restoration and Development? Major Processes

We are presenting the model of practice included in this chapter as the guide that we are using for our current work. Through continuing practice and study, we expect to develop it to its fullest potential. The project and its work are done within the context of activities of a movement in which symbols, myth, campaign, and slogans are significant in involving people to secure their emotional investment as well as their commitments.

The model will be presented in three phases and our work in PRODUCIR, INC., Cubuy and Lomas, Puerto Rico will be used to demonstrate our philosophy, principles, and methods of work. The following illustration represents the community development model as it is operationalized in Producir, Inc. Each of the four organizational components was developed with the community functional areas in mind. While each organizational component may carry aspects of all seven functions, each has a primary function.

- Phase I: Contract-making between community development worker and community.
- Phase II: Development of political awareness and the decolonization process within the action planning body.
- Phase III: Activities of community development/community restoration within the total community.

Phase I: Contract-Making

This phase involves the introduction of the community development worker to the community. We prefer that the worker be a member of the community where the work is to take place. In our case, we are residents. In the case of

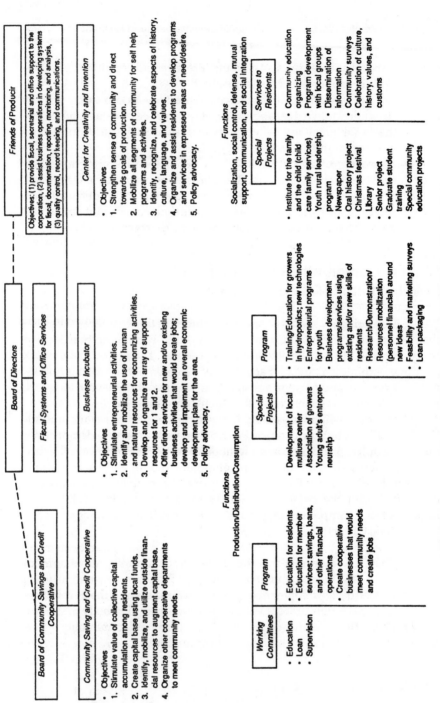

FIGURE 11.2 • Community Development Model for Producir, Inc.

students of the Graduate School,[4] all learners were residents who had to receive approval and endorsement from a community agency for themselves and the basic idea for an educational plan.

The important consideration is that the community development worker must have an invitation and an endorsement for the work to be done. The worker must be accepted as a member of the community with a compatible base of the experiences, values, and affiliations. As a member of the community, she or he must have the freedom to work with residents who may be challenging the legitimacy of the existing power arrangements. The worker's decision to work in community must be legitimized by (1) residents who suffer some problem that they wish to change and (2) a group that makes a commitment for comprehensive work that will require their time and energies.

Community development work cannot be undertaken by agencies controlled by outside entities or heavily funded by government. Examples of these are: agencies heavily staffed by professionals whose commitments and interests are outside the area; agencies whose missions are rooted in social welfare programs; and agencies whose personnel or past activities/ accomplishments are questioned by residents.

Once a decision is made by a worker and a community group to begin working together, it is necessary to have direct and clear discussions about the mutual responsibilities and expectations. At this time, decisions are made regarding objectives, organizational base, legal considerations, funding sources, manner of working, representative nature for the working group, accountability, and communication with the community.

Phase II: Development of Political Awareness (Phases II and III may occur concurrently)

No work can be expected to be lasting or continued by community members unless they have grown in awareness and understanding, adopting additional skills of analyzing, planning, acting, and evaluating; secured a working relationship among themselves; tested themselves and grown in understanding, commitment and operationalizing the mission, goals, and objectives for the work.

In the case of Producir, this phase has taken almost a year of weekly and ongoing meetings with a core group of ten persons selected by the local social and civic association, and it still continues with board members, personnel, and residents. Meetings were held with us and with others who handled information, content, or skill areas. During this time, the group was also engaged in activities such as writing bylaws and articles of incorporation; obtaining legal incorporation and tax exempt status; developmental

TABLE 11.5 • Major Phases in Community Development Work

	Phase I	Phase II	Phase III
OBJECTIVE A N D	Contract Making • Have worker and community introduction; establish agreements for work together; to form an action group (a committee or a corporation)	Developing Political Awareness • Secure the organizing body • Prepare a planning action committee for work to be undertaken • Assess the scope and parameters of work and to make a plan of work	Community Development Activities • Implement a plan of action with goals and products • Organize and establish community participation beyond initial core group • Add other resources to extend the core group activity
MAJOR EMPHASES	• Establish consent; roles of mutuality; defining work mission and goals; expectations for products and outcomes	• Legitimize activity in community • Refine and initiate a plan of work • Resource development • Collect information from inside/outside community • Analysis of information circumstances re: community	• Legitimize entity • Provide services and activities • Creation of new production and distribution ventures in cooperative modes • Establish or reopen service, cultural, educational, artistic institutions
PARTICIPANTS	• Community • Community development worker • Community group to undertake project	• Community • Community development worker • Outside resources	• Established business entities through their delegates • Community through multiple strategies of services, board membership, community activities, task groups
MAJOR ACTIVITIES	• Community meetings for education and information		

SOME BASIC PRODUCTS-OUTCOMES

- Identification and meeting with leadership
- Identifying members of a committee or corporation composed of community members
- Preparing profiles of community from census data
- Agreement to work together with a philosophy that works
- Clearly stated objectives and products to be pursued
- Statistical profile of community

- Legally established entity for sponsoring work

- Community meetings for education and information
- Data collection and analysis
- Resource development
- Communicating with community and establishing processes
- Augmenting initial core with personnel, others

- Assessment and analysis of functions of the community
- A model for work and action
- An action body informed and ready to involve others in implementing plan

- Community development worker
- Community sponsoring entity
- Other entities providing resources
- New businesses open and producing
- Services and activities
- Community meetings for education and information
- Board and sector planning committees, meetings, and projects
- Resource development
- Institution building and leadership development
- A number of cooperative and worker/owner businesses
- New buildings, housing, businesses, services, and recreation
- Specific products and goals as indicated in action plan
- Community mobilized and in action through multiple strategies to realize goals and objectives as planned

and organizational structure; acquiring an office; securing a first grant; program planning; visiting government agencies; gaining friends and supporters; fighting off takeovers by a larger established entity; hiring personnel; establishing program and service priorities; and developing a process for expanding the planning/action base by adding members to the board.

The development of political awareness involves the acquisition of various types of information and content that are internalized and applied in concrete activities and for concrete goals:

- Information from residents through community surveys, available from census data, municipal data, other surveys, and local leadership, and information that allows them to analyze the situation of their community.
- A community profile of resources, institutions, services, businesses, leadership base, organization groups, needs, deficiencies, and discussions that allow for an understanding of the social stratifications within and outside the community.
- Governmental planning and economic policies regarding the area (intentions, projections, plans, uses) and beyond that have consequences for the area and allow for controls over residents.
- Basic content and conceptual lenses for the community development work (definitions, origins, nature of community, nature of social problems, nature of power, concepts of leadership, systems theory, social policy formulation, nature of human person, and belief systems about people).
- Basic skill learning—planning, fund raising, data gathering, policy development and analysis, budgeting, grantsmanship, public presentation, analysis of information, and communication skills.
- The emphasis on this phase is always on the acquisition of information and skills; its analysis and decision making regarding the use of the information for policy, programs and activities; and decisions regarding the methods to be used. In this process, analysis of information and experiences is constant for members to learn the differences between reality, gossip, and hearsay; individual experiences as contrasted with group experiences; prior indoctrinations as contrasted with newly acquired information; and community development goals as contrasted with the development of social service programs and activities.

This phase must culminate with the community development worker engaging the core group in deciding if they wish to continue in this activity. Do they have the disposition, interest, time, and energy? Can they hold themselves in accountability to the community? Do they view themselves and their lives as being intimately connected to the well-being of the community? Can they risk and/or protect the interest of their community?

Phase III: Activities of Community Development and Community Restoration within the Total Community

This is the phase that has major characteristics of need assessment; augmenting the core base to include personnel and others; program planning/development; resource mobilization; setting in place the evaluating and feedback mechanism; securing the philosophy and methodology through the system; community organizing and educating for participation in the work; providing services and activities to residents; and legitimizing the entity and integrating new persons (personnel, consultants, residents, community groups).

In this model, Phase III is continuing and has no end as one usually sees in organizing models. Since the worker is a member of the community, there is no traditional exit process for her or him and there is no final transfer of power/control/authority from a professional worker to a community group. The central role of the worker is constantly shifting as new leadership constantly emerges through board membership, personnel, and neighborhood and/or community committees that assume different responsibilities for sustaining the philosophy and implementing the owner-worker work plans. New organizations, businesses, and worker-owner ventures and cooperatives are developed by residents. The board of the entity is expanding and changing with representation from various segments of the community. Because communities change, the activities of the work will change. Since the processes of destruction and deterioration are constants, the work of community development must be continuous.

Endnotes

1. This point of view was developed in the 1950s, when progressive social scientists renewed the concept of community and analyzed the circumstances under which a community can be destroyed (Joyce Lardner, Charles Hampden-Turner, Robert Blauner, Thomas Gosset, Franz Fannon, Albert Memmi, and others).

2. We wish to acknowledge the writings of Ronald Warren, *The Community in America*; Melville Herskovitz, *Economic Anthropology*; Frederick Engels, *The Origin of the Family, Private Property and the State*, with an Introduction by Eleanor Burke Leacock; among others, for assisting us in organizing our ideas on functions of community. These writings are listed in the references that follow.

3. We have added the concept restoration to community development to recognize that, even under the most destroyed circumstances, many functions continue to exist.

4. Doctor Pantoja and Doctor Perry established a Graduate School for Community Development, in San Diego, California that existed from 1974 to 1983.

References

Peter L. Berger and Thomas Lockman, *The Social Reconstruction of Reality* (Garden City, New York: Doubleday & Company, Inc., 1966).

Robert Blauner, *Racial Oppression in America* (New York: Harper and Row, Publishers, 1982).

Frederick Engels, *The Origin of the Family, Private Property and the State* Eleanor Burke Leacock, ed. (New York: International Publishers Co., Inc., 1972).

Paulo Freire, *Pedogogy of the Oppressed* (New York: Seabury Press, 1970).

Thomas S. Gossett, *RACE: The History of an Idea in America* (New York: Schoken Books, 1971).

Charles Hampden-Turner, *From Poverty to Dignity* (Garden City, N.Y.: Anchor Books Paperback, Anchor Press/Doubleday, 1975).

Jacquetta Hawkes and Sir Leonard Woolley, *History of Mankind, Cultural and Scientific Development, Volume 1, Prehistory and the Beginnings of Civilization* (New York: Harper and Row, Publishers for UNESCO, 1963).

Melville J. Herskovits, *Economic Anthropology, The Economic Life of Primitive Peoples* (New York: W.W. Norton and Company, Inc., 1952).

Inter-American Development Bank, *Community Development Theory and Practice* (Mexico City, Round Table, Inter-American Development Bank, 1966).

Thomas S. Kuhn, *The Structure of Scientific Revolutions* 2nd ed., (Chicago: The University of Chicago Press, 1970).

Joyce A. Lardner, *The Death of White Sociology* (New York: Vintage Books, A Division of Random House, 1972).

Albert Memmi, *The Colonizer and the Colonized* (Boston: Beacon Press, 1967).

Albert Memmi, *The Dominated Man* (Boston: Beacon Press, 1971).

Michael Novak, *The Rise of the Unmeltable Ethnics* (New York: The Macmillan Company, 1972).

Jose Ortega y Gasset, *The Revolt of the Masses* (New York: W.W. Norton & Company Inc., 1957).

Antonia Pantoja, Wilhelmina Perry and Barbara Blourock, "Towards the Development of Theory: Cultural Pluralism Redefined" *Journal of Sociology and Social Welfare*, 4 (September, 1976) 125–146.

David Ricci, *Community Power and Democratic Theory* (New York: Random House, Inc., 1971).

Walter Rodney, *How Europe Underdeveloped Africa*, Revised edition (Wash., D.C.: Howard University Press, 1981).

William K. Tabb, *The Political Economy of the Black Ghetto* (New York: W.W. Norton & Company, Inc., 1970).

Ronald L. Warren, *The Community in America*[1] 2nd ed., (Chicago: Rand McNally College Publishing Company, 1972).

Richard Weisskoff, *Factories and Food Stamps, The Puerto Rico Model of Development* (Baltimore: The Johns Hopkins University Press, 1985).

These references are a partial listing of a collection of readings that we consider essential for developing a political and theoretical perspective for community development/restoration work.

CHAPTER TWELVE

The 1990s: Fraud in the Inducement?

FELIX G. RIVERA   JOHN L. ERLICH

Introduction

"As long as some citizens live in houses and others live on the streets, the Civil War is still going on, it's still to be fought," said African-American historian Barbara Fields in Ken Burns' documentary, *The Civil War*. The struggles being waged by communities of color are some of the greatest challenges confronting us in the 1990s. When we look at the recent reversal of many of the modest gains made during the 1960s and early 1970s, the challenge to organizers is clear. The deep commitment required all too often leads to disenchantment, burnout, and a movement toward "safe" community organizing and less threatening social work practice in general. Like the homeless with too many problems—economic; drug and/or alcohol-related; other health problems, psychiatric and the like—for comfortable intervention, communities of color demand much from us.

The Urban Centralization of Problems: Persisting Racial Inequality

It is by no accident that the changing and emerging communities are a largely urban phenomenon. It is the inner cities within the inner cities that continue to offer shelter to new arrivals, mainly because of housing costs, employment possibilities, and ethnic support structures. It is these neogemeinschaft pockets that have been particularly victimized by dramatically increasing poverty rates.[12] Census data demonstrates this pattern in urban ghettos and barrios.[8] There was a 59 percent rise in poverty between 1969 and 1982; from 8 to 12.7 million. For example, poor, inner-city African-Americans increased by 74 percent; from 3.1 million in 1969 to 5.4 million in 1982.

Those people of color who have managed to escape the inner cities since the 1960s have been more than replaced by a wide variety of immigrant and migrant populations—refugees from China, Hong Kong, and Taiwan; those escaping political and economic oppression in South and Central America; Native Americans seeking employment off reservations; and the like. This "crystallization" of the underclass is supported by the secondary labor market with its underpaid service occupations and other menial employment.[16] Massey has also shown that, indeed, a majority of the most recent immigrants and refugees tend to come from Latin America and Asian countries.[5] Direct connections between home countries and inner cities are supported by bridges to family or group economic and social ties.

The economics of these little Havanas and Hong Kongs helps to support the growth of inequality in the United States. Race is and continues to be the main determinant for inequality. Whites continue to be overrepresented in the white-collar jobs. They are almost twice as likely as African-Americans (1.71 times) and Latinos (1.97 times) to hold these kinds of jobs. Forty-seven percent of African-Americans and 43 percent of Latinos work in the service sector, compared to only 27 percent of the white community.[14]

The research by Tienda also suggests the growing evidence of poverty among people of color.[11] She identifies three general conditions for the exclusion of people of color from the labor market: (1) limited access to education, (2) the role played by ascription (discrediting by blaming) as a method of placement that triggers racism and exclusion from participation in political, social, and economic systems, and (3) uneven distribution of opportunities for social advancement.

A telling illustration of inequality is death rates. Table 12.1 shows death rates for persons under 45 years of age. African-American and Native American death rates are compared with those of whites. For virtually every type of disease (except cancer for Indians and injuries for African Americans), people of color have significantly higher death rates.[1, 13] There can be little doubt that increasing rates of poverty bring with them a host of associated problems: political, cultural, and social.

Differences and Similarities

Differences in cultures, languages, economic, political, and social histories, and the disparate ways the communities of color see their agendas for the future, presents a picture of diversity. This section of the epilogue addresses

TABLE 12.1 • Percent of Average Annual Deaths of Persons Under 45 Years of Age that Are Excess Deaths.* 1979–1981.

	African Americans		Native Americans	
	Male	Female	Male	Female
Cardiovascular disease	58.6	67.8	16.5	29.0
Cancer	24.1	23.7	−80.0	−49.0
Cirrhosis	73.0	76.3	83.2	90.1
Infant mortality	48.9	51.6	18.6	24.0
Diabetes	5.2	58.2	50.0	0.1
Injuries	−1.0	−4.0	50.9	56.7
Homicide	84.3	76.9	53.5	60.0
Other	45.7	50.1	51.7	42.0
Total	46.7	47.2	43.2	41.1
Number of deaths	31,094	17,232	1.738	872
*Excess deaths	14,578	8.134	751	358

the similarities and differences of the communities as presented by the authors. The information is not intended to be used as somehow assuring entry into communities or as "correct" organizing rhetoric. It is intended to serve as one key place for *beginning* the understanding of communities of color from a social change perspective. It would be presumptuous to assume that a thorough understanding of any culture can be garnered from a single exposition or book chapter.

The editors have adopted Teresa Sullivan's multipurpose model of distinctive populations and subpopulations as a design for their discussion.[10] Sullivan identified minority status, race, time of arrival in the United States, language, and national origin as the most important variables affecting a group's identity with their attendant implications for community organizing.

Race Although the concept of race is useful in the discussion of different skin characteristics (African-American, Asian, etc.), it does not endure in a more analytical look at these communities. For example, in African-American communities there are all gradations of skin tone, from the blackest to the lightest of color differentiation. For an outsider looking at the community, there is no easy skin-color label. The African-American community does not have any unique surnames that may automatically be used for purposes of identification. Many names that have descended through the years were given by masters during the times of slavery. The phenomenon of taking Moslem names is an added variable that must be assessed, for it lends another important dimension to the identifiable characteristics of the group.

The confusion this causes in those unaware may prove embarrassing, for there is a potential problem of mistaking one group for another by surname alone.

The issue of color as an indicator of race in the Asian community is further complicated by distinctive physiological characteristics. Again, to the uninitiated it is possible that they will fail to make a distinction among Japanese-Americans, Korean-Americans, Filipino-Americans, Vietnamese, Cambodians, and Laotians. However, to members of those distinct cultural and racially *different* groups, the uniqueness are readily apparent. It is particularly dangerous to think of the Asian community as monolithic. The chapter on the Southeast Asians, for example, addressed the problems faced by ethnic Chinese in Vietnam who are culturally, linguistically, and racially different from the majority population, yet, upon arriving in the United States, they are lumped into the "Vietnamese" grouping. Add skin hue to the picture and there are too many differences to permit one to make an assessment of race alone.

Native Americans are also difficult to identify by racial characteristics alone. Some have been mistaken for Latinos, some as Asians, some for Moslems, and some as being white. Most Native Americans have "white" names, unless they, like many African-Americans, have resumed their tribal or ancestral names.

The Latino community represents an even more complex phenomenon. Because of the Spanish colonization, the slave trade from Africa and the mingling of Indian and Moorish blood, racial characteristics are not easily described. Add to this confusion the immigration in the Nineteenth and Twentieth Centuries of Europeans to Latin America and the problem becomes even more complicated. And, if these racial characteristics were not confusing enough, add Asian racial features to many segments of the population. The Japanese-Peruvian elected to the presidency of Peru is an excellent example of this. Differences among the Latino population range from black to the fairest of individuals. Further complicating this reality is the use of surnames which reflect Irish, German, Spanish, Italian, Chinese, or Japanese ancestry. The resulting racial mixtures have led to some exotic names in an attempt to classify them, such as mulatto, mestizo, coyote, zambaigo, lobno, chamiso, morisco, cafe con leche, castizo, etc.[7] In an attempt to unify the various Latin-American racial groups, Vasconcelos identifies Latin Americans as belonging to "La Raza Cosmica."[15] Thus, although there are national differences, language and cultural ethos serve to bind Latin Americans into one cosmic identity. However, when asked who they are, they do not answer "Latino." Rather, their answers reflect their cultural nationalism. Thus, they often say they are "Cubano," or "Chicano," or "Salvadoreno."

In summarizing this section of the model, it is important for community organizers not to lump cultural and ethnic groups together by skin color alone. There are more differences than there are similarities when the issue of race is addressed. All too often, organizers work from a stereotype of what they have been socialized to believe is a "typical" individual of color. That stereotype would soon be challenged by an African-Cuban-American whose last name is O'Reardon!

Language of Choice   Another significant variable is language. This identifying characteristic was formerly relatively simple until the heavy migrations from Southeast Asia began. Communities of color generally spoke English or some variation, or else they spoke Spanish or some variation of it. However, as the model presented in Chapter One indicates, the Primary and Secondary Levels of Intensity of Contact make speaking in the native language of the communities a must. The southeast Asian community presents new and unique issues for organizers. The many languages represented in these communities is a challenge, even for those individuals from that cultural group who have been somewhat removed from the community and have partially lost language fluency. As was also mentioned in Chapter 1, organizers must be sensitive to the dialect or parallel language spoken in each neighborhood or area. Some of the nuances of language may be class-specific, thereby possibly offending someone from another class, or, what is accepted parlance in one community may be insulting or derogatory in another community. In summarizing the role played by language, it behooves organizers to be aware of the language levels, nuances, idiomatic expressions, and accepted slang. Organizers using the accepted mode of speaking will find this an important asset.

Time of Arrival in What Is Now the United States   Time of entry into the United States is significant both for historical and strategic purposes. The implications of time of arrival are germane to issues of pride and self-esteem, citizenship, and questions of turf and proprietorship. Organizers need to understand the dynamics of time of arrival—both historical and contemporary—so as to better analyze the ethos and sense of community shared by specific communities of color and subgroups within that community.

Native Americans were here long before the arrival of the whites and their "Manifest Dynasty." The Indians lost virtually all their lands, thereby making them special victims of an external oppressive force. The resultant loss of self-esteem and control continues today as described in the chapter by Edwards and Egbert-Edwards. Organizers cannot join in the struggle with Native Americans without sensitivity to the issues surrounding lands and tribal histories.

The Spanish influence on this country has also been significant. Mexicans in the United States have felt a sense of proprietorship—many still believing that the white man is living illegally on their lands. The heavy influx of Latinos from Cuba and Central American countries in the last fifteen years has caused a backlash on the part of the dominant society. Border crossings have become quasi-armed camps, and the Immigration and Naturalization Service has assumed an air of control beyond the mandates of its office. The result has been responsible, in part, for the demise of bilingual and ethnic studies programs across the country.

The Cuban experience has been markedly different. The more recent political refugees have been victimized by the earlier, more affluent anti-communist refugees in places like Dade County, Florida. The 1980 Mariel immigrants received harsh treatment at the hands of the non-Hispanic population as well as some conservative Cuban-Americans. The fact that many of these new arrivals were African-Cuban, male and young cannot be ignored, for it has played a significant role in the racism and xenophobia experienced by them.

The Puerto-Rican experience, as discussed by Morales in his chapter, is unique. Being part of a Commonwealth has given Puerto Ricans citizenship that permits them to move back and forth between the mainland and the island. Much of their rancor toward the United States has to do with what they see as preferential treatment of many Cubans and Central Americans because of their political refugee status which has permitted these groups to obtain social services more readily than the Puerto Ricans. Another difference is the fact that Puerto Ricans, while experiencing a diaspora which began in the 1940s, are still treated as second-class citizens, even decades after their arrival in the United States. It is difficult for them to accept that very recent arrivals have not had to tolerate the intensity and length of discrimination suffered by much older communities.

The Asian community's time of arrival in the United States is also wrought with strong feelings about preferential treatment of one group over another. The classic example, of course, was discussed by Murase in his chapter on the Japanese-American experience in this country. It was the West Coast Japanese Americans who were put in concentration camps during World War II, not the then allied Chinese. Similarly, the Vietnamese friends of the United States government were given preferential treatment in resettlement and social services, again causing resentments in other Asian communities. However, the Boat People have been special victims of gross racism, because they were not a part of any preferred group and also because these newest arrivals were poor and politically unconnected. The African-American experience has been well-documented. As Devore notes, African-Americans began arriving in this country in the 17th Century, and have been treated as second-class citizens ever since. Their struggles for liberation and self-esteem have sometimes become embittered when African-Americans see new arrivals being given preferential treatment. The recent reparation settlements for the Japanese-

American community has come under attack by some African-Americans, their position being that experiencing slavery for hundreds of years should make them eligible for some kind of reparations.

In summarizing this section of the model, it must be repeated that organizers cannot get involved with a community without knowing the history of the community within the United States, and the implications of that history for organizing strategies. The similarities and differences of the experiences of the various communities are deeply ingrained in their attitudes toward wishing to be part of the mainstream. The longer a group has been present in this country, the more reliance organizers can place on broader values, a sense of current place and recent history, and the roles each group can and should play within those communities. It is important to understand the frequent double oppression they have experienced from both inside and outside of their communities. The implications of not having citizenship status is critical. Experience has shown that people without citizenship are much more reluctant to involve themselves in a public struggle. And, if they entered the United States without papers, then it is safe to assume that their fears, negative self-esteem, and unwillingness to involve themselves in a struggle toward self-determination and social justice will be greater than those with citizenship or "documented" status.

National Origin   National origin is an important variable because, as has already been noted, organizers cannot group Asians, Latin Americans, or African-Americans into one monolithic lump, assuming that their oppression experiences are more or less the same. Each country of origin has its unique culture, history, political ethos, art forms, and social makeup. One cannot assume that, for example, all Central Americans are similar. In comparing the neighboring countries of Costa Rica and Nicaragua, Harrison has pointed out a multitude of differences that one must recognize and respect.[4]

The many national origins of Asian communities are diverse with languages, cultures, and social systems being very different. Some of the histories of these countries are intertwined with World War II, Korea, and Vietnam, with distrust and even hatred that have abated but little. Similarly with the Native American nations, their tribal customs, languages, and traditions are unique, and it is a requisite for successful organizers to be aware of these differences.

Citizenship status has not helped the quality of life experienced by African-Americans and Puerto Ricans who are typically born citizens of the United States. Their continued oppression and exploitation has been well documented by Devore and Morales in their respective chapters. A brief observation is in order, however. Many individuals within these communities believe that programs benefitting other communities of color should be available to them. Programs for political refugees, for example, have come under attack.

Minority Status   The confusion between minority and ethnic status has not been resolved by social scientists, planners, or politicians. Traditional definitions of minorities as signifying "fewer than" is no longer valid in such large and diversified states as California, with a population that will be more than 50 percent people of color by the year 2000. Part of the problem with the term is that it has taken on a meaning that is convenient for those interested in identifying communities of color as comprised of second-class citizens by using this label. To identify persons as belonging to an "ethnic" group means that the community has a specific uniqueness—culturally and often linguistically—that is used to place them with many mainstream groups of the country. Thus, Italian, Irish, Jewish, and Polish neighborhoods are often seen as "ethnic," while Chinese, Vietnamese, Nicaraguan, and other communities of color are perceived as "minority" neighborhoods. What distinguishes one from the other? If judged by the degree of cultural uniqueness, those communities of recent arrivals are more "ethnically pure" in relation to the traditional variables of customs and language. Yet, the differences played by color and racial diversity often feed into the racist views of people who wish to regard themselves as superior.

This racism and xenophobia continues to manifest themselves in the media. During the Gulf War, many individuals who looked "Arab-like" were taken for Iraqis, and thus victimized by this stereotyping process. Foreign accents unfortunately tend to be tolerated only if they are identified as Western European in origin.

Imagine the reactions of people of color experiencing the racism and xenophobia of the United States for the first time. Latinos, if they are African-Cuban, African-Puerto Rican, or Mexican or Central Americans of Indian descent, report unfavorable experiences. Similarly, white Puerto Ricans or other Latinos who have never perceived themselves as minorities within their countries are shocked when they come to the United States and are victimized by a society intolerant of their accents. What is especially difficult for organizers in assessing the Latino experience, for example, is the awareness that, notwithstanding the similar experiences of racism and exploitation, not all Latinos identify themselves as minorities. Some are given that status while others are not.[10]

Vietnamese, Cambodians, Chinese, and other Asian groups continue to be perceived as minorities rather than ethnic groups. Nevertheless, whatever the perceptions of the dominant society, American whites are treating groups that have been the majority in their countries (with some exceptions, such as ethnic subgroups within a country, the Chinese in Vietnam, for example) as second-class citizens within the United States.

The implications of perceptions of minority status require that organizers be very sensitive to the ethos, and possibly stigma, shared by the community, especially with recent arrivals. The education that must take place hinges on the notion that these communities need to be made to feel as "subjects" rather than "objects." They must be helped to believe that they can affect meaningful change in their lives and for their communities.[3] They must be encouraged to develop a sense of empowerment that leads to productive actions.

An Agenda for the 1990s

When asked, as the authors have pointed out, communities of color are clear on what they need: jobs, housing, economic revival of inner cities, better health systems, education, and the like. What is less clear, however, are the strategies and tactics deemed likely to be most effective in achieving these goals.

Although there are similarities in the basic needs perceived by many communities, some of their cultural and sociopolitical experiences have led to differences in the ways they perceive their situations and the ways in which to alleviate their problems. Political attitudes range from the extreme right to the extreme left. Some cultural nuances discourage public behavior, while other groups are hampered by so many of their communities being monolingual in languages other than English. Recent arrivals tend to be less willing to engage in any self-help activities that may thrust them into the public arena, especially if many people are undocumented. Further confounding organizers is the generational differences found in these communities. With these limitations in mind, the editors will discuss some strategies and tactics that seem the most viable for the 1990s.

Based on the conditions described throughout the book, the editors have identified coalition building; increasing the community's power base through political and legislative reform; working toward ending racism in all its manifestations; and nurturing the growth of true cultural pluralism as key components of such an effort.

Coalition Building It is clear that for disenfranchised communities to be heard, often they need to join together, identifying common concerns and issues, and present a united front to external political forces. It is also clear that the communities need advocates, brokers, and leadership that is able to hold together diverse interests, agendas, and strategies for change.

One major problem in coalition building arises in trying to identify the cadre responsible for forming the coalition and issues of self-determination within each community as this impacts the coalition.

Historically, coalitions have had problems staying together, even when the group consisted of relatively homogeneous individuals. In working with communities of color, there are so many problems and so many generational, race, ethnic, and sociopolitical issues that the idea of keeping a coalition together seems rather formidable. Add to these problems concerns surrounding short-versus long-range issues and one begins to appreciate the challenges for the coalitions and their organizers.

Dluhy has identified some of the organizing principles of coalitions as consisting of the following: bread and butter, consciousness raising, networking, preassociation, prefederation, and presocial movement.[2] Depending on the rationale for forming the group, there are then structural, political, ideological, resource, staff, membership recruitment, and communications issues that need to be resolved. Thus, organizers interested in forming and working with coalitions must be cognizant of the dynamics and difficulties in working with them at the various task levels. Given the nature of fear and caution in many communities of color, the process will necessarily be a difficult one.

To say that coalitions are best served with single, winnable issues is too simple. The many concerns intrinsic to communities of color are such that the isolation of single "most important" issues around which to organize is both dangerous and difficult. While it may be necessary (and most effective) to address one issue at a time, a focus on the broad range of issues identified by each community must be sustained if major, long-term changes are to be achieved.

Should white people work with communities of color through coalitions? As has been pointed out in the introduction of the book, there have been many instances in the history of social change where organizers from outside the community served specific and successful roles in bringing about meaningful change. Different today, however, are the dynamics of the inner cities, with their racial and ethnic representations. The editors tend to rely on the Organizer's Contact Intensity and Influence Model from Chapter 1. The organizer must determine the level of coalition building within which he or she is functioning. Simply stated, it is foolish for an organizer not from the community—racially, linguistically, or culturally—to attempt to gain the full confidence and trust of the community. The organizer will have many strikes against her or him to start with. However, there will always be exceptions to the preference stated here. This is particularly the case in circumstances where the coalition includes white organizations or multicultural organizations (which include whites). In sum, the coalition-building task has to be assessed within the unique context presented by each organizing situation.

Politics and Legislative Reform   The decade of the 1990s presents challenges to communities of color that are comparable to the civil rights work of the 1960s. The steady erosion of civil rights since Ronald Reagan became President has been steady and thorough. President Bush's veto of the 1990 Civil Rights Act does not augur well for the years ahead. Also, the appointment of more conservatives to the Supreme Court presents a special challenge to communities of color for decades to come. Each community has its own agenda. That is understandable and to be encouraged. However, organizers working within these communities need to develop more of a shared vision of the struggles ahead and set limits to compromises that lead to partial victories.

> Political actors must be careful not to let secondary issues, such as the filling of affirmative action quotas, deflect attention from the more fundamental issues of economic bifurcation and rising poverty among some minority groups.[11]

Although there have been some isolated victories around the country, like the Japanese-American movement for reparations, the struggle for social justice is floundering because the onslaught of the conservative trend is so strong. Author Vu-Duc Vuong ran for the Board of Supervisors in San Francisco, California. Although he lost his bid for the seat, he helped raise the consciousness of the white community about the plight of Southeast Asians in the Bay Area. This was the first time a Southeast Asian had ever run for political office in San Francisco. That in itself was an important victory.

At the same time, this increased visibility of Southeast Asians and their needs has stimulated a series of meetings between Southeast Asian leaders and leaders of a number of other Bay Area communities of color. Despite this example and a few others like it, the movement toward broader visions seems slow and haphazard at best.

Racism Communities of color must get together to fight and reduce racism; that is, the racism experienced by them from both outside the community and from other communities of color. Kenji Murase, in his chapter on the Japanese Americans warns against "exceptionalism," where the white community defines a particular community of color as being a "model minority" because it embraces the values of the white middle class. What follows, of course, is the logical conclusion that the other communities of color are lacking.

Also, we caution against the malignancy of intracommunity of color racism. Several of the authors have addressed this sad dilemma. Organizers need to be prepared to deal with it, especially organizers from a different cultural and racial group who have gained the confidence of groups other than their own. Tienda notes:

The looming question for the 1990s revolves around the course of political participation of minority groups, and the viability of rainbow coalitions to provide economic and social concessions to minority constituencies, as well as protecting the gains achieved during the 1960s and early 1970s. But in defining and striving for collective economic and social goals through "rainbow" political strategies, it is important to recognize that growing divisions within and between groups, with their deep class and regional underpinnings, almost certainly will undermine the formulation of collective minority agendas designed to improve the economic position of *all* people of color.

Social Work   How might social work respond more effectively to the challenges presented by communities of color and those wanting to work in them?

Are schools of social work (and others who prepare students for the human services) responsible for offering training to those who want to work in these communities? The editors believe they are. Either they are, or the rhetoric of support for diversity, equality, and social justice needs to be made consistent with what is offered. Otherwise, to maintain the rhetoric without the community involvement is to perpetuate a fraud, a fraud born of promises all too often in the past honored by avoidance and sidestepping of issues that bring the academic program into conflict with universities, powerful welfare programs, institutions, or governmental bodies.

For social work—educational programs and local units of the National Association of Social Workers—this means actively and aggressively recruiting students of color, building appropriate support structures so that these students can be retained, and finding the scholarships, paid field work, and loan funds that will make it possible for these students to survive economically. Without a strong base of economic support, the commitment to diversity and community organization is mostly hot air. Indeed, social work's pretentious language without action to support it makes a mockery of what we say we believe, and undermines our recruitment of minority students who truly want to serve their communities.

At the same time, there is much that can be done to support research, especially ethnographically sound research, in communities of color. There is little reason why our assistance cannot be put at the service of ethnic enclaves as it has been put at the service of welfare departments, mental health agencies, and public schools.

The curricula of schools of social work can be greatly enriched by the documented experiences of both established and emerging communities of color. Indeed, this should be regarded as a marvelous opportunity for the growth and development of what we know about people of color. But in this case very clearly adjusted to take account of local—state, city, and neighborhood—conditions.

The issue of multicultural education in schools of social work needs to be addressed. It is imperative that the curriculum be sensitive to the inclusion of materials on communities of color. Even though the Council on Social Work Education has an accreditation standard that requires such material to be present in the curriculum, there exists a move in some schools of social work to make the material—watered down at best—an elective course. We take the position that the material be taught in a required course, but that it also be disseminated throughout all the curriculum. In that way students will learn about communities of color from a total social work perspective that is clearly needed in a society that is reluctant to pay the critical attention that is so badly needed in understanding and working with communities of color.

At the same time, basic definitional problems will need to be more effectively addressed. Although Meenaghan suggests, "(Community organization) may be seen as a set of activities primarily directed toward building or maintaining groups who are ultimately capable of deciding what they want," the definition of community development offered by Spergel is much more typical of the 18th Edition of the Encyclopedia of Social Work:

> Community development has a variety of interrelated meanings for different groups, disciplines, and professions and for the public, voluntary, and sectarian agencies.[6, 9]

Given the limitations of the job market for organizers and community developers, academic programs need to better reflect not only full-time roles for organizers, but part-time (or "own time") opportunities as well. However, such efforts are no substitute or excuse for not vigorously seeking to develop employment opportunities for students of color (and white students) who want to help empower emerging and changing communities of color. An unscientific, but fairly comprehensive survey of a national sample of schools of social work recently completed suggests that such efforts on any major scale are virtually nonexistent. Surely, there is room for a great deal of work in this arena.

There is also a sense, as noted by a number of our authors, that many people of color continue to feel that their interests are the last attended to, regardless of the economic situation. As one young Latino put it, "Upturn or downturn, somehow it's never our turn." The political conservatism that has extended from the 1980s into the 1990s suggests an extension of a celebration of "diversity" with a lot of rhetoric, modest high visibility programs (filled with "photo opportunities") and very limited medium and long-term financial commitments. Given the budgetary constraints that now appear likely to extend well into the mid 1990s, especially in light of the huge expenses associated with the War in the Persian Gulf, this problem is not going to take care of itself. It would appear, then, that one part of the social work commitment to the maintenance of effort in minority communities will involve working with those communities (and other local organizations like the Urban League) to secure public and private external funding.

There will be no quick fix or easy answers. The rapid changes occurring in many of these communities will require sustained vigilence if anything approaching full advantage of the opportunities to back social work's rhetoric with action is to be taken.

Conclusion

An agenda has been set throughout the chapters of this book for community organizers with a commitment to working in communities of color. Issues and problems have been identified, along with strategies and tactics that may bring about meaningful change.

Organizers must work toward re-establishing a sense of dignity and freedom within their communities. What is needed is a new vision, or perhaps, a series of new visions. If empowerment means anything, it means that communities of color must be supported in taking control of their own visions of the future and be aided in the difficult struggle to bring those visions to realization. But this challenge should not be thought of as being a strictly localor regional phenomenon. As Vu-Duc Vuong and John Duong Huynh pointed out in their chapter on Southeast Asians, their struggles have very important global implications. These larger connections need to be emphasized by organizers, for it is partly through creating bridges back to home countries that a continued sense of pride and belonging can occur. This, in turn, will build a sense of empowerment, pride, and a view toward the future that is embraced by a sense of meaningful social change.

Endnotes

1. Edna Bonacich, "Inequality in America: The Failure of the American System for People of Color," *Sociological Spectrum* 9 (1989):77–101.

2. J. Milan Dluhy, with the assistance of Sanford L. Kravitz, *Building Coalitions in the Human Services* (Newbury Park: 1990), 7.

3. Paolo Freire, *Pedagogy of the Oppressed* (New York: Seabury Press, 1972).

4. Lawrence E. Harrison, *Underdevelopment is a State of Mind* (Cambridge, The Center for International Affairs: Harvard University and the University Press of America, 1985).

5. D. S. Massey, "Dimensions of the New Immigration to the United States and the Prospects for Assimilation," *Annual Review of Sociology* 7 (1981):57–85.

6. Thomas Meenaghan, "Macro Practice: Current Trends and Issues," in National Association of Social Workers *Encyclopedia of Social Work* 18th ed. (Silver Spring, MD: NASW, 1987), 85.

7. Magnus Morner, *La Merzcia de Razas en la Historia de America Latina* (Buenos

Aires: Paidos, 1969). Translated from the original title, Jorge Piatigorsky, *Race Mixture in the History of Latin America* (London: Little, Brown & Co.).

8. F. G. Rivera and J. L. Erlich, "Neogemeinschaft Minority Communities: Implications for Community Organization in the United States, *Community Development Journal* 16 (October 1981):189–200.

9. Irving Spergel, "Community Development," in National Association of Social Workers *Encyclopedia of Social Work* 18 ed. (Silver Spring, MD: NASW 1987), 299.

10. Teresa A. Sullivan, "A Democratic Portrait," in Pastora San Juan Cafferty and William C. McReady, eds. *Hispanics in the United States: A New Social Agenda* (New Brunswick, NJ: Transaction Books, 1965), 10.

11. Marta Tienda, "Race, Ethnicity, and the Portrait on Inequality: Approaching the 1990s," *Sociological Spectrum* 9 (1989):23–52.

12. U.S. Bureau of the Census, *Current Population Reports*. Series P–60, "Characteristics of the Population below the Poverty Level," 1982 (Washington, D.C.: Government Printing Office, 1984).

13. U.S. Department of Health and Human Services, Report of the Secretary's Task Force, *Black and Minority Health*, Vol. 1, Executive Summary, Washington, D.C. USGPO August 1985:71–80.

14. U.S. Department of Labor, Bureau of Labor Statistics, *Employment and Earnings*, Vol. 34, Washington, D.C. USGPO 1987:212.

15. Jose Vasconcelos, *La Raza Cosmica* 4th ed. (Mexico, Espasa-Calpe Mexicana, S. A. 1976).

16. William J. Wilson, *The Truly Disadvantaged* (Chicago: University of Chicago, 1987).

Index